WPP$$

Ballinger Series in
BUSINESS IN A GLOBAL ENVIRONMENT
S. Prakash Sethi, Series Editor
Baruch College, City University of New York

WPP$$
Who Is to Blame for the WPPSS Disaster

JAMES LEIGLAND
ROBERT LAMB

BALLINGER PUBLISHING COMPANY
Cambridge, Massachusetts
A Subsidiary of Harper & Row, Publishers, Inc.

International Standard Book Number: 0-88730-127-4

Library of Congress Catalog Card Number: 86-7924

Printed in the United States of America

Library of Congress Cataloging-in-Publication Data

Leigland, James.
  WPP$$: who is to blame for the WPPSS disaster.

  Bibliography: p.
  Includes index.
  1. Washington Public Power Supply System—Finance.
2. Electric utilities—Washington (State)—Finance.
I. Lamb, Robert, 1941-   II. Title. III. Title:
WPPSS. IV. Title: Who is to blame for the WPPSS disaster.
HD9685.U7W3445 1986   363.6'2'09797   86-7924
ISBN 0-88730-127-4

CONTENTS

FOREWORD

This book explores with surgical precision a case of disastrous management. The issues that it analyzes are critical to our future as an economy, as a society, and as a nation. As a body politic we have found it very difficult to find the optimum balance between total socialism with all-encompassing government management at one extreme and a completely unregulated, free-enterprise, market-driven economy at the other.

In 1971, amid high hopes and great fanfare, the Washington Public Power Supply System began building the first of five nuclear power plants. By the spring of 1983 the acronym *WPPSS* had become synonymous with the largest municipal financial disaster of all time. Tens of thousands of WPPSS bondholders will likely lose billions of dollars due to the bad judgment, mismanagement, and greed of others.

James Leigland and Robert Lamb have tried to produce the most objective, thoroughly documented account of why and how WPPSS experienced project collapse and, eventually, default. Their goal was to take a cold, hard look at WPPSS, without many personal anecdotes or much emotion—to present an unimpeachable source of information that clearly was not biased and begged no questions. The authors have avoided excessive legal detail in the book (indeed, many legal questions associated with WPPSS may not be resolved for years), but they have tried to build a legal-style case, avoiding hearsay and exaggeration whenever possible—not an easy task in the aftermath of the WPPSS default.

The result is an enlightening case study of public management failure. It is an excellent book—a monumental work worthy of the investment of deep thought about its implications by anyone interested in public finance, public administration, or organizational management in general. It is of course required reading for anyone interested in WPPSS.

There are a few extremely large enterprises on the border line between private finance and management and public management and finance. When very large projects fail we can often learn more about our economic and social system dynamics than we can from apparent successes. The WPPSS disaster may provide us with clinical insight that we otherwise would not have.

The reader should start with the question: "How did it happen, and why did it end the way that it did?" Then the book should be reread with a second basic question as the frame of reference: "If it could all be done again then what would have been the optimum way to reach the same goal with the least risk and the most benefit to those who undertook the project and those who financed it?"

If we can learn from our mistakes we may salvage something from WPPSS.

—Bruce D. Henderson, Vanderbilt University,
Founder, the Boston Consulting Group

ACKNOWLEDGMENTS

The following individuals were kind enough to assist us in the preparation of our manuscript, either through interviews or through critical comments on draft sections of the manuscript: Stephen M. Buck, Assistant Treasurer of WPPSS; Gary Petersen, Deputy Director, Public Affairs and Information, WPPSS; James Boldt, Director of the Washington Public Utility District Association; Charles Komanoff, Komanoff Energy Associates; Richard Carlson, QED Research Inc.; Arthur J. Hausker and William J. McCarthy, Fitch Investors Service, Inc.; Hyman Grossman, Standard & Poor's, Inc.; H. Russell Fraser, Nicholas Moy, Thomas Dorsey, and Joan Perry, AMBAC Indemnity Corp.; David J. Olson and Kai N. Lee, University of Washington; Curtis Eschels and Jeannie Hale, formerly with the Washington State Senate Energy and Utilities Committee; Herman R. Charbonneau, Chemical Bank; Arthur Hoffer, C. Richard Lehmann, and Merton Freeman, National WPPSS 4 and 5 Bondholders Committee; Eileen V. Austen, Drexel Burnham Lambert, Inc.; Prakash Sethi, Baruch College and City University of New York Graduate Center; Richard M. Pious, Barnard College and Columbia University; "Sidney Smith"; and Bruce D. Henderson, Vanderbilt University.

Some of the research that went into the writing of this book was funded by the Institute of Public Administration. The authors wish to thank Annmarie H. Walsh, president of IPA, Xenia W. Duisin, director of the IPA Research Library, and others on the IPA staff for their generous assistance.

Not all of the individuals or organizations mentioned above agree with the views and conclusions expressed in this book, but all have helped us to sharpen our focus on a large and difficult subject. Needless to say, the book's views and conclusions—as well as any mistakes or omissions—are solely the responsibility of the authors.

1 THE CONCENTRIC RINGS OF WPPSS

In the summer of 1983, after years of deepening problems, the Washington Public Power Supply System defaulted on interest payments due on $2.25 billion in outstanding bonds. WPPSS made it clear that it did not expect to make interest payments on those bonds in the future, and it did not expect to be able to pay back the principal to the tens of thousands of bondholders who had invested in Project 4 and 5 bonds. As a disruption of the municipal bond market, the WPPSS default is unmatched by any event since the Great Depression. In terms of the volume of debt involved, the default far surpasses any public agency Depression default. Of the five WPPSS nuclear plant projects for which over $8 billion has been borrowed, only one has begun limited operation; the rest have been terminated or indefinitely delayed.

Charges of responsibility for WPPSS' difficulties have been volleyed among all of the principal actors in the WPPSS drama — ratepayers, bondholders, underwriters, financial advisers, bond counsel, rating agencies, the Bonneville Power Administration (an agency of the federal government), the state of Washington, project participants, the courts, and others. Dozens of lawsuits have been brought to settle these claims and in the process are writing their own chapters about WPPSS almost daily.

The specific purpose of most of these suits is to determine who is legally responsible for the financial problems caused by the Supply System's default on outstanding bonds. Only the courts can answer

1

this question because the answer depends largely on a review of the many legal agreements binding WPPSS, project participants, the federal government, officials of the Washington State government, members of the investment community, bondholders, ratepayers, and others.

But the facts of who did what to engender the WPPSS project crisis and bond default are already reasonably clear in documents available from the WPPSS organization itself, studies by independent consultants who have examined WPPSS and its operations since the early 1970s, and investigations by state and federal officials.

CONCENTRIC RINGS OF RESPONSIBILITY

In order to make sense of the complicated WPPSS default, it is helpful to impose an overall conceptual order on the WPPSS drama. One way to do this is to think of all of the actors involved as constituting a series of concentric rings of power, influence, and responsibility, both formal and informal. At the center of these rings is the WPPSS organization itself. Surrounding it are the entities and organizations that have exercised varying degrees of influence over Supply System activities—the state of Washington, the federal government, the general public, the news media, the investment community, and the like.

A hierarchical organization of all of the actors and their interrelationships may also come to mind, but a hierarchy implies formal, superior-subordinate relationships, or chains of command. Imposing a series of hierarchical relationships on the WPPSS situation would beg the question of who is responsible, especially since those kinds of relationships did not always exist in the case of WPPSS. The courts will decide the extent to which formal and informal influence (or the lack of either) implies legal liability. This book will be confined to questions of responsibility resulting from cause and effect relationships. It will sort out which groups among the concentric rings, both inside and outside of WPPSS, seem to be most accountable for the disaster that WPPSS has become.

WHAT IS WPPSS?

Before investigating the WPPSS disaster, it will be helpful to take a brief historical look at exactly what WPPSS is. The Supply System has functioned as a corporate subsidiary of the state of Washington for three decades. Over that period, WPPSS has taken on a variety of different functions, hired and supervised thousands of personnel, interacted with hundreds of private contractors and other governmental entities, and borrowed billions of dollars. An outline of this history will provide the background for an understanding of how, after those three decades, WPPSS has become a nationally recognized symbol of government folly and financial disaster. The glossary at the end of this chapter summarizes the key players and issues discussed below.

The Empire of Public Power

The men who created and managed WPPSS were ambitious builders of empire. In the Pacific Northwest the empire was one of public power created in the 1930s when state laws were changed to help farmers and others create their own power utilities and break the grip of the eastern conglomerates that had supplied the area's power needs. Three things motivated the empire builders. The first was a desire to avoid electric power shortages that could inhibit economic growth in the region. The second was the realization that the availability of power over and above the region's needs at any given time could lower power prices, attract new industries, and generally drive economic growth. The third was the desire to see cheap power distributed fairly. In the Northwest this meant that power ought to be generated and sold by public entities.

The empire builders were more successful in Washington State than anywhere else in the region. Washington's laws allowing the organization of public utilities were far more liberal than in any other nearby state, and public support for New Deal progressivism was exceptionally strong there.

Although World War II signaled a decline in hostilities between private and public power in the region, the battle raged on and off into the 1960s. From the 1930s to the early 1950s rural electric cooperatives, public utility districts, and municipal lighting companies maintained their empire against most efforts by the investor-owned utilities to build their customer bases at the expense of the public utilities. The federal government helped by building the world's largest hydroelectric generating system in the area. Through the Bonneville Power Administration (BPA), created especially for the purpose, the federal power was marketed at low cost, and preference was given to the power needs of BPA's public power customers.

But by the early 1950s private, investor-owned utilities had made a comeback by capturing a significant share of the business in supplying electricity to the industries that had been attracted to the area during the 1940s by cheap power and the needs of Boeing's aircraft plants. By the mid-1950s these investor-owned utilities threatened the empire of public power in two ways. First, they had begun to develop cooperative arrangements among themselves to build and operate their own hydroelectric projects. In 1952 four private utilities in the area formed the first of these consortia. Second, at the direction of President Eisenhower, himself an opponent of the federal role as power project developer, the federal government stopped authorizing new federal projects in the area, and even considered selling some of its federal dams to private interests.

WPPSS was created to ensure that the region would continue to have its growing power needs satisfied and that those needs would be met by a public entity. In 1957 seventeen public utility districts borrowed the concept of the construction consortium from the private sector and established WPPSS as a joint action agency (JAA) to purchase existing federal dams or build new power generating facilities. Under Washington State laws JAAs are empowered to buy, build, own, and operate electrical generation and transmission facilities. They can be formed by two or more Public Utility Districts (PUDs) or municipalities, and they exist as political subdivisions and public corporations of the state. By the time of the default in 1983, WPPSS participants numbered nineteen PUDs and four cities (Ellensburg, Richland, Seattle, and Tacoma). Each member was represented on the board of directors, the Supply System's highest formal governing body, although by the mid-1970s an executive committee of the board was approving most of the important management decisions.

Early Projects

Eisenhower's administration authorized no new federal power projects, but neither did it sell any dams. WPPSS began building its own facilities in 1962, when it started construction of a 27.5 megawatt hydroelectric project at Packwood Lake, Washington. To finance this construction WPPSS sold revenue bonds at an interest rate of 2.6 percent. But the project quickly fell months behind schedule and eventually ran 25 percent over the original $10 million budget. The plant began operation on June 1, 1964, seven months late (roughly a 50 percent schedule delay). But WPPSS' problems with the plant were not over. A construction contractor sued the Supply System for errors in design and work description that necessitated 130 change orders and a 60 percent increase in the cost of its job. After counter-suing, WPPSS settled out of court.

In 1966 a second WPPSS project began commercial operation, after a construction process that was again plagued by schedule delays but by little if any cost overrun. This system generated electricity using by-product steam from the federal government's nuclear reactor at Hanford, Washington. The Hanford facility had been built during World War II to produce plutonium for weapons; in the mid-1950s interest arose in using the facility to produce electricity as well. In 1958, after earlier rejections, Congress and President Eisenhower approved the construction of a special reactor at Hanford that eventually could be converted for electric power generation. But there was still considerable resistance in Congress to the use of federal funds for the development of public power in the Pacific Northwest, and the funds for conversion were never actually approved.

After President Kennedy failed to persuade Congress to appropriate $60 million for the conversion, Washington Governor Albert Rosellini initiated discussions among the Atomic Energy Commission, the Bonneville Power Authority, the Washington Public Utility Districts Association, and the State Power Advisory Committee concerning the possibility that the state itself could proceed with the conversion. The discussants concluded that the Washington Public Power Supply System was the natural choice to finance and manage the construction necessary, as well as to operate the converted facility. In 1962 Congress and President Kennedy approved electrical generation at Hanford. Bonneville agreed to transmit the power and arrange special power exchange agreements with participating utilities, which facilitated WPPSS's efforts to raise money for construction in the tax-exempt bond market. But by the same token, BPA used the exchange agreements as a lever to force cost control on the Supply System.

In 1963 seventy-one PUDs and a number of private utilities contracted for shares of the power output. Construction financing was arranged through the issuance of $122 million in revenue bonds. By the end of November 1966 the conversion of the Hanford reactor was complete (one year over schedule), and the plant, operated by the federal government with a rated capacity of 860 megawatts, began producing electric power for commercial customers.

The Public Power Environment

It is noteworthy that the Supply System's early projects were somewhat different from those of traditional power generating facilities in the Pacific Northwest. Since the construction of Grand Coulee Dam in 1933, the region had relied heavily on the hydroelectric power provided by the Columbia River and its tributaries. This abundant, low-cost electricity transformed the physical and economic character of the area.

In the 1940s area residents paid less than half the national average for their electricity and used more than twice as much. Through the next two decades the cost of the region's power declined as new generating capacity was built. Even after a score of price increases during the 1960s and 1970s, by 1980 the average monthly electric bill in Seattle was still just one-sixth of that in New York City—and residential use in Seattle was four times as high as in New York (Lee, Klemka, and Marts 1980: 6).

This was the public power environment into which WPPSS entered in the mid-1960s. The Northwest was accustomed to cheap power, and lots of it. There was no history of power conservation or experience with nuclear or coal power generating technology. Indeed, the area did not even possess other natural energy sources. Neither crude oil nor natural gas has ever been commercially produced in the area. Petroleum products must be imported, and until recently there was no coal mining in the area.

The Pacific Northwest also had in place certain generally accepted ideological assumptions that were important components in its philosophy of hydropower development. The first and most important of these assumptions was that the more power generated, the lower its cost would be.

The Bonneville Power Authority

Although Eisenhower's administration began to slow federal hydropower development in the Northwest, a federal agency continued to dominate the Northwest power planning process for the next two decades. That agency was the Bonneville Power Administration. Now an agency of the U.S. Department of Energy, BPA was created by the Bonneville Power Act in 1937 as a marketing and transmission agency for power generated at the Bonneville Dam. Over the ensuing years BPA was authorized to market and transmit power sold on a wholesale basis from thirty hydroelectric dams that were built and are still owned by the U.S. Army Corps of Engineers and the U.S. Bureau of Reclamation. BPA was never authorized to own or build additional generating capacity; nonetheless, it played an influential role in the region's power business. By the early 1970s BPA was supplying about half of the electric power produced in the region and providing some 80 percent of the high voltage transmission capacity (Lee, Klemka, and Marts 1980: 32–33). BPA's influence in regional planning was attributable to the fact that it set rates for the acquisition and transmission of that power and dealt with about 150 utility, industrial, and government customers in eight western states.

By the late 1960s one thing was clear to BPA officials and others responsible for supplying the region's public power needs. If the demand for power continued to grow at over 7.5 percent annually, new power generating facilities would be urgently needed, and needed quickly. In 1968 BPA initiated discussions of area power needs by the Joint Power Planning Council, a group headed by BPA and including 108 public and private utilities. The result of these discussions was the development and implementation in 1968 of the Ten Year Hydro-Thermal Power Program, a plan designed to meet the region's future electricity needs through the completion of large power generating plants during the early 1980s. Looking toward the end of the century, the plan's sponsors saw the need for the construction of over 41,000 megawatts of thermal and hydroelectric generating capacity, including at least twenty nuclear power plants, at a total cost of about $16 billion.

On October 18, 1968, BPA presented the program to Congress. That same year, Secretary of the Interior Stewart L. Udall and the

Bureau of the Budget approved complex billing contract procedures that would allow BPA to provide a measure of security for the tax-exempt financing necessary to carry out the hydro-thermal program. BPA's charter helped to determine what entity of state government would make use of that security and manage the actual construction. The Bonneville Project Act of 1937 and subsequent legislation and executive orders required the agency to give preference in the disposition of electric energy to public bodies and cooperatives. As a joint action agency, WPPSS was such a public body, and one that had already issued tax-exempt bonds to successfully build power generating facilities—including the region's first use of nuclear power to generate electricity. In addition, WPPSS Managing Director Owen Hurd had been aggressively promoting the Supply System's ability to build a 1,000 megawatt nuclear plant since late 1966. In early 1967 Hurd told Bonneville's advisors to the Joint Power Planning Council that with immediate delivery of a turbine generator, WPPSS could have such a plant built by July 1972 at a cost of roughly $156 million (Gleckman 1984: 5).

The Joint Power Planning Council worked in cooperation with the Public Power Council, a regional public utility planning organization whose leadership included most of the WPPSS members. The council formally requested WPPSS to make a contribution to the grand regional program of power development by initiating construction of a nuclear power plant. On March 27, 1969, Owen Hurd informed a meeting of the council that WPPSS would indeed build one of the plants.

Projects 1, 2, and 3

In August 1971 engineering began on the first plant, which was to be built on the Hanford Federal Reservation near Richland, Washington, some 140 miles southeast of Seattle. This was designated Project 2 because of plans, later scrapped, to upgrade the Supply System's Hanford project and rename it Plant 1. The boiling water reactor for Project 2 was designed by General Electric to have a net generating capability of about 1,100 megawatts. Construction was originally estimated to take seventy-three months, with the plant to begin commercial operation in September of 1977; the total cost was estimated at $397.5 million.

In 1972 the Public Power Council asked WPPSS to build two more plants. Work began on Project 1, also located on the Hanford Reservation, in July 1974. This was to be a pressurized water reactor, designed by Babcock and Wilcox, with a net generating capability of about 1,250 megawatts. Construction on this project was originally estimated to take seventy-four months, with the plant initiating commercial operation in September 1980. The total cost was originally estimated at $632.9 million.

Project 3 was started in July 1975 at a location in Grays Harbor County near Satsop, Washington, sixty-six miles southwest of Seattle. Its pressurized-water reactor was designed by Combustion Engineering to have 1,240 megawatts of net generating capacity. Construction was originally estimated to take seventy-four months, with commercial operation to begin in September of 1981. The project's total cost was estimated at $581.4 million. Unlike the first two projects, 70 percent of Project 3 is owned by WPPSS and 30 percent by investor-owned utilities.

The participation of investor-owned utilities was the result of a compromise made by the region's public power interests to attract financial help for plant construction. In response to that need WPPSS—still only a consortium of small rural public utility districts—also offered membership in its organization to four large Washington State cities, Seattle, Tacoma, Richland, and Ellensburg. A seven-member executive committee was created to make day-to-day decisions for the Supply System.

Since each project reactor was designed to produce more electricity than the combined normal usage of the twenty-three members of the Supply System, shares in the projects were offered to public and investor-owned utilities in Idaho, Oregon, and Montana, as well as in Washington. All of the utilities were customers of BPA, and with that agency's firm prediction that the power from the three plants would soon be needed, 104 utilities (including members of the Supply System itself), and 5 investor-owned utilities contracted to purchase the full power output of Projects 1 and 2 and the 70 percent share of Project 3 owned by WPPSS.

Projects 4 and 5

Given assurances by BPA Administrator Donald Hodel that the power from the three plants would be incapable of meeting the region's needs in the 1980s, WPPSS agreed in 1974 to take on the construction of two more plants. BPA's claim was formalized by a notice of insufficiency issued to its customers in 1976, which claimed that the federal agency might be unable to meet their power needs after July 1, 1983. But for a variety of reasons, the complicated financial arrangements that allowed BPA to assist in the financing of the first three projects were no longer feasible. WPPSS itself would have to find participants willing to help fund the two additional projects. Under considerable pressure by WPPSS and BPA, eighty-eight utilities, most of which were participants in the first three projects, signed participants' agreements to back the construction of Projects 4 and 5.

Projects 4 and 5 were designed to take advantage of "twinning arrangements" with two of the first three projects. Project 4 would be built as a twin of Project 1 (1,250 megawatts) and would be situated on the same Hanford location. Project 5 would be built as a twin of Project 3 (1,240 megawatts) and would be located at Satsop, Washington. Projects 4 and 5 were scheduled for completion by 1982.

Schedule Delays and Cost Overruns

The original informal estimated total cost of the five projects was $4.1 billion. This was a guesstimate of the kind often made in statements to the local press by utility managers and consulting engineers when projects of this kind are first conceived. WPPSS now disavows such figures, but it should be remembered that these estimates were part of the basis for decisions to sign participants' agreements and initiate engineering and construction. By the time WPPSS started Projects 4 and 5 in 1976, estimated total cost for the five projects had grown to $6.67 billion, including $2.3 billion for Projects 4 and 5. Across the nation the signs of rising costs of nuclear power projects were growing even more ominous. Costs were rising precipitously, at nearly twice the rate of inflation. By 1974, when WPPSS first agreed to build Projects 4 and 5, plans for over a dozen similar nuclear power plants outside of the Pacific Northwest had already been canceled. Scores of plants were being delayed. Cost overruns and schedule delays for the five WPPSS projects began to mushroom, spurred on by a host of factors including regulatory changes, inflation, design refinements, labor problems, and management problems. In 1979 the total budget had risen to $11.9 billion. In January 1981 a new managing director initiated an extensive review of WPPSS budgets. Using a variation of the zero-based budgeting concept to reassess all WPPSS project cost components, the reviewers generated a new and up-to-date total project cost estimate. In May of 1981 the results were issued, showing a total project cost for all five plants of $23.8 billion, a sixfold increase over the 1974 budget estimate. The total cost for Project 2 alone had risen from $397.5 million estimated in 1971 to $3.2 billion, and its projected date of completion had been moved back seven years to 1984, more than doubling the original estimated seventy-three month duration.

Financing Problems

As the May 1981 budget figures indicated, a huge amount of additional financing would be required to finish all five projects. For Projects 1, 2, and 3, an additional $4.3 billion would be needed, and $8.9 billion would be needed to finish Projects 4 and 5, which were only 24.2 percent and 13.7 percent complete, respectively.

But by averaging $200 million in bonds issued every ninety days, WPPSS had already become the nation's leading issuer of tax-exempt revenue bonds, with $6.1 billion worth issued by the spring of 1981. In the spring of 1980 it became clear that institutional investors were beginning to limit purchases of WPPSS bonds because of portfolio saturation. Institutional portfolio managers typically provide a limited space in their portfolios for any one kind of issuer. When the space is filled, as it had been in many institutional portfolios, saturation occurs. WPPSS faced the possibility that it might eventually be unable to raise funds at acceptable interest rates, especially with the dramatic increase during the late 1970s in the number of joint-action agencies issuing long-term debt.

Other Difficulties

Along with the specter of portfolio saturation, WPPSS was confronted in late 1981 with a growing list of power demand forecasts that predicted much lower future demand than the 7.5 percent annual increase figure that had justified the huge Hydro-Thermal Power Program. A study commissioned by the Washington State Legislature and issued in late 1981 predicted a 1.5 percent annual growth rate well into the future.

Wall Street investment firms also began to question the need for Projects 4 and 5. In spring of 1981 Wertheim and Company suggested that Projects 4 and 5 be terminated. Drexel Burnham Lambert issued a report in June 1981 predicting that the projects would never be completed. Since the late 1970s a small but steadily growing number of the region's ratepayers were also opposed to the completion of Projects 4 and 5, partly because BPA was forced to raise its electric rates to pay debt service on WPPSS bonds. That debt service had been capitalized, or paid for out of the proceeds of bond sales. But according to the original financing agreements for Projects 1, 2, and 3, as the predicted completion dates for the plants were reached, BPA had to take over that debt service—whether or not the plants were actually finished. Beginning in June 1977 BPA assumed debt service on bonds for Project 2. Debt service on bonds for Projects 1 and 3 was to be paid by BPA starting in July 1980 and July 1981, respectively. Since none of the plants was even close to being operational, BPA was forced to begin making debt service payments by raising its rates to all of its customers in the region—an 88 percent average wholesale rate increase in late 1979 and a 59 percent increase in July 1981.

Despite the fact that in 1981 electric rates in the Pacific Northwest were still the lowest in the nation, ratepayers reacted bitterly to the announced increases. Conservation group membership grew and became more vocal in their criticism of the nuclear plants. Activist ratepayer associations were created to fight rate increases, and in some cases they called for cancellation of the plants. And voters in the state of Washington passed an initiative in November of 1981 that required future WPPSS bond sales to be approved by a public vote. Although ultimately successful, the legal battle by WPPSS, BPA, and bond trustees to overturn the initiative intensified and publicized anti-WPPSS sentiment.

The Termination of Projects 4 and 5

Beginning in May of 1981, at the urging of WPPSS Managing Director Robert Ferguson, the Supply System began to explore the possibility of delaying, or mothballing, construction on Projects 4 and 5, that is, to perform minimal maintenance on the plants until construction could be resumed. The alternative was to borrow a total of $1.65 billion during FY 1982 for all five plants. But a $750 million bond sale was already planned for September 1981, and the Supply System's financial advisers stated flatly that the $1.65 figure was unrealistic.

Accordingly, a construction slowdown was imposed on July 1, and WPPSS began to negotiate with the participants to put a mothballing plan into effect. The key to the proposed plan was to borrow $150 million from the participants—the eighty-eight utilities were to contribute 50 percent of that sum, four investor-owned utilities were to pay 29 percent, and the group of seventeen industrial users, 21 percent. The plan was given special support in a September 1981 report by a three-member panel of businessmen appointed by the governors of Washington and Oregon to study WPPSS. The panel suggested that the alternatives to mothballing might be an immediate uncontrolled collapse of Projects 4 and 5 and a serious threat to future financing for the other three projects.

But after eight months of negotiations, about 35 percent of the public utilities and one of the four investor-owned utilities turned the plan down. The direct-service customers balked at contributing after a lawsuit was brought against them by fourteen of the same WPPSS participants who were seeking their cooperation in realizing the mothballing plan. The lawsuit challenged new contracts signed by the direct-service customers that appeared to give them more secure access to BPA power than allowed by law. Other serious disagreements involved the questions of how much each participant should pay to compensate for the refusal to pay by others and how quickly the money would be repaid.

Underlying much of the hesitation to back the mothballing scheme was the growing realization that Bonneville was unlikely to purchase any significant share of the capability of the plants, as many of the 4 and 5 participants assumed would be the case when they began work on those plants. Since Bonneville would be unable to help complete the plants and a growing number of demand forecasts were predicting that plants would not be needed until far into the future, many Project 4 and 5 participants began to believe that WPPSS should try to cut its losses rather than continue construction.

Some of the eighty-eight participants who had refused to back the mothballing plan had already offered their support for termination of Projects 4 and 5. On January 22, 1982, the WPPSS board of directors voted to set in motion a termination plan. But termination was not by any means a money saving alternative. The board's plan would cost $531 million: $188 million spent since the July 1981 slowdown had been imposed and $343 million to terminate over 150 separate contracts, with $192 million specified to be spent during the following 12 months. At least $70.5 million, and as much as $94.6 million, was to come in the form of a loan from the eighty-eight participants, and $121.7 million was to come from a variety of sources, including cash reserves. The participants were contractually obligated to begin paying the remaining plant costs one year after formal termination.

By the end of February WPPSS was virtually assured of raising the $70.5 million figure, but twenty-nine of the eighty-eight participating utilities had refused to participate in the termination plan. In addition, a dozen small utilities began contemplating lawsuits to release them from WPPSS debt obligations.

The Mothballing of Project 1

Financing continued to be a considerable problem. Because of cost-saving efficiencies lost with the termination of Projects 4 and 5, estimates of costs for the remaining three plants jumped by $1.8 billion. WPPSS had sold $850 million in bonds in February at a tax-exempt interest rate of 15.12 percent—a rate second only to that of the WPPSS September bond sale. The February sale increased the total debt outstanding for the three remaining plants to $5.3 billion, not including interest costs. An additional $1 to $1.37 billion had to be borrowed to ensure that construction would continue until Initiative 394 could be overturned in court. If the initiative were upheld, the money would be needed to keep construction going until a referendum was held and the voters could authorize or deny further financing.

Dozens of activist ratepayer organizations began to appear throughout Washington, Oregon, and Idaho in late 1981. Their activities included movements to recall public utility commissioners (including those on the WPPSS board of directors), election of dissident commissioners, and withholding of utility payments. A boycott of a bank acting as WPPSS bond trustee resulted in the loss of over 145 accounts and $600,000 in deposits.

On March 18, 1982, a bipartisan group of eighteen Washington State legislators called on WPPSS to mothball another plant because of the low power demand forecast, huge additional financing requirements, and ratepayer protests. They suggested a work stoppage at Project 3, which was only 50 percent complete and would be the last of the remaining plants to become operational. On the basis of its own reduced power demand forecasts BPA requested in April that WPPSS mothball Project 1 for up to five years. The WPPSS board accepted the suggestion.

Project 1 was selected because, although it was closer to completion than Project 3 (60 percent versus 50 percent complete), 30 percent of Project 3 was owned by four investor-owned utilities—a situation that entails legal and financial problems for mothballing. Ironically, the placement of Project 3 had been somewhat unpopular with residents of Grays Harbor County where the plant was being constructed, whereas the residents of the Hanford area stood more solidly behind continued construction of Project 1. Responding to the announcement by WPPSS that 6,000 jobs would be lost as a result of mothballing Project 1, over 10,000 enraged area residents marched in protest.

By March Project 2 was 90 percent finished and required only about $556 million for completion. The mothballing plan, expected to cost $250 million a year during a two- to four-year delay, meant that WPPSS would need only $600 to $700 million before July—a figure that financial advisers indicated was the upper limit of acceptability to investors.

Additional Financing Needs

In late 1982 WPPSS announced that by fall of 1983 it would need an additional $146 million to complete Project 2 and that it was considering a June bond sale to raise the necessary funds. WPPSS also announced that it needed $981 million to complete Project 3 and that it was tentatively planning a series of four bond offerings, from June 1983 through 1984, to raise that money. In terms of estimated total costs, the WPPSS budget had fallen from $23.8 billion for five plants to $8.2 billion for the remaining two plants. However, these budget figures for the two remaining plants represented a $500 million increase over those announced a year earlier.

Default

In October 1982 an Oregon court voided all Project 4 and 5 contracts signed by utilities in that state on the grounds that those participants exceeded their authority in signing them. The contracts included step up provisions, which required remaining participants to pay an increased share of the debt to make up the loss, but these provisions were soon challenged in court as well. In October a King County Superior Court judge ruled that Project 4 and 5 participants did have the authority to enter into their take-or-pay contracts, but in December the same judge ruled that the step up provisions did not apply to cases in which participants were freed from debt obligations by state courts. Also in December the first bankruptcy among the eighty-eight participants was declared. A number of other participants filed suit to bar the Supply System from forcing them to pay for power not received.

On January 25, 1983, the eighty-eight participants in Projects 4 and 5 were obligated to turn over a total of $19 million to the Supply System. This was the first monthly installment of their respective shares of what was supposed to be a $190 million interest payment to bondholders by July 1. But by the end of January WPPSS had received payments from only two utilities, totalling just $9,435. WPPSS planned to make the July 1 debt service payment, even if reserve funds had to be used. In the meantime, the WPPSS board decided to slow construction on Project 3 for a minimum of three years.

But the question of how to make future debt service payments suddenly became moot June 15, 1983, when the Washington State Supreme Court in effect reversed the November 1982 decision of the King County Superior Court. The State Supreme Court ruled, in a seven to two decision, that twenty-nine Public Utility Districts in

Washington had acted outside their contractual authority by signing power sales agreements for shares in Projects 4 and 5. With those contracts voided, WPPSS had no alternative but to admit that it could not pay back Project 4 and 5 bondholders. In August of 1983 Chemical Bank, acting as bond trustee, made the default official by asking for immediate repayment of the outstanding Project 4 and 5 debt. Stunned bank officials and WPPSS executives alike realized that the $2.25 billion in Project 4 and 5 bonds would probably never be repaid.

FATED VISIONS OF EMPIRE

The WPPSS default is by far the largest default in the history of tax-exempt bond markets, and the extent of project failure—the cancellation of two projects and the indefinite delay of two more—is simply staggering. A variety of motives for its apparent headlong rush toward disaster have been attributed to, and admitted by, the WPPSS organization, its members, and the project participants. One motive not to be discounted was an overwhelming desire to maintain and extend the public power empire that had held sway in the region since the 1930s. Not only did WPPSS represent a weapon in the battle of public power interests against private investor-owned utilities, but it came to be seen by some regional public power advocates as a possible alternative to the federal presence of the Bonneville Power Administration (Gleckman 1984: 9).

The Pacific Northwest public power constituency considered itself a distinct and important group, many of whose members possessed a populist belief in the "rightness" of public ownership of electric power. At the base of their competitive spirit was a fear that public utilities might someday be unable to supply the growing power needs of a rapidly expanding regional economy and that customers would turn to investor-owned utilities for electric power, thereby allowing private power to invade the public power service areas.

Early on, Bonneville was a partner of regional interests that sought to protect and extend the rule of public power. But Bonneville had its own agenda as well. New Dealers had originally hoped for a Columbia Valley Authority, comparable to the Tennessee Valley Authority, to plan and operate a basinwide federal power system. But private utility interests successfully blocked such comprehensive powers, and the resulting compromise led to BPA—an agency with marketing responsibilities but no congressional authorization to build its own projects.

Since the 1930s BPA has fought for its own version of the public power empire. Waging bureaucratic battles with the Corps of Engineers and the Bureau of Reclamation, BPA struggled long and hard to successfully expand its marketing powers and service area, finally becoming the leading actor in the Northwest's federal electrical system and an unmatched force in regional power planning. Bonneville already had a long history of association with regional public utilities when WPPSS was formed. But when BPA and WPPSS worked together on the Hanford project, tension surfaced over Bonneville's insistence on stringent cost control. Regional utilities that constituted WPPSS membership, and others who became participants on WPPSS projects, worked again with BPA to begin implementation of the Hydro-Thermal Power Program. But by the late 1970s, as WPPSS teetered on the brink of disaster, tension between the two organizations flared up once again. As we shall see, the constructive partnership of two organizations that had once shared a vision of the empire of public power disintegrated into bickering and backbiting as each fought to preserve its power and prestige. In the end, their visions of empire were not the same.

GLOSSARY

WPPSS. The Washington Public Power Supply System, or simply the Supply System, is a municipal corporation and joint operating agency of the state of Washington. It has the authority, among other things, to acquire, construct, and operate plants for the generation and transmission of electric power. WPPSS was formed in 1957 as the supply arm of its members.

WPPSS Members. WPPSS membership numbers nineteen Public Utility Districts (PUDs) and the cities of Ellensburg, Richland, Seattle, and Tacoma. Because WPPSS is a municipal corporation of the state of Washington, all members must be in that state.

The WPPSS Board. The WPPSS board of directors is responsible for the management and control of WPPSS. It is composed of representatives from each of the twenty-three member utilities.

WPPSS Projects. Beginning in the early 1970s WPPSS embarked on a nuclear power plant construction program. By 1976 WPPSS was responsible for the construction of five nuclear power plants known as Projects 1, 2, 3, 4, and 5. In 1982 WPPSS terminated construction on Projects 4 and 5. One year later WPPSS defaulted on payments to Project 4 and 5 bondholders. In 1982 construction on Project 1 was stopped for up to five years. In 1983 construction on Project 3 was halted for three years. Neither Project 1 nor Project 3 are likely to produce any revenues to repay bondholders in the foreseeable future. In 1984 Project 2 began commercial operation.

WPPSS Participants. These are the various municipal utilities, public utility districts, and rural electric cooperatives in several Pacific Northwest states that purchased in advance the generating capability of the WPPSS nuclear plants. There are 104 Project 1, 2, and 3 participants, and 88 Project 4 and 5 participants. Most Project 4 and 5 participants are also participants on Projects 1, 2, and 3.

Project Owners. WPPSS owns Projects 1, 2, and 4. It shares ownership of Projects 3 with four privately owned utilities (which own 30 percent), and Project 5 with one privately owned utility (Pacific Power and Light, which owns 10 percent).

Bonneville Power Administration (BPA). BPA is a federal agency that markets and transmits power generated at federal hydroelectric projects in the Pacific Northwest. BPA helped to facilitate financing of Projects 1, 2, and 3 through special net-billing agreements with participants, which provide extra security for the bonds issued by WPPSS. BPA exercised considerable influence to help WPPSS persuade most of the eighty-eight Project 4 and 5 participants to sign agreements to back those projects.

BPA Customers. By the early 1980s BPA sold electric power to 116 public and cooperative utilities and 15 industrial customers, all in the Pacific Northwest. BPA supplied all or nearly all of the electric power requirements of those customers. In addition, it sold power to fifteen customers outside that region. Nearly all of the WPPSS participants are BPA customers.

Net-Billing Agreements. These are complicated legal agreements between BPA and Project 1, 2, and 3 participants in which BPA committed itself, prior to plant completion, to the purchase of each participant's share of the electric output of those plants. BPA would then, in effect, sell the power back to those participants. BPA's role as a kind of middleman increased the likelihood, in the eyes of investors, that the bonds used to finance construction would be paid back in timely fashion. If a participant for some reason could not or would not pay for its share of Project 1, 2, and 3 output, that cost would not fall directly on other participants or on bondholders. Instead it would be BPA's responsibility. BPA could spread that cost across its customer base, which included more than just WPPSS participants or members. In other words, these agreements facilitated the financing of Projects 1, 2, and 3. For a number of reasons, such agreements were prohibited after 1972 and could not be used on Projects 4 and 5.

Take-or-Pay Agreements. These were agreements by which the Project 4 and 5 participants committed themselves, prior to plant completion, to purchase the entire power output of those plants. Without BPA serving as middleman, the Project 4 and 5 participants had to take extra measures to convince investors that bonds for this project were secure. The extra measures involved promising to pay for their shares, and thus the costs of construction, whether or not Projects 4 and 5 were ever finished or capable of generating power. It was this promise to pay for something (power plant output) that might never exist, that the Washington State utilities did not have the authority to make, according to the State supreme court decision that precipitated default.

The Washington State Supreme Court Decision. On June 15, 1983, this court ruled that Washington State's utility participants in Projects 4 and 5 did not have proper legal authority to enter into the take-or-pay agreements. The court ruled that, in effect, those utilities had no authority to pay back their 70 percent share of Project 4 and 5 debts.

Default. Prompted by the state supreme court decision, WPPSS admitted on July 22, 1983, that it could not pay back any of the obligations it had incurred for Projects 4 and 5. This meant that it could not pay bondholders either the interest or the $2.25 billion principal due them. The representative of the bondholders, or bond fund trustee, Chemical Bank, then demanded immediate repayment of the interest and principal. According to the bond resolution, an event of default had occurred. One month later when WPPSS could not comply, Projects 4 and 5 officially registered the largest municipal bond default in history.

WPPSS Bondholders. These are the thousands of investors, either institutional or individual, who paid for WPPSS bonds with the expectation of an essentiallly risk-free investment. WPPSS bondholders are spread across the country and include large insurance companies, wealthy individual investors, individuals who purchase shares in investment trusts managed by large investment companies, and the proverbial widows and retirees who purchase bonds because they seem to provide the best combination of return and security. After the default, Project 4 and 5 bondholders saw their $5,000 bonds drop to prices as low as $500. It is estimated that Project 4 and 5 bondholders number around 75,000.

WPPSS Ratepayers. These are the individuals or businesses who purchase power from WPPSS members or participants. The number of ratepaying customers per utility (municipal system, utility district, or rural cooperative) ranges from one (PUD No. 1 of Whatcom County, Washington) to 288,000 (Seattle City Light). (Ratepayers purchasing power from the non-WPPSS utility customers of BPA, or directly from BPA in a few cases, must share to some extent the costs for Projects 1, 2, and 3 with WPPSS ratepayers because of BPA's net-billing agreements.) WPPSS ratepayers still bear the ultimate burden of paying for WPPSS Projects 1, 2, and 3.

REFERENCES

Gleckman, Howard. 1984. *WPPSS: From Dream to Default.* New York: Credit Markets.

Lee, Kai N.; Donna Lee Klemka; and Marion E. Marts. 1980. *Electric Power and the Future of the Pacific Northwest.* Seattle: University of Washington Press.

2 WPPSS MANAGEMENT

Even though the WPPSS default occurred as a direct result of a decision by the Washington State Supreme Court, enormous construction cost increases and schedule delays motivated participants to turn to the courts for a way out of their contractual obligations. Without those cost increases and schedule delays, the state supreme court never would have rendered a decision. And even had the decision not voided the take-or-pay power supply contracts, at least a short-term or technical default would have resulted from participants' failure to hand over to WPPSS their shares of debt service payments.

One of the most confusing aspects of the WPPSS drama has been management's role in the Supply System's difficulties. Part of the problem has been a proliferation of definitions. The responsibilities of WPPSS management have been defined in many different ways. Perhaps most confusing has been the ongoing disagreement, even within the WPPSS organization during the most of the 1970s, about who is responsible for managing WPPSS and its projects: the board, the managing director and his appointees, or the private contractors.

THE CHALLENGE OF
ORGANIZATIONAL GROWTH

Perhaps the greatest challenges facing the Supply System during the 1970s were those brought on by rapid organizational growth. WPPSS was not originally created and organized to undertake projects as monumental as the simultaneous construction of five 1,200 megawatt nuclear power plants. For the first fourteen years of its existence the Supply System occupied itself with the construction and operation, one after the other, of the Packwood and Hanford projects, which today operate at a combined rated capacity of only 890 megawatts. In 1971, when WPPSS began work on the first of the five nuclear power plants (Project 2), the possibility of constructing other plants was still officially remote, and WPPSS had only eighty-one employees. By 1977 that figure had risen to over 922, with thousands of construction personnel building each of the individual projects. And by 1979 WPPSS had 1,701 employees. In 1972 annual administrative and general expenses amounted to just over $1 million; by 1976 that figure had grown to over $33 million. With Projects 4 and 5 fully under construction, it was clear that both administrative costs and the number of personnel would continue to soar. In fact, by 1981 the number of WPPSS employees exceeded 2,000, with an additional 14,000 construction personnel working under contract.

Along with this rapid growth in size and complexity had come a tremendous growth in the complexity of the operating environment of WPPSS. When the first project was planned in 1971, similar types of projects that had been built or were under construction had achieved acceptable cost and schedule performance. Inflation had been stable, as had been the costs of supplies, labor, and so on. Interest rates were low. There was relatively little public interest in environmental and safety concerns related to nuclear power. Largely because of all of these factors, BPA voluntarily exercised almost no oversight with regard to WPPSS activities. As BPA's own consultants reported in 1979, the net billing and project agreements drawn up by BPA involved little attention to construction details such as budget formats, progress reports, or expenditure justifications (Theodore Barry & Associates 1979).

By 1976, all of this had changed. Five plants were now being constructed simultaneously, and there were no other projects of that scale against which WPPSS construction performance could be realistically measured. (WPPSS still ranks as the largest nuclear power plant construction project of all time.) Other, smaller nuclear projects were already experiencing schedule delays and cost overruns, and projects were being delayed or cancelled. Inflation, interest rates, and the costs of materials, labor, and the like were rising precipitously. Public concern about nuclear safety and environmental quality was intensifying and putting increased pressure on individual WPPSS board members, who represented a conflicting variety of public utility district and municipal constituencies.

By 1975 the complex net-billing agreements could no longer allow BPA's involvement to help cut costs of additional plants. WPPSS was forced to draw up its own contracts for the power from Projects 4 and 5, with no formal guarantee that BPA would ever be able to participate in the financing or construction of those plants. Extensive environmental impact statements were now required. The power use projections sponsored by BPA were being openly challenged by the Environmental Research Center at the University of Washington, the first in a long succession of such critics. And complicating the vague role of BPA in the construction of Projects 4 and 5 was the fact that by late 1977, BPA would have to start paying debt service on Project 2 from its own revenues. Those payments were supposed to have been made out of the operating revenues of Project 2, which was scheduled to begin commercial operation in September of 1977. With that project already far behind schedule, BPA officials suddenly, frantically tried to become more actively involved in the affairs of WPPSS.

HOW CAN WPPSS MANAGEMENT
BE EVALUATED?

For our purposes we will define WPPSS management to include the board of directors, the managing director and his senior staff, and the major contractors on the projects. We will include all forms of strategic planning and policymaking in our definition of management, along with directing the day-to-day operations of the organization.

In examining WPPSS management we will work our way through the concentric circles of the WPPSS organization itself. People normally think of a formal corporate structure as organized hierarchically, with chains of command, written job descriptions, and so on. In such a system, theoretically it would be possible to document each directive sent down the hierarchy by any manager and determine if that directive was proper or not, if he or she was a "good manager" or not. But the essence of effective management tends to

be something fundamentally different from control. As two management experts have put it;

> Management functions arise in the face of organizationally important circum-
> stances that are important because they are not under control. . . . Contrary
> to the proverbs of the day, there is an inverse relationship between the abil-
> ity to control and the necessity to manage. A controlled situation is one in
> which there exists both well-defined objectives and a technology capable of
> achieving them—it is, as the phrase goes, a closed set. But management is
> informed by a task environment that is unregulated, risk-bearing, and prob-
> lematical. The idea is to search out solutions to problems that materially
> threaten organizational capacity (Landau and Stout 1979: 149).

This statement may push the distinction between control and
management too far, but the point is that effective management is
not always simply the control of subordinates or the enforcement of
compliance with rules and regulations, where discretion is the equivalent of error. Effective management requires the adoption of a management style that is appropriate for the size of the organization and
the challenges the organization faces from its operating environment.
An inappropriate management style can cripple the operations of an
organization by inhibiting its responsiveness to challenges, even
though it may be impossible to identify a single directive that is
"wrong." In this sense, a grossly inappropriate management style
constitutes mismanagement.

Management style is associated with many intangible characteristics of large organizations. Sometimes equated with management philosophy or corporate culture, the term is the subject of articles in
academic journals as well as courses at leading business school. Corporate culture usually refers to the broad system of shared values and
beliefs that most large organizations possess. Management philosophy
or style usually refers to the managerial values, beliefs, and habits
exhibited by the leaders of these organizations, most often the
sources for, and best examples of, organization-wide corporate culture. WPPSS top management had a distinct management style, and
it had a significant impact of the Supply System's organizational
structures and control systems. Board members did not act as managers, nor were they supposed to, but they selected top WPPSS executives and generally accepted, and implicitly approved, the kind of
management style exhibited by those executives. That style includes
the manner in which top executives communicated with subordi-

nates, hired new employees, identified and acted on problems, planned for the future, dealt with the press and public, delegated authority, and so forth. Management style thus becomes the outermost concentric circle of power and influence that existed within the WPPSS organization itself.

The efforts by the WPPSS board of directors and the various managing directors and their senior staffs to effectively manage the Supply System organization have been documented in a series of studies and reports completed by management consultants hired by the Supply System and, in one case, the Bonneville Power Administration. By 1979 WPPSS had commissioned and received eleven such reports, offering over 400 suggestions. These reports and their recommendations provide a window on the management activities of WPPSS.

APPROPRIATE MANAGERIAL RESPONSES TO RAPID ORGANIZATIONAL GROWTH

The management consultants who worked for WPPSS and BPA during the 1970s identified problems that are by no means unique in rapidly growing organizations, especially public authorities like WPPSS, which can be legislated into existence virtually overnight. But the growth-related challenges facing WPPSS are even more common, if typically less extreme, in the private sector. In the mid-1970s, particularly, management consulting firms were routinely brought in to help companies manage growth. The growth problem was so common in fact that one of the largest consulting firms, McKinsey & Co., began research on appropriate managerial responses to rapid organizational growth. The research was eventually summarized in *Managing the Threshold Company*, a report written by McKinsey consultant Donald Clifford (1973) and distributed privately by the company. The report is reviewed here for its insights into problems similar to those faced by WPPSS.

Clifford's study reported on a McKinsey analysis of the problems faced by over 100 clients and by 700 other investor-owned threshold companies. Under the McKinsey definition, a threshold company is one with $20 million to $200 million in sales volume, which typically means that the company stands at the threshold of leadership in its industry. In order to avoid stagnation, such a company must shed many of its past characteristics and adopt a new managerial structure and style. As the report notes, most of these companies have the size and complexity of market leaders of the 1960s but lack the resources and intangible factors that allowed market leaders to cope with large-scale management problems.

The successful pre-threshold company, according to the report, is often characterized by a personal and informal style of management and is often under the primary control of a single executive. The product line is usually small and the markets limited; consequently, there are few decisions to be made, most of which can be made by top management. Communications are direct and informal, and the organization is generally characterized by an uncomplicated hierarchical framework. In short, there is little need for formal management structure and processes.

But managerial and organizational requirements change as the company increases in size and approaches the leadership threshold. Fast-paced growth quickly compounds the number and complexity of decisions that must be made. As the company becomes more highly leveraged, effective financial management becomes more important. And the growing complexity of product lines and markets are compounded by mushrooming environmental pressures from labor, government, and social forces. The result of this growth is the need for more formal management structure and processes and, above all, a new style of management.

The McKinsey report outlines a number of ways in which these managerial and organizational changes must be made.

1. The chief executive must alter his own role. He must delegate power and rely on others to make decisions. He must spend more time selecting, motivating, and evaluating key talent. He must spend more time on strategic planning, and he must be more conscious of and willing to deal with outsiders.

2. New skills must be brought in from outside the company. This means recruiting more highly skilled, highly paid executives for top-level jobs.

3. The organizational structure itself must be changed to accommodate new skills and responsibilities. This involves the delegation of authority and the clear and formal definition of responsibilities. This step usually includes the establishment of sophisticated planning functions, management information systems, and specialist staffs.

4. Top executives often must "face up to people issues." "Almost without question, the threshold companies have to face up to replacing or building around certain executives who can no longer meet the requirements of their jobs" (Clifford 1973: 30).

As the report notes, if these kinds of changes are not made by management, then it is the responsibility of the board of directors to replace the chief executive officer with someone who is capable of taking the appropriate steps.

WPPSS MANAGEMENT STYLE

The management consultants who worked with WPPSS during the 1970s recognized that the organization faced growth-threshold challenges, but that it lacked a management style that would facilitate passage beyond the growth threshold. The consulting firm of Cresap, McCormick and Paget, Inc. was brought in to help adapt WPPSS management and organizational structure to the needs of constructing one nuclear power plant in 1971. Five years later, after Projects 1 and 3 were under construction and engineering had begun on Projects 4 and 5, Cresap was again brought in to suggest organizational and managerial changes.

What Cresap consultants found in 1976 was an organization that was still being managed as if its size and responsibilities remained at 1971 levels. The huge growth in organizational size, complexity, and responsibility had not been accommodated by managerial and organizational changes. WPPSS in 1976 was an organization that had quite literally grown out of control.

As all of the WPPSS consultants noted, there was no single, quantitatively identifiable, major shortcoming of WPPSS management. Instead, there was an unprecedented series of smaller inadequacies that existed singly or in combinations in many similar kinds of projects. The difference at WPPSS was that these inadequacies existed all together, reflecting above all else a failure of management style. This failure set the tone for breakdowns of effective control throughout the organization. As the Cresap consultants pointed out in 1976, a number of steps would have to be taken immediately by WPPSS management in order to ensure that the organization would be able to cope with the growth in the number and complexity of executive responsibilities since 1971 and the continued growth that was expected by the end of the decade. But the steps taken were too little and too late.

The Management Staff

The Cresap report portrays the top management of WPPSS as exercising a conservative style characterized by concentration of authority and accountability at the top levels. Communication among members of this group was open and informal, but communication with other levels of the organization, including the board of directors, tended to be infrequent as well as informal. This leadership group was slow to delegate to middle and lower levels of management the authority to handle anything more than routine matters. As a result, lower level management remained underdeveloped and underutilized. The effects of this underutilization were compounded by a lack of effort focused on recruiting or developing new management talent. And because of a lack of time, capability, or what the Cresap report referred to as a "desire to be responsive to the WPPSS membership rather than to appear to be advancing its own interests," top management showed a distinct hesitance to involve themselves in overall organizational governance or policy planning (Cresap, McCormick and Paget 1976: III-17).

The Cresap consultants noted that this style had been appropriate in the past, but "if left unchanged, there is considerable risk that this pattern could break down under the weight of future management burdens" (Cresap, McCormick and Paget 1976: II-3). More responsibility and accountability had to be delegated to middle and lower management, managerial talent had to be recruited and developed, channels of communication had to be formalized, and more strategic planning had to be undertaken by top management.

The Cresap consultants also emphasized what the McKinsey report would call a failure to deal adequately with people issues. "As is true of many rapidly growing organizations, WPPSS has found it necessary to promote or to hire individuals rapidly just to maintain operations, and to make the compromises that are inevitable under such conditions (Cresap, McCormick and Paget 1976: III-14-15). The Cresap judgment was confirmed years later by the somewhat more candid admission of the Supply System's own administrative auditor that prior to 1979, "the type of staff required to manage the growing giant of a program was simply not 'in place' '' (Washington Public Power Supply System 1980: 1-1). Decisions about management personnel were being handled informally by the managing director and his assistants. Cresap consultants recommended a more rigorous and formalized personnel planning and recruiting system as a first step to upgrade the quality of management personnel.

Other personnel actions were put more diplomatically. It was suggested, for example, that certain top management positions be eliminated and that, in the jargon of management consultants, certain personnel be worked around. The problem being hinted at stemmed from the WPPSS tradition of promoting from within whenever possible or hiring personnel or contractors with whom the Supply System had previous working experience, rather than recruiting top outside executives with extensive experience in large nuclear projects. Many top WPPSS executives had been drawn from the Army Corps of Engineers because of their experience on area hydropower projects. Many others had been kept on after the early Supply System projects. The first managing director, Owen Hurd (1957–1971), had been with the Supply System since its beginning. Hurd had managed the Benton County Public Utility District for nine years before joining WPPSS. Although his experience with nuclear power was limited to the WPPSS Hanford project, which of course did not involve the construction by WPPSS of a nuclear reactor, Hurd was an outspoken advocate of nuclear power, as well as the Supply System's ability to construct large nuclear power plants at minimal cost.

Hurd retired in 1971, the same year that ninety-four public utilities signed contracts to participate in WPPSS construction of Project 2. He was replaced by J.J. ("Jack") Stein (1971-1977), a member of the WPPSS executive committee and manager of Grays Harbor County PUD. Stein was a former Navy officer who had twenty years of experience with Grays Harbor but virtually no experience with nuclear engineering or planning, staffing, or managing major construction projects. WPPSS board members recall that Stein was regarded as a no-nonsense man who made decisions, gave orders, and expected them to be carried out. When he retired in 1977, Stein was receiving a salary of $55,000 a year.

Neil O. Strand, managing director during the crucial years from 1977 to 1980, had been trained as an engineer and had spent nineteen years in that capacity with General Electric, where he worked in the early 1960s on G.E.'s Oyster Creek, New Jersey project—famous both as a ground-breaking nuclear power plant project and as a project plagued with construction problems and immense cost overruns. He had joined the Supply System as an engineer before any nuclear plants were actually under construction and for another seven years worked his way up through the organizational hierarchy, spending most of his time as project manager of Plant 2.

At the time of Strand's selection to succeed Stein, the board had undertaken an executive search and interviewed a number of highly experienced project engineers. The board had also commissioned a salary survey of the industry and found to its surprise that managing directors in other, similar jobs were receiving $150,000 annually. Strand was ultimately chosen because he demanded less money than the other finalists (about $70,000, as opposed to the $100,000 or more demanded by experienced outsiders) and because he was familiar to, and liked by, members of the board (Anderson 1985: 106). He was described as a quiet and deliberate person who sought to avoid conflicts and tried to get things done by seeking consensus.

The Cresap report recommended that the managing director delegate most of the responsibility for operating management that had remained centralized in his office and receive high-level assistance with the increasingly important responsibilities that had suffered neglect up to that time—external relations and coordination and administrative supervision of executive staff activities. In something of an understatement, the Cresap report called for a more sophisticated approach to the top-level direction of such a large and politically sensitive public organization: "To assume that WPPSS can effectively be managed by a single individual whose sole concern is internal matters ignores the inseparability of political and operating considerations. . . ." (Cresap, McCormick and Paget 1976: IV-5).

The Board of Directors

The shortcomings of the management style exercised by top WPPSS executives were exacerbated by the board's own style, as documented in a series of management consulting studies beginning with Cresap report in 1976. The Supply System's 1957 charter placed ultimate responsibility for management and control of the organization with the board, which met quarterly and consisted of nineteen elected commissioners of the member public utility districts (PUDs) plus officials of the four city-owned member utilities.[1] But the board consistently failed to exercise management oversight for a variety of reasons.

One major reason stemmed from the managerial values, beliefs, and habits that board members typically brought to their job. The institutional character of the WPPSS board was similar to that of the Washington State Public Utility District boards of commissioners from which most of its members came. Across the United States, the local utility board is a common administrative device used to provide a kind of democratic control over local utility planning and management. Typically, these boards consist of three to five unsalaried members with three- to five-year overlapping terms. Their function is to appoint a professional utility manager, approve budgets, and participate in basic planning. But the manager is usually delegated full operating authority, and the most important function of the board is to promote the interests of the utility and act as a liaison between utility management, elected officials, and the public.

PUD commissioners in Washington State are themselves elected and have traditionally served in the roles of spokesmen, liaisons, and promoters with considerable vigor. Since the 1950s, when public utilities began to take a more active role in the area's hydropower development, PUD commissioners constituted an old boy network that very successfully served as a collective spokesman for and promoter of the virtues of public power expansion in the area. It was not uncommon in the 1970s to find PUD commissioners who had been active in area public power development since the 1940s.

In other words, most WPPSS directors were successful small businessmen whose public power management experience was generally limited to approving budgets for local utilities and promoting local power use. At various times the board was made up of wheat ranchers, apple orchard owners, veterinarians, muffler shop owners, and refrigerator salesmen. Only a few board members were power professionals, and virtually none had high-level managerial experience or experience with nuclear power. They were not appointed, but in most cases they represented two constituencies—the voters of their utility district and their fellow utility board members who had sent them to the WPPSS board. Perhaps most important was the fact that all they knew about being board members was what they had learned from their experiences as local PUD commissioners.

Boards may evolve through fairly distinct stages as their organizations face the normal challenges brought on by growth. In the legitimizing stage the board simply rubber stamps the decisions of management. The auditing stage is one in which the board becomes fully aware of its legal responsibilities and actively seeks out reliable information on organizational performance. The directing stage is when the board actively establishes strategic policy goals and identifies organizational problems that could interfere with the attainment of those goals.[2]

Decisive action by the board of directors is sometimes the last chance for a rapidly growing company to avoid stagnation and successfully cross the threshold to industry leadership. A board that exercises a directing function, or one that is able to make the transition quickly from auditing to directing in response to crisis is needed. The same would hold true for public authorities such as WPPSS, which exist as public-sector counterparts of the threshold company. But the WPPSS board was clearly locked into a legitimizing stage. All of the consulting studies of WPPSS management from 1976 to 1980 reflect the necessity that the board make a rapid transition to more active oversight of Supply System affairs.

On paper the executive decisionmaking responsibilities of the board appeared impressive. The board, or its executive committee, was required to approve all individual vouchers, contracts, and procurements over $15,000. All contract change orders above $250,000 were reviewed by the board in advance. The directors were also formally responsible for the selection of contractors and for approving bond resolutions, including bond terms, prices, and interest rates. The board was legally responsible for payment of principal and interest from Supply System revenues. Finally, it had the duty of monitoring the efficiency of construction and operation, taking part in power development planning with the WPPSS participants, and assuring plant safety.

In reality most of these decisions were determined by others, and the board was overwhelmed by a mixed deluge of trivia and issues beyond its ability to understand or handle. The Cresap report implies that the board was unwilling or unable to provide even the most basic direction for WPPSS management—even less so than the typically passive public authority or public corporation board (Walsh 1978: 171-208). The report notes that the directors felt growing pressure to represent the interests of their different area constituencies and to deal with the criticisms and demands of outsiders as well. The directors were unwilling to fuel this pressure by indicating any sign of disagreement or controversy in the public meetings.

Board meetings were largely devoted to approvals of construction change orders and other matters in which the members lacked technical expertise. In a typical two and one-half hour meeting, Cresap consultants noted that only about three minutes were devoted to policy considerations (Cresap, McCormick and Paget 1976: III-17). In a survey administered by the Institute of Public Administration in 1979, board respondents indicated that they spent an average of twenty-seven hours per month on matters relating to WPPSS. But four to one, they indicated that board members should be more involved in policy issues than they had been (Institute of Public Administration 1979: 1). And as the board minutes indicate, it was not until 1978 that board members began questioning managerial decisions or requesting detailed information about project management from the top management staff.

Other examples drawn from the board minutes illuminate the nature of board concerns. In a regular executive committee meeting on June 23, 1978, in two hours and twelve minutes the members approved more than 500 claim vouchers, discussed litigation, and heard project progress reports that described pipefitters' pickets at Project 1, a work stoppage necessitated by defective weld rod control procedures, teamsters picketing one contractor at Project 2, and a planned march by the Crabshell Alliance on the Grays Harbor site. The directors passed nineteen resolutions, some rejecting bids, most awarding contracts and approving change orders without information on their cost impacts. The board heard a report that a $150 million bond issue had been sold at a net interest cost of 6.8 percent on May 23, 1978, and that sale of a $180 million bond issue would take place on July 11. They voted to send two board members to New York for an investors' information meeting.

In a five-hour meeting on June 27, 1980, the executive committee approved over 1000 vouchers and passed over 30 resolutions, all by unanimous vote. Project discussions covered a notice of violation from the Nuclear Regulatory Commission carrying a $161,000 penalty, performance problems with contract number 215, collapse of a crane at Project 3, rejection of the sole bid received for a bond issue the prior April because of high interest cost, and plans for an emergency response facility. One of the resolutions appointed Robert Ferguson the new managing director. Another authorized a new bond sale of $180 million for Projects 4 and 5. Many of the resolutions were akin to the following: "A RESOLUTION APPROVING THE EXECUTION OF CHANGE ORDER NO. 2 TO CONTRACT NO. C-0072, METEOROLOGICAL MONITORING PROGRAM, WITH ENVIROSPHERE COMPANY" (Washington Public Power Supply System 1980a). Labor representatives requested the board to pressure the contractors about negotiations at Hanford. But the longest discussion involved completion of new WPPSS office space in Seattle, including the color of the carpeting, the shape and size of the new board room table, and location of future meetings while completion of new office space was delayed.

By the late 1970s major issues were coming into the board room through staff reports forced out by public knowledge of problems such as safety violations, construction site accidents, labor troubles, rate increases, and so forth. But the board members were also still regularly embroiled in confusing discussions of technical details such as changes in specifications for red head bolts and whether or not some issue currently being discussed had already been discussed at a previous meeting (and if so, what the conclusion of that earlier discussion was). The sheer volume of items coming before them, the thin information, and the short decisionmaking time allowed the board members little opportunity for significant influence on progress and performance.

As many subsequent consulting reports were to do, the Cresap report implored the WPPSS board to leave small, technically oriented decisions to management and to concentrate instead on two crucial questions. The first was whether or not the overall WPPSS policies and plans were actually in the best interest of the Supply System members and project participants. The report put the second question more bluntly: "Is WPPSS well managed?" (Cresap, McCormick and Paget 1976: IV-2).

PLANNING AND BUDGETING

Management style alone does not dictate the success or failure of organizational performance. It is possible that if an organization operates in a relatively unchallenging environment, or if its top management is exceptionally capable in a few crucial ways, then the kind of overall management style possessed by top management may not make much difference. The so-called rules or principles of the science of management are constantly being violated, with success. But unfortunately in the case of WPPSS, the operational environment was highly complex and challenging. The overly centralized management style that had worked well for a few years quickly outgrew its usefulness as the organization began to expand rapidly. The existing management structure and control systems could not meet the challenges of growth and were not adapted in appropriate ways.

Throughout most of the 1970s WPPSS activity was divided into three general areas, all of which were subject to the direct supervision of top management. The Finance and Administration Division was the foremost division in that the efficient work of the more technical divisions presupposed a hospitable financial and administrative environment. Finance and Administration facilitated activities such as budgeting, auditing, labor relations, data systems, and general administrative services. Its budget activity created the Supply System's operating budget, which established the general and administrative, or owner's, costs (as opposed to construction costs) for the subsequent year's operation.

The second major division, which also facilitated the achievement of the organization's primary goals, was the Generation and Technology Division. It carried out general engineering and quality assurance efforts, as well as preparations for the eventual liscensing and operation of the plants.

Finally, the heart of activity was the Projects Division, through which WPPSS participated directly in the construction of the five nuclear power plants. One important way was in the creation of construction budgets, which projected expenditures to the date of commercial operation for each project. Thus, the operating budget and the construction budget were produced by separate functional areas of WPPSS and combined only in later stages of the yearly budget process.

Operational Planning and Budgeting

The management style of WPPSS was manifested in weaknesses in all three divisions. The inadequacies of the Project Division, which were reflected in dramatic cost overruns and schedule delays, were ultimately the most damaging to WPPSS. However, an appropriate place to begin a discussion of the practical shortcomings of the management style is in its effects on the activities of the Finance and Administration Division. This is so because in the planning, budgeting, and implementation of management control systems, this division was charged with providing ways to identify and communicate to top management the problems of the other divisions. Of course, some communication from the bottom to the top levels of management should go on constantly, but formal planning and budgeting processes typically provide opportunities for broadening a corporation's perspective on its problems—for identifying, linking, and creating long-term solutions to problems that are otherwise dealt with on a day-to-day, reactive basis. If the engineering department needs more engineers to review design changes, it formally presents its request—and identifies the associated problem—as part of the planning and budgeting process.

In an organization the size of WPPSS in 1975 and after, it is imperative that strategic planning and operational planning and budgeting complement each other. Strategic planning is essential for providing overall direction for operational planning and budgeting through the establishment of organizational goals and programs to attain them. Without feedback from the latter processes, it is impossible for strategic planners to have a realistic understanding of the kinds of organizational problems and capabilities that may affect the attainment of those goals.

At WPPSS operational planning and budgeting were carried out in keeping with the pre-threshold management style that emphasized little delegation of authority, poor bottom-to-top communication of information, and a corresponding effort by top management to control as many operational details as possible. Top management neglected strategic planning for more immediate problems. To the extent that any long-range planning was done at this level, it involved an almost complete reliance on information supplied by the outside regional planning organizations that were closely associated with BPA.

Operational planning was totally separate from and unrelated to strategic planning, and in any case almost nonexistent. Technically, it was to be done in the various operational departments and then functionally coordinated by the budget office. But because of the extreme centralization of the budgetary process at WPPSS, little operational planning was done, and, as a result, top management was effectively cut off from important sources of information about operating problems.

The WPPSS budget process resembled that of a state or local government much more than it did that of a large, profit-oriented business. It emphasized financial control and accountability rather than planning and performance improvement. In a state or municipal government, the budget process typically begins with the communication by top management down the organizational hierarchy of the organization's basic objectives. Goals, programs, and budget requests are then formulated at the departmental level. Next, the requests are communicated back to top management, which typically spends most of its time paring the requests to fit predetermined overall budget levels. The predetermined levels are represented by a projection of revenue limits for the coming fiscal year. The governor or mayor usually must also submit his executive budget to a legislative body for approval.

At WPPSS all of the worst features of this kind of budgeting seem to have been realized. As the Cresap study pointed out, top management involved itself only at the beginning and end of the process, making budgeting decisions seemingly without serious consideration of the goals or programs developed at the departmental level. Consequently, top management was generally unaware of the departmental rationales for their budget requests. In fact, the only formalized part of the planning and budgeting process at the departmental level was the actual preparation of the budget document. The Cresap report noted that budget reductions by top management, as a result of its review of department budget requests, were decided upon "without any input from department managers on budget requirements as they relate[d] to departmental goals" (Cresap, McCormick and Paget 1976: III-13). It is not surprising that department managers tended to deemphasize planning and concentrate instead on expenditure levels. Nor is it surprising that their commitment to the plans and programs that resulted from the budget process was weakened by their perception that budget decisions were arbitrary (Cresap, McCormick and Paget 1976: IV-20).

There were reasons for the use of this kind of highly centralized, control-oriented budget style at WPPSS. First, it is the kind of budget process typical of much smaller organizations in which communication between upper and lower executive levels is easy and informal, where top management has a more direct hand in operations and is more immediately aware of operational problems. Because it was not until 1980 that WPPSS hired a managing director with managerial experience in an organization the size of WPPSS, this style of budgeting was probably the only kind that WPPSS management knew through the late 1970s.

Also, developments at WPPSS during the mid-1970s made the situation of top management comparable to that of a governor or mayor beleaguered by revenue shortfalls and a watchdog legislative body. As cost overruns and schedule delays began to appear in the construction budget figures, it became necessary to practice expenditure control, and to do so wherever possible. The operating budget was a natural place for top management to exercise its control over expenditures, for it had little control over construction costs or the construction budget process, for that matter. And indeed, this reasoning may have worked in the sense that in 1975 general and administrative cost expenditures came in at nearly one-third below budget.

One result of the WPPSS budget style was what the Cresap report referred to as a "penny-wise and pound-foolish" effect on the management of WPPSS activities (Cresap, McCormick and Paget 1976: IV-8). By concentrating on cutting expenditures, top management ignored some of the broader organizational problems facing WPPSS. It also tended to leave unsolved certain problems that might have been meliorated with modestly larger allocations in the operating budget. Administrative delays, such as those that occurred in WPPSS engineering reviews of design changes, often resulted in construction schedule delays and subsequent cost increases that were ultimately many times more costly than would have been appropriate corrective administrative measures, such as the hiring of a few more WPPSS engineers.

The emphasis on expenditure control also meant that other possible functions of budgeting were ignored. Specifically, budgeting was not used as a management control or performance measurement tool. Accounting and internal auditing staffs were only marginally involved in the budget process, and thus could not exercise the kinds of checks that they do in many similar organizations. Mid-year budget adjustments reflecting changes in project schedules, for example, were not made, and thus little attention could be paid to justifying variances. The Cresap opinion of the operating budget process was quite clear:

... the approach does not serve to build a sense of responsibility and accountability on the part of lower level managers for achieving maximum progress within budgetary constraints. It also does not sufficiently tap reservoirs of knowledge at lower levels, nor promote a healthy interchange between management levels prior to detailed budgeting. Finally, the process places a burden on upper levels of management that may soon become unmanageable and that diverts them from the more important tasks of planning and coordination (Cresap, McCormick and Paget 1976: III-13-14).

Construction Budgets

An additional crucial shortcoming of the WPPSS budget process as carried out by the Administration and Finance Division was that it had little to do with the all-important construction budget process. The annually updated project construction budget at WPPSS was a revised statement of each project's total construction expenditures forecast to the time of project completion. The revised construction budgets might reflect changes in designs, schedule delays, or changes in the owner's costs (overhead or administrative and general costs), as noted in the annual operating budget. Operating costs and direct construction costs were consolidated during the process when the former were distributed among the five projects, the Hanford and Packwood plants, and any special programs that might be undertaken at a given time (for example, the Uranium Exploration Program).

At WPPSS the determination of operating or administrative costs and of direct construction project costs arose from two completely separate budget processes. As noted, until 1979 the operating budget process was coordinated by the Planning and Budgets Office of the Administration and Finance Division. The construction budgets process, prior to the allocation of owner costs, was coordinated by the Planning and Measurements Office of the Projects Division. Interaction between the two budget processes was minimal until the costs were consolidated in the final stages of preparing the total budget. In other words, the staff of the Administration and Finance Division was not delegated the authority to oversee any aspects of budget preparation by the project managers.

This lack of control by the finance staff resulted in the absence of a single set of construction budget policies and procedures, as well as expenditure forecast assumptions. In fact, there was little coordination of the construction budget process even by the Projects Division. Because of special management difficulties that will be discussed in a later section, the construction budget process relied heavily on information supplied by the construction engineers and contractors. A number of different construction engineers were involved in the projects, and each tended to use his own cost and performance status reporting system. Thus, cost data for the projects was often inconsistent and not comparable. In addition, few cost reports included any trend analysis that projected future effects of ongoing activities. The construction budget process was not even automated, as was the operating budget process (the Data Systems Office was in the Administration and Finance Division).

This lack of central coordination of the budget process led to poor construction cost data. It also reinforced the failure to use the overall WPPSS budget for performance evaluation. In a 1979 report to BPA by the management consulting firm of Theodore Barry & Associates, the following characteristics of the typical WPPSS budget report were noted as being inconsistent with any serious attempt at performance evaluation:

1. The reports omitted the original budget.
2. Budget adjustments were to prior budget rather than a base-line budget.
3. Controllable and uncontrollable costs were not distinguished.
4. Budget variance analysis was in absolute dollar amounts with no percentage calculations to indicate a level of variance significance.
5. Variance analysis was also restricted to budget amounts rather than actual expenditures.
6. Variance analyses performed by the construction engineers were not even included in managerial reports to the board of directors (Theodore Barry & Associates 1979: VIII-18).

Once again, the shortcomings of the WPPSS budget process give evidence that the management style of WPPSS was inappropriate for the organization's size and complexity. The top managers failed to delegate authority to coordinate and oversee the construction budget process because of their overly centralized approach to their responsibilities. The self-sustaining qualities of this style are evident in its impact on budgeting. That process, as carried out at WPPSS, required a great deal of attention to detail by top management—if no one has been delegated the responsibility for a needed function, it is the responsibility of top management. And because of the amount of attention the budget required, top managers had little time or energy to adopt a larger and longer-term perspective of organizational problems. In the case of budgeting, most of top management's time was devoted to cutting costs on a line-item basis, and not enough time was spent evaluating the nature and distribution of corporate resources. In cases where this style of management fails to identify and deal effectively with major organizational problems, embattled management typically increases control, centralization, and distrust of lower management and outside groups. All of this befell WPPSS in the late 1970s.

PROJECT MANAGEMENT AND PROJECT COSTS

We have reviewed the management style favored by WPPSS top management and some of the ways in which that style manifested itself in organizational activities such as budgeting. But even though that style had major impacts on some organizational activities, it does not necessarily follow that the Supply System's serious cost-related problems can all be attributed to managerial inadequacies. There were other significant factors responsible for construction cost increases and schedule delays that fell beyond the control of WPPSS management. But it also appears that WPPSS management failed to recognize and take steps to contain many costs that were largely under their control. This failure seems to have resulted, at least in part, from the management style practiced by WPPSS top executives and from the awkward organization structure and functions produced by that style.

The following description of the WPPSS project cost problems divides the issue into two parts: the Supply System's own description and explanation of the cost and schedule problems, and the Supply System's efforts to manage the construction projects and control project costs.

The WPPSS Explanation of Construction
Cost Increases

Although costs and schedule delays had increased steadily since engineering on the first project began in 1971, no one outside the Supply System itself seems to have been seriously concerned until 1977, when the commercial operation of Plant 2 had been originally scheduled to begin. That was also when BPA was required to assume the responsibility for Plant 2 debt service payments. With none of the anticipated revenues coming in from the plant, BPA was forced to begin raising rates for electricity it sold to utilities in the region. It was at this time that BPA retained Theodore Barry & Associates to examine WPPSS management practices and suggest ways in which money might be saved, as well as ways in which BPA might more effectively carry out its oversight responsibilities.

The local news media began bringing WPPSS cost overruns to the attention of the public on a consistent basis in August 1978, after heavy rains caused most of the Project 5 construction site to slide into nearby creeks. Because construction on the site had started at the onset of the area's rainy season, which routinely yields more than ninety inches of rain a year, the mishap was viewed by the press as a gross miscalculation. It was estimated to have cost $51 million in increased project costs, and it became the subject of the first of many highly critical investigative reports on Supply System management and finances.

Estimating the size of WPPSS cost increases has always been difficult because of problems in determining the original estimated cost figures for any of the five plants. In each case, preliminary estimates were made before significant amounts of engineering work had been completed. Although presumably these figures were extremely important in the original decisions to undertake the projects, WPPSS has always maintained that only later, and much higher, official estimates should be used in determining the sizes of cost increases.

The Supply System explained cost increases in a number of ways. One way was by pointing to the fact, already widely recognized in the mid-1970s, that the nuclear power industry in general had seriously underestimated the rate of inflation and the rapid climb in interest costs that plagued utility construction projects across the country. Inflation alone had more than doubled construction costs by the end of the 1970s. WPPSS hired United Engineers to conduct a study of the industry as a whole, and the result was a report that found WPPSS cost increases to be typical of the industy (Vann 1978). WPPSS also claimed that statutory and regulatory requirements for power plant design and construction were responsible for large increases in its plant costs. In 1979 WPPSS put the percent of cost increase due to regulatory change at 30 percent. The Supply System's contention was supported by EBASCO Services, engineers for Projects 3 and 5 who conducted their own study of the industry. EBASCO found that between 1969 and 1978, 78 percent of the increase in power plant costs across the country was due to statutory and regulatory changes (Bennett and Kettler 1978: 2).

WPPSS also pointed to factors unique to the Pacific Northwest as important contributors to cost increases. One factor was the high cost of labor in the region. In response to criticism about cost increases in early 1979, WPPSS noted that composite wage rates for skilled craftsmen and laborers on WPPSS projects amounted to $18.27 an hour, including fringe benefits. This rate contrasted sharply with that of Duke Power Company, a large east coast utility that paid a wage rate of about $8.83 an hour (Washington Public Power Supply System 1979: Ex. 8).

WPPSS also had to respond to more critical, independent studies, and these provoked other kinds of defensive arguments. In response to a request by U.S. Representative (and vocal WPPSS critic) Jim Weaver, the General Accounting Office conducted a study of WPPSS construction cost estimates. In the spring of 1979 the GAO concluded that, compared to a selected group of other public and private nuclear power plant construction projects, WPPSS capital costs were higher by at least 30 percent, making its projects "among the most expensive under construction" (Peach 1979: 4). The management consulting study conducted by Theodore Barry for BPA produced figures showing that the Supply System's final installed costs were very near the upper limit of costs experienced by nuclear power plants of the same vintage across the country (Theodore Barry & Associates 1979: IV-32). A standard WPPSS defense against these kinds of studies was to contend that costs were usually measured differently on other projects. WPPSS executives claimed that, unlike similar projects, WPPSS included in its total all of its interest costs, some of the costs for uranium fuel, and all of its corporate overhead costs.

Despite the Supply System's attempts to portray most of its cost increases as beyond the control of management, some of the external factors that were said to push costs up either were not totally beyond WPPSS control or did not exist to a significant degree. A number of other reasons for cost increases were simply not identified, possibly because top management had not yet realized their importance. Finally, when considering WPPSS' explanations of cost increases and schedule delays, it is useful to note that an investigation by the Washington State Senate Energy and Utilities Committee (1981: 44) found that WPPSS had maintained no records of the causes of these overruns and delays.

Labor Costs. Labor costs were certainly not beyond the control of WPPSS management. The Theodore Barry report pointed out that there were alternatives to accepting prevailing national and local trade agreements. Such agreements often produce high labor costs because they are negotiated under the assumption that workers are only temporarily employed on a given project and risk long periods of unemployment. However, in the cases of large, long-term projects such as those being built by WPPSS, this assumption can be and often is questioned for certain specific contracts. The risk of worker unemployment is reduced somewhat, and unions are sometimes willing to recognize this. Moreover, because of the complexities of such projects, it is in the owner's interest to coordinate more closely the activities of various crafts. In these situations, separate contracts are often negotiated for specific construction projects. Somewhat less common is the merit shop arrangement under which no contract is negotiated and fringe benefits and add-on payments are somewhat lower than they would be otherwise, although the wage rate itself is not typically lower.

Probably because of a past practice of negotiating lump-sum contracts with individual construction firms (already generally discontinued by the time of the Theodore Barry report), WPPSS had a policy of not participating in negotiations with unions regarding labor contracts. WPPSS construction sites were not even represented at local labor negotiations. Rather, individual contractors administered labor contracts and interacted with the unions. But whatever the reason for remaining uninvolved in local labor negotiations, this policy virtually assured that the Supply System faced the highest labor costs in the region.

In addition, although the Supply System complained about high labor costs, its executives admitted that low labor productivity was the fault of WPPSS management rather than of labor. In his 1980 testimony before the Washington State Senate Energy Committee, WPPSS Assistant Director for Projects said, "We have never claimed that low productivity is the fault of labor. The low productivity is generally our fault, management; either the material is not available when and where it should be, or the engineering is not available when and where it should be, or our planning is incomplete, or what have you" (Washington State Senate Energy and Utilities Committee 1981: 45).

Regulatory Changes. There is no question that high labor costs contributed to the overall project cost increases experienced by WPPSS. Regulatory changes certainly increased costs as well, but it is difficult to separate the direct and unmitigated impact of those changes from contributing effects of WPPSS managerial inadequacy. There were instances in which regulatory changes did indeed result in cost increases. And although over 1,000 new regulations were imposed on the nuclear power industry during the 1970s, the vast majority did not directly result in huge cost increases. WPPSS executives, however, were exceptionally liberal in determining which cost increases were caused by changes in regulatory requirements. An investigation by the Washington State Senate Energy and Utilities Committee found, for example, that the cost of repairing $56 million in site damage from erosion was attributed to changed regulatory requirements. The committee noted that the regulations related to site erosions had not changed, and if existing regulations had been followed, the damage most likely would never have occurred in the first place. The reliability of such WPPSS explanations could not be documented by the committee, and a WPPSS official later testified that such explanations for cost increases were indeed opinions of management—that WPPSS had never maintained any records of the causes of cost overruns and schedule delays (Washington State Senate Energy and Utilities Committee 1981: 44).

A few observations about the relationship between cost increases and regulatory changes can be made with some certainty. Regulatory changes do not appear to have been a major reason for change orders—the most obvious and immediate cause of construction cost increases. Change orders are adjustments to or modifications of al-

ready awarded contracts. Their main purpose is to compensate contractors for work, in addition to that contracted for, which is necessitated by some change in project scope beyond the contractor's
control. By January of 1976 over 518 change orders had been approved on Project 2 alone, representing a total cost increase of $440
million. And this dollar figure did not even take into account the
associated administrative costs or the fact that top management and
the board of directors were spending much of their time reviewing
and approving change orders. Through 1976 the board approved
every change order over $50,000. In the case of Project 2, this num-
ber represented about 91 percent of the total dollar amount of all
change orders approved through 1976. The excessive amount of time
and attention spent on this problem may have been especially costly
since the board had limited technical expertise and could have more
profitably devoted its time to policy and planning issues.

The report by Theodore Barry, completed in early 1979, found
that detailed, comprehensive studies of the cost and schedule impacts
of change orders had never been undertaken by WPPSS. But the report went on to say that limited research on Projects 1 and 2, conducted by the Supply System itself, indicated that an average of only
7.5 percent of the number of change orders for those two projects
could be attributed to regulatory changes (Theodore Barry & Associates 1979: IV-13). The Theodore Barry report estimated that this
number more accurately represented about 12 percent of the total
cost of change orders. The report urged that studies be initiated immediately to determine the precise causes and impacts of change
orders.

Various Nuclear Regulatory Commission reports and letters to
WPPSS indicate that many of the Supply System's problems were
actually due to repeated violations of the same kind, failure to document whether work completed had been done according to NRC
specifications, delays (of up to eighteen months in one case) in ad-
justing work procedures after being notified that finished work might
not meet standards, and industry building codes that lagged years
behind NRC regulations. In 1980 the NRC noted that it had identified improper pipe support installation eleven times since 1977; failure to maintain component cleanliness, including material left in
pipes, had been identified five times between 1978 and 1980. The
Washington State Senate Energy and Utilities Committee found
that noncompliance with NRC regulations was twice as frequent at

WPPSS Projects 1, 3, 4, and 5 as at two other West Coast plants during the eighteen months prior to July 1980. Noncompliance at Project 2 was found four times as often (Washington State Senate Energy and Utilities Committee 1981: 45).

Other Reasons for Cost Increases. As in the case of labor costs, a large proportion of the change orders and general cost overruns was due to a combination of factors that were not beyond the significant influence of WPPSS management. Of crucial importance was the combination of WPPSS construction contracting and project design procedures. Until the spring of 1977, when WPPSS executives finally lobbied Washington State legislators for a change in the process, construction contracts were generally of the fixed-cost, lump-sum, or hard money variety. This meant that contractors were paid a fixed amount for doing a specific job, the scope of which was defined ahead of time. When costs are accurately predefined, these kinds of contracts usually work to the advantage of the owner. Unforeseen increases (or decreases) in costs are absorbed by the contractor. However, if construction costs increase because of circumstances beyond the contractor's control, the contract can be modified through the submission and approval of a change order. Depending on the exact wording of the contract, these circumstances can include project design changes, interferences that prevent a contractor from carrying out his work, and construction schedule revisions.

Design changes were common on WPPSS projects because of the use of what the construction industry calls fast-track design procedures. Fast track is a fairly common time-saving engineering design practice in which project designs are not fully completed before construction is begun. It is only appropriate, however, under certain conditions and, as one consultant noted, only when at least 60 to 70 percent of the project design is completed before construction contracts are let (Cresap, McCormick and Paget 1976: IV-14). WPPSS construction was initiated at a much earlier stage of design and involved a technology that was constantly changing. WPPSS architect-engineers generally favored what one consultant referred to as a state-of-the-art philosophy that called for continually updated design features for the plants, as the technology evolved. Because incomplete designs were routinely used as a basis for advertising and awarding WPPSS construction contracts, a proliferation of change orders was inevitable.

Another feature of WPPSS contracting procedure combined with fixed-price contracts and fast-track design to virtually ensure an exponential growth in change orders. Another state law required competitive bidding on all contracts over $10,000—an idea long promoted by a depressed regional construction industry. The result of this practice was that forty to sixty-five contractors worked on each project, in contrast to the six to ten on other, similar projects. By the end of 1978 WPPSS had awarded over 440 contracts. As part of a special manpower staffing diagnostic conducted for the Supply System in 1979, Management Analysis Company reported that the large number of contractors was causing chaos at project sites. Scaffolding, cranes, and construction specialty equipment were used inefficiently, and many contractors were simply unable to fulfill contractual commitments (Management Analysis Company 1980: III-2). This confusion led in turn to a flood of change orders.

Because of WPPSS concern to forestall criticism from oversight groups, both formal and informal, for the large number of change orders approved, change orders of all sizes and varieties were subjected to complex administrative processing and review. Members of the WPPSS project teams had little delegated authority to approve even the most minor change orders (Cresap, McCormick and Paget 1976: IV-14). The lengthy process created backlogs and delays. As one contractor submitted a change order, one or more others were often forced to do the same. And administrative delays engendered by the lengthy review of basic design changes by an understaffed engineering department resulted in still more change orders and schedule delays.

The combination of competitive bidding and fixed-price contracting increased the number of change orders in another way—by encouraging low-ball bids by contractors. Because design changes could be expected, contractors had a strong incentive to bid low to win a contract and then submit change orders to raise their fees up to or beyond what they might have been paid under other contracting procedures. It was often impossible to separate the low-ball characteristics of a successful bid from the sources of cost increase beyond the contractor's control. And it only increased costs more to replace a contracting firm that had already started a job, even if low-ball bidding was suspected.

Other Perspectives on WPPSS Costs. In spite of WPPSS claims that its project costs were simply examples of industry trends, two perspectives on the WPPSS cost problem suggest otherwise. The first involves comparisons of WPPSS costs with those of other nuclear power plants still under construction. Extensive research of this kind has been carried out by energy economist Charles Komanoff, who was called on by the Washington State Attorney General to examine WPPSS costs in the spring of 1982. Komanoff concluded that costs per kilowatt for the five WPPSS plants were 42 percent higher than the industry average, after excluding financing costs. In constant dollars, the plants were 81 percent more expensive. Komanoff concluded that WPPSS costs above the industry average "were not primarily attributable to factors that WPPSS considers inherent in nuclear construction costs in Washington State and which WPPSS management contends it was powerless to avoid" (Komanoff 1982: 2).

A second perspective on WPPSS construction cost increases suggests that WPPSS problems were indeed similar to those of other utilities building nuclear power plants in the 1970s but questions why WPPSS continued to build plants and incur costs while many of these other utilities opted instead to cancel or defer construction. Studies by various federal agencies indicate that during the mid-1970s, even before WPPSS began construction on Projects 4 and 5, information was available to the effect that dozens of utilities across the country were already deferring or cancelling nuclear power plant construction.[3]

Finally, between May and November of 1980 the Washington State Senate Energy and Utilities Committee held an inquiry into the cost and schedule problems at WPPSS. Thirteen public hearings were held, and the committee conducted an additional 184 interviews with WPPSS and BPA personnel, representatives of labor, contractors, the architect-engineers, and officials from consulting firms and investment banking organizations. The committee concluded that " . . . WPPSS mismanagement has been the most significant cause of cost overruns and schedule delays on the WPPSS projects" (Washington State Senate Energy and Utilities Committee 1981: 40).

WPPSS Project Management and Cost Control

If the preceding analysis of the major reasons for construction costs increases is correct, then efforts to contain costs should have begun at the policy planning level. In other words, general contracting and design procedures should have been reviewed and possibly changed.

Efforts should have been made to change laws that restricted efforts to contain costs and to carefully identify basic problems by distinguishing them from their operational manifestations, and then plan for their solution.

Substantial savings probably could have been made by more carefully selecting and using a variety of contracting methods. But by the time management began extensively realigning construction contracts in 1978, the overall effect on project costs was much less than it would have been earlier.

It was not until 1980 that WPPSS management undertook changing the state law requiring competitive bidding. Ken Billington, the executive director of the Washington Public Utility Districts Association until 1978, and probably the most influential public power lobbyist in the state (known popularly as "Mr. Public Power"), claims that before 1980 WPPSS managing directors had never even mentioned the problems caused by the competitive bidding law (Connelly 1982).

As late as 1979, as the Theodore Barry report points out, WPPSS had not conducted comprehensive studies of the cost and schedule impacts of change orders. In effect, the Supply System's board and top management could not yet fully explain cost increases even to themselves. In 1980 the Washington State Senate Energy and Utilities Committee found that WPPSS was still making no attempt to monitor the cause of cost overruns and schedule delays.

Instead of confronting the problem of costs at the level of policy, WPPSS top management pursued a strategy consistent with the management style that prevailed at the organization through the 1970s. And if management style was as important and pervasive in the WPPSS organization as seems to have been the case, then the correction of certain specific, individual problems would be difficult without first altering that management style. In fact, even the timely and accurate identification of problems might be difficult.

The earliest reaction of WPPSS top management to the problem of increasing costs was based on its identification of the problem in strictly operational terms. Construction cost increases and schedule delays pointed to the need for closer Supply System supervision of design and construction activities. In 1976 management determined to play a greater role in project design and construction management. There was an obvious need for improvement in this area, but top management acted without recognizing that simply taking tighter control of the projects would solve nothing; it needed to define responsibilities, delegate authority, carefully realign and adjust construction contracting, improve management communications, and concentrate its own efforts on overall planning and policy approaches to the problems. The following subsections define the construction management challenge that WPPSS faced and assess the Supply System's responses to those challenges.

The Construction Management Problem. One way to describe the basic construction problem facing WPPSS is as a failure to adapt WPPSS' methods of managing construction to the needs of the particular design procedures being used on the projects. The manner in which this problem manifested itself on WPPSS construction sites has been discussed by industry experts for some time. The 1970s saw the widespread adoption of the construction management concept in the delivery of construction, especially in cases where design was not finished by the time construction began. A 1973 article in the *Harvard Business Review* noted that the concept of construction management had been applied for many years in a wide variety of situations, and it seemed to produce generally good—sometimes spectacular—results. The authors of the article stated that the concept

> is one of the more exciting and promising developments in the field of facilities construction, and it represents an alternative to traditional procedures of which all potential construction *owners* should have the right to be aware. (Davis and White 1973: 93).

The construction management concept has always been associated with fast-track construction, also sometimes called design-build construction, or phased construction. All of these terms refer to an alternative to the traditional design-then-build approach, which calls for plans and specifications to be completed before field work begins. Builders such as WPPSS, pressured to save time and money, decide not to wait until all design documents are completed before letting bids, and try to integrate actual construction with design. In effect, this fast-track method calls for the phasing of construction with design completion. Although this usually means that construction begins with less than half of the plans and specifications for the entire project completed, the plans and specifications for the work that contractors start on (foundations and site work, for example) should be at least 60 percent complete, according to the Supply

System's own consultants (Cresap, McCormick and Paget 1976: IV-14), or 80 percent according to other experts (Squires and Murphy 1983: 57).

Construction management in the context of this design-build concept refers to more than the routine oversight and coordination of construction by owners, architect-engineers, or general contractors, although any of these can practice construction management. It usually involves the practice of employing a professional management firm that provides clients with a service designed to control and coordinate all phases of construction project development. The decision to hire a professional firm that specializes in construction management is often made when:

1. the complicated nature of fast-track construction requires a high degree of knowledge and skill to provide cost/effective project coordination;

2. neither the owner, the general contractors nor the architect-engineers have the kind of knowledge and skill to manage the project; and/or

3. the owner prefers to have his own representative managing construction—someone who reports directly to the owner, and whose responsibilities involve project management exclusively.[4]

In addition to sophisticated construction management, large and complicated fast-track projects require careful adjustment of construction contract formats, methods, and terms to the style of management, the degree of construction phasing, and the type of construction manager (owner, architect-engineer, or general contractor). For example, if cost-plus construction contracts are used on a project (and contracts very similar to these were used on WPPSS projects after 1979), then the responsibility for covering future cost increases tends to fall heavily on the owner. In this situation, it is especially important for the owner (or someone) to exercise tight overall project coordination and control—to make certain that contractors have every opportunity to perform their work in a cost-effective manner.

WPPSS, faced with the largest and most complicated fast-track construction effort that the nuclear power industry has ever seen, required the most sophisticated approach to construction management available. It made use of a variety of different designs, hundreds of contractors, a state-of-the-art design philosophy that required constant design changes—even after construction was begun—and initial designs and specifications that were less complete than would be normal on many other fast-track projects.

But throughout the 1970s WPPSS projects benefitted from neither the sophisticated project management nor the appropriate contracting procedures required by its fast-track construction process. The overall management style at WPPSS, which ignored the policy dimension of management, dictated against efforts to modify existing state legislation that complicated project management and construction contracting. The WPPSS management style emphasized control instead of management, and top management treated the organization like a small, pre-threshold organization. This attitude frowned upon the delegation of authority necessary for WPPSS to exercise its own project management, as it tried to do throughout most of the 1970s. It also meant that WPPSS top management tended to behave like intuitive managers of small commercial firms, who believe that they have an accurate sense of the condition of their businesses and therefore do not need computerized management information systems. The failure of WPPSS executives to install adequate computerized systems, in spite of repeated recommendations by management consultants throughout the 1970s, all but guaranteed that management would be incapable of carefully monitoring and coordinating construction project activities.

The WPPSS Response—Background. The Supply System's response to construction management can be summed up by saying that through the 1970s, top executives did not fully understand how important it was, how it should be carried out, or who should do it. In 1970, when engineering was begun on Project 2, WPPSS had no project management staff. Design and construction management responsibilities were assumed to be the responsibility of a single architect-engineer (AE), Burns and Roe. However by state law, the status of the AE was that of an independent contractor—it could not act as an agent for WPPSS. Thus WPPSS actually maintained the responsibility for individual construction contracts. And because WPPSS was contemplating only one nuclear plant at that time, the managing director and his assistants could indeed function in a project management capacity.

But as WPPSS took on the responsibilities for the additional four plants, these project management arrangements proved to be seriously inadequate. In compliance with the state law requiring competitive bidding on all WPPSS contracts, different AEs and different designs were used for each of the first three plants. The absence of a centralized project management office with the staff size, expertise, and delegated authority to coordinate design and construction resulted in the loss of economies of scale.

WPPSS did have its own engineering staff, which was supposed to review plant designs in terms of safety, reliability, constructability, and the like and to provide some coordination among the different projects. However, the staff's actual influence on design was minimal. Under the matrix staffing arrangement, engineers were assigned to individual projects while supposedly maintaining their responsibility to report to superiors in the Engineering Department (which was part of the Generation and Technology Division). But the WPPSS engineers had poorly defined responsibilities and little delegated authority. Because of cost-cutting budgeting decisions by top management, the Engineering Department was seriously understaffed. Virtually all of the engineers were assigned project-specific duties, leaving few supervisory personnel to provide coordination or direction. The Cresap report noted in 1976 that as a result of this situation, engineering personnel tended to become "totally absorbed into the project organizations" to which they were assigned (Cresap, McCormick and Paget 1976: III-6).

This absorption afforded little communication of technical experience and information among the projects; in effect, AEs were unable to learn from each othèrs' mistakes. It also complicated the determination of when a design mistake had in fact been made. The WPPSS engineers failed to document any consistent set of design standards that could be used to guide the AEs and against which their work could be reviewed. Moreover, because the AEs functioned informally as construction managers, the identification and correction of serious design errors was not always done in a timely manner. Incredibly, omissions in AE contracts for Plants 1 and 2 left WPPSS with financial responsibility for redesign work needed as a result of AE errors—even if those errors could be identified.

Because of a lack of supervision and coordination, as well as other contract omissions, the cost and schedule information supplied by AEs was often inconsistent and was almost never presented succinctly or in terms that allowed comparison among the different projects. The lack of involvement in project management meant that the

WPPSS construction budget process relied heavily on information supplied by the AEs and contractors.

As noted, because of the requirement for competitive bidding, the number of contracts for each project soared. The effect on project costs due to change orders of forty to sixty-five contractors per project has also been discussed. But competitive bidding was also responsible for awarding contracts to inexperienced contractors and for breaking the continuity and ultimately increasing costs when a reliable contractor lost a bid for a component of a project he had already initiated. WPPSS project managers blamed competitive bidding and multiple contractors for a lack of cooperative spirit on the projects. The large number of contractors posed special problems for the AEs in terms of coordinating access, scheduling work, and so on. The confusion was compounded by the fact that the AEs were somewhat inexperienced with the kind of fixed-price contracts used by WPPSS. As a result, the AEs at each site essentially became unnecessarily large management staffs that duplicated much of the work done by the contractors' non-manual staffs. Above all, the plethora of contractors exacerbated the lack of centralized control on the projects.

Because state law stipulated that AEs not act as agents of WPPSS, their contractual responsibilities were stated primarily in terms of staff functions such as monitoring, recommending, and reviewing. In other words, the AEs were not even contractually responsible for the full range of managerial functions—including those relating to schedules, costs, and quality control—that WPPSS top management had failed to formally delegate to anyone in its own organization.

When WPPSS operated on a relatively small scale, top management could maintain some responsibility for project-related details, or the AE could be expected to handle informally some of the responsibility. Direct but informal lines of communication could exist between AEs and top management. Many of the AE contracts and the project agreements with BPA seem to have been created in an atmosphere that favored informal arrangements. But as the organization grew, information channels had to be formalized, and crucial management responsibilities had to be carefully defined and delegated to offices with the appropriate personnel to carry them out.

If such changes are not made at the proper stages in the growth of an organization, they become much more difficult to implement later. In 1976, after construction on all five nuclear plants was well under way, top management finally began to increase the Supply System's involvement in project management. But it did so in the spirit of taking tighter control of the projects rather than of recognizing the need to carefully establish lower level management positions within WPPSS to which project control could be delegated. By taking more control over the projects, but not delegating some of it, top management again preoccupied itself with the performance of staff functions and precommitted even more of the time and energy that should have been devoted to more generic policy questions about project performance.

The Failure of Integrated Management.   By the time attention began to focus on overall construction management, WPPSS executives found themselves confronted with an overwhelming organizational and staffing problem—the need to develop, virtually out of thin air, an effective project management capability for five nuclear power plant construction projects. WPPSS had neither the personnel nor an existing management information system capable of speedily taking on these new responsibilities.

Because of these formidable obstacles, and because of existing contractual relationships, a kind of compromise arrangement had to be made—integrated management, in which a single WPPSS division-level manager was assigned to each project and given the responsibility for project costs, schedules, and quality. The project managers joined with the AEs to form joint project management teams. Under the team concept contractors still were to receive direction from the AE site manager. The AE's project control staff was to receive administrative direction from the AEs and functional guidance from the WPPSS project management.

However, the steps that were required to turn functional guidance into true construction management were not taken, for reasons evident both to the Cresap consultants in 1976 and the Theodore Barry consultants two years later. Both reports describe the reasons in terms of a failure to recognize the importance of total project management (Cresap), or the systems approach to project management (Theodore Barry). The point was that in order to effectively manage each of the five huge construction projects, it was necessary to view them as microcosms of the entire enterprise. The management of each required a vision of the total project system—a simultaneous awareness of the status of a large, complicated collection of interrelated and interdependent activities. The Cresap report pointed out that decisions about seemingly trivial direct expenditures can have tremendous consequences for scheduling and hence total project cost. For example, a one-day scheduling delay incurred by a lack of personnel to review a design change could increase total project costs by hundreds of thousands of dollars (Cresap, McCormick and Paget 1976: IV-8). The Theodore Barry report noted that without a management approach that appreciates the systematic character of such interrelated activities, "the total project cannot be visualized in sufficient detail to plan, schedule and control" (Theodore Barry & Associates 1979: IV-5). The total or system approach to project control is of course the essence of sophisticated construction management as defined above.

Integrated management was never fully realized at WPPSS. The concentration of WPPSS directors and top management on change orders and other secondary manifestations of deeper problems seriously delayed their full attention to problems associated with project management. This same shortsightedness prevented top management from fully identifying the real problems of project management. Unable to appreciate the systematic character of WPPSS itself, top management failed in a number of crucial ways to make systems management possible at the project level, and this failure resulted, among other things, in the collapse of integrated management.

First and most important, and perfectly in keeping with the WPPSS pre-threshold management tradition, decisionmaking authority was not adequately delegated to WPPSS project managers. Delegation was a necessary requirement of the systems approach at WPPSS because top management simply did not have the time or the perspective to monitor and control adequately all of the interrelated project components. But delegation was not implemented because of a lack of clarification of project roles, responsibilities, and departmental relationships prior to project management integration. Even when Theodore Barry consultants came on the scene two years after the integration process had been started, this clarification had not been made. Theodore Barry personnel found that flowcharts describing document flows were incomplete and that organization charts had not been issued at some sites (Theodore Barry & Associates 1979: V-35). Because WPPSS project managers could not effectively make or enforce many project decisions, most of the work continued under the complete direction of the AEs and contractors.

Another problem was the fact that integration was not even contemplated in some areas crucial to a total project management approach. WPPSS project managers could not provide functional guidance in the areas of work-force management and materials procurement and management. Centralized project control over the latter was especially crucial since the availability of material resources is an obvious necessity for effective scheduling and coordination of construction activities. And as late as 1979 many of the activities normally associated with materials management simply were not done at some WPPSS sites (Theodore Barry & Associates 1979: VII-28).

Underlying all of the other requirements for an effective total management approach to project control is the need for computer-based monitoring of schedule and cost factors. Project managers need it to maintain visibility over all aspects of a project, and top management needs it to monitor the performance of project managers. If decisionmaking authority is not delegated to project managers, top management has more direct responsibility for project control, and thus a greater need for such a system.

As part of the project management integration, WPPSS acquired a computerized information system developed by the Tennessee Valley Authority (TVA) and augmented it with parts of a system developed by Kaiser engineers. But WPPSS had difficulties using the system in project management. Vast quantities of data were produced, but neither project management personnel nor top management learned to summarize and use the information effectively for decisionmaking purposes. Theodore Barry consultants found user manuals incomplete and employee training minimal. They found summary-level reporting to be fragmented and informal, and they discovered most of the data produced by both computerized and manual systems filed away at the project sites rather than summarized and reported to upper levels of management.

The Cresap report noted in 1976 that WPPSS top management had not begun delegating authority to its project managers because the project information system was not yet capable of providing adequate visibility over the managers' performance. Apparently, top management did not comprehend the seriousness of the need to fully implement and use the system so that delegation could proceed. In 1976, well after system implementation had begun, WPPSS top management had not yet established a formal review group to set priorities for and evaluate the results of project systems development by the Data Systems Office (Cresap, McCormick and Paget 1976: III-15, 16). The Cresap report clearly stated the nature of the situation and the risks involved:

> Management information flows and reports on the progress of major contracts are not sufficient to generate confidence that an ineffective use of authority would be identified and the specific manager held accountable. Nevertheless, the inadequacy of delegation is costly and only reinforces the need to proceed rapidly with full installation of the automated project control system (Cresap, McCormick and Paget 1976: III-10).

As the Theodore Barry report attests, both the project control system and the consolidation of project management were in disarray by 1978. And ironically, in its efforts to control costs by increasing control over the projects, WPPSS management had succeeded only in increasing costs. The Theodore Barry consultants found that project management costs had continued increasing at a higher rate than other construction costs.

> Such increases have resulted primarily from the increase in WPPSS staff without any decrease in the A/E staff. This is contrary to the expected benefits resulting from the consolidation of A/E-CM [Architect/Engineer-Construction Manager] and WPPSS organizations at the WNP projects. With increased involvement in project management, a reduction in A/E-CM efforts should have been expected (Theodore Barry & Associates 1979: V-7).

Beginning in 1978 and continuing into 1979, WPPSS extended integrated management to all five projects in spite of the warnings and questions posed by Theodore Barry, growing AE protests, and a May 1978 report by Coopers and Lybrand (p. XI) that recommended the immediate definition of the roles and responsibilities of AEs and WPPSS personnel at each project site. However, WPPSS project managers continued to have little formal authority to make decisions and remained subject to an array of bureaucratic controls. Under these conditions, the attempt to extend integrated management simply engendered further interference with project management as it was actually being carried out (albeit haphazardly) by the AEs. Not only were all aspects of project administration confused and slowed, but the accountability and responsibility of the AEs was further diluted.

Construction Contracting and Construction Management. The selection of appropriate contract formats, methods, and terms is crucial to fast-track construction. A series of inappropriate contract formats used on the WPPSS projects only exacerbated the kinds of problems described above.

Construction contracts, especially those related to fast-track projects, are shining examples of the art of risk allocation and avoidance that is at the heart of every contract negotiation and drafting process. Ideally, these contracts allocate both foreseeable and unforeseeable risks between the parties. Because fast-track construction is essentially a cooperative process, it is important for the contracts involved to encourage the flow of information up and down the contractual chain and to help ensure that the contracting parties are free of constant pressure to protect themselves against liability.

Fast-track construction involves a great deal of risk for the following reasons:

1. Litigation between owner and contractor is fairly common over the issue of whether finally completed designs and specifications represent a change in scope from preliminary drawings, or simply completion of the originals.

2. Work scheduling problems are much more common on fast-track projects and lead to many more cases of litigation concerning damages for delay.

3. A contractor may perform work not specifically outlined in the preliminary designs. The question then arises of whether or not such work was actually needed or authorized by the owner.

4. A similar problem arises when a contractor believes that an item of work was, or should be, completed by another contractor (Squires and Murphy 1983: 58–59).

Issues such as these can create severe problems for owners and contractors involved in fast-track construction. In cases where construction management is not adequate, where coordination and quality control are substandard, those problems can become nightmares. Construction contracts should be carefully drafted to form a legal foundation for coordination and quality control by explicitly detailing the roles and responsibilities of the various parties. Then should problems arise and parties turn to litigation, the contracts bear the full weight of the problem resolution process. Even in cases where construction management is adequate, if the contracts do not clearly identify who is in charge in various situations, then persistent problems with project chains of command result. Of course, owners, AEs, and other potential participants in the construction process, such as construction managers and general contractors, must come to mutual agreement about their respective roles in project management. Those roles must be carried out in practice if construction contracts are to delineate adequately chains of command. Unfortunately, that was not done on the WPPSS projects until after 1980; at no time during the 1970s was construction contracting carefully integrated into the construction management process.

As we have already noted, WPPSS contracting procedures were determined by Washington State laws, but WPPSS officials possessed the influence necessary to get those laws changed. In 1977 WPPSS officials finally lobbied to have the Washington State legislature amend the organization's construction contracting procedures. Because of the large number of contractors working at each site and the constant flow of change orders resulting from the fast-track construction process, the lump-sum contracts used to that time seemed exceptionally hard to manage. Part of the problem, of course, was the fact that construction management in general had been inadequate. Another problem was that the contracting method used was better suited to a fully designed, firm-price job—a common problem in fast-track construction (Squires and Murphy 1983: 62).

As noted above in the discussion of cost increases, lump-sum contracts required contractors to do a designated job for a specific amount of money (a lump sum). The job is described ahead of time, and any increases in cost are the responsibility of the contractor, unless they result from design changes or other factors outside the control of the contractor. Given the Supply System's design and construction management procedures (or lack of them), an enormous number of change orders were generated by this contracting method. Many large, reputable construction firms were unwilling even to bid for these jobs because of the high stakes involved—either the contractor had to complete the work at or below designated cost or he had to be willing and able to spend the time and effort necessary to prove that cost increases were not his fault.

When WPPSS executives finally decided to have the contracting procedures changed, they did so without effectively distinguishing the underlying causes of the construction problem from its manifestations. Construction management was the underlying problem. It led to excessive design changes, poor work coordination, and poor quality control. Lump-sum contracts were inappropriate for fast-track work, but they were not the sole or even the primary reasons for change orders and cost increases.

This became evident to everyone upon the failure of the next contractual format based on a target man-hour concept. Here, contractors included the total number of man-hours that they estimated would be necessary for the job. Contractor performance was then measured against this target, and the contractor was rewarded with incentive fees for reducing this man-hour total. WPPSS executives thought they could allay cost increases by encouraging contractors to hold down the number of man-hours expended on specific jobs.

As the AEs pointed out, this format would unwittingly give contractors a different incentive to increase costs. In order to complete jobs under the man-hour targets, contractors could simply reduce the number (and quality) of personnel working. Each contract also involved work schedules, but most of these could not be met anyway because of poor construction management by WPPSS. In other words, change orders proliferated under the old lump-sum format not just because of inept or unscrupulous contractors. Target man-hour contracts did not solve the change order problem—change orders continued to be necessary. As pointed out by the Washington State Senate Energy and Utilities Committee, " . . . in almost every instance, the contractors had valid, well-documented claims demonstrating that WPPSS' failure to perform its contractual obligations made it impossible for the contractors to perform on schedule" (1981: 28).

The target man-hour contract format simply exposed another facet of the underlying problem—poor construction management. By late 1979, after completing the revision of all construction contracts for the five projects to the target man-hour format, WPPSS executives realized they would have to change again. This time they chose another format that would maximize their own risk in terms of future cost increases, in exchange for the unquestioned right to direct the contractor's work. These were unit-price-level-of-effort-plus-fixed-fee contracts. As the Washington State Senate Energy and Utilities Committee later pointed out, these contracts were almost indistinguishable from cost-plus contracts, under which the contractor receives the basic cost of the job (whatever that might turn out to be) plus a fee.

The adoption of this format in 1979 coincided with the extension of the integrated construction management technique to all five project sites. Both techniques represented an effort by the Supply System to increase its control of the projects. Of course, both integrated management and the unit-price-fixed-fee contract format required that WPPSS be capable of effective and comprehensive construction management. This might have been possible if WPPSS top executives had been willing to delegate decisionmaking authority to project-level personnel, if the organization had an effective computerized management information system (which had been urged on WPPSS by six different management consulting firms between 1978 and 1980), or if it had a project monitoring system that interrelated costs and schedules, a basic component of any large construction management effort. Without these techniques and tools, and appropriate experience using them, WPPSS should have considered either returning project management responsibilities to the AEs and holding the AEs fully responsible for carrying out those tasks, or hiring a professional construction management firm.

WPPSS did neither. According to a Washington State Senate investigation in 1981, integrated management negatively affected "all aspects of project administration and, therefore, construction" (Washington State Senate Energy and Utilities Committee 1981: 34). This in turn meant that the unit-price-fixed-fee contract format exposed the Supply System to risks of construction cost increases that the organization had no way of controlling. As the Supply System's own administrative auditor pointed out, "Contractors obviously appreciate the removal of risks from their operations" (Washington State Senate Energy and Utilities Committee 1981: 28). The Supply System's willingness to take over contractor risk is evidenced by its payments to contractors during labor disputes. The contracts were designed to pay overhead and profits in regular monthly installments. During labor strikes, contractors continued to receive these payments and could submit change orders later to extend their contract completion dates. But since WPPSS had never been fully involved in dealings with labor, the contractors were also the ones negotiating with striking workers. The results of this arrangement, formalized in contracts designed to give WPPSS control over contractors, were higher profits and overhead payments to contractors and a distinct lack of incentive for contractors to reach early settlements in labor disputes.

A New Managing Director and a New Management Style

In February 1980 the WPPSS board dismissed Managing Director Neil Strand. On August 1, 1980, after a six-month search, the board hired Robert Ferguson—the "no-nonsense manager." He was a veteran of the nuclear power industry, having spent five years as director of the Department of Energy's test reactor at Hanford, and two years as Deputy Assistant Secretary of Energy for nuclear reactor programs. Ferguson was the first managing director in WPPSS history who had not previously worked with the Supply System in some close capacity. His salary, unlike those of his predecessors, was close to the industry standard for an experienced managing director, about $125,000.

Ferguson found problem after problem awaiting his attention. By the time of his appointment WPPSS had signed from forty-five to sixty-five construction contracts for each of its plants and used a change order system that would have had difficulty passing a professional audit, according to a team of management experts (Boeing Engineering and Construction Company 1979). Later in August Ferguson was confronted by a report from the administrative auditor, recommending that integrated management be ended and that the AEs again be given responsibility for the projects and held accountable for their performance. On August 15 he received a memorandum from his assistant director for projects, admitting that "The existing computerized scheduling and cost systems are inadequate. . . . Our project control system has been put together piecemeal and is not designed in relation to minimum essential requirements for effective project management (Washington State Senate Energy and Utilities Committee 1981: 36).

Ferguson's response to these problems indicated a management style appropriate to the requirements of an organization of size and complexity of WPPSS. He began by admitting that integrated management was probably a mistake, and he appointed an engineering task force to conduct a comprehensive evaluation of construction management and make recommendations for improvement. One of the most important recommendations that Ferguson carried out was the termination, in January 1981, of the Supply System's participation in joint construction management. Bechtel Power Corporation, the giant of the nuclear power plant construction industry and probably the world's leading construction management firm, was hired to provide construction management services for Projects 1, 2, and 4. Bechtel also assumed responsibilities for labor relations. EBASCO Services entered into a new contract with the Supply System to take over independent engineering and construction management at Projects 3 and 5. Thus, Ferguson addressed the problem of construction management at WPPSS with an understanding of the available options and the reasons for using each.

Other task force recommendations that were substantially followed include the clarification of the project responsibilities of WPPSS project personnel, AEs, and construction managers; the delegation of more authority to lower level WPPSS managers; and substantial contract realignments. Ferguson also successfully lobbied the state legislature to change the competitive bidding law and insisted on no-strike site agreements with labor unions working on Projects 1, 2, and 3.

Admitting that the WPPSS change order process was a "nightmare" (Washington State Senate Energy and Utilities Committee 1981: 40), Ferguson began simplifying procedures. His first move was to disregard the traditionally conservative interpretation of state laws that the Supply System had used to justify its overly complicated contracting and change order approval processes. As the Washington State Senate Energy and Utilities Committee noted at about the same time, "There is no state law which requires the change management procedures which WPPSS chose to adopt" (1981: 39).

Most important, Ferguson initiated a complete review of total project costs. This was a policy planning method that had not been used at WPPSS since the earliest cost estimates. It was very different from the traditional Supply System practice of simply computing total costs by adding recent individual cost increases to previous, often outdated estimates. Ferguson's totals led to a reassessment of the need for all five plants and the eventual termination of Projects 4 and 5.

THE WPPSS MANAGEMENT VACUUM—WHY?

Consultants' reports and other documents provide some of the details of how WPPSS management shortcomings contributed to project cost increases and schedule delays. The question of why all of this happened, however, is an entirely different matter—consulting reports do not speculate about motivation. It does seem clear in retrospect that at least two factors played significant roles in the paralysis of WPPSS management. One was the fact that WPPSS was a public authority; the other has to do with the complex origins of the unique management style possessed by WPPSS board members and top managers.

The Public Authority Device

WPPSS is a public authority or municipal corporation, one of the corporate subsidiaries of state and local government that now number over 8000 in the United States. Such entities are given special legal and administrative independence so that they can function outside of the regular executive structure of state or municipal government. Defenders of the concept argue that this independence and flexibility is required for government to act in a businesslike fashion to finance, construct, and often operate revenue-producing public enterprises—usually thought of as the most businesslike of all government activities. But over the last decade it has become fashionable to argue that public authorities tend to be governmental bodies out of control.[5] Some political observers charge that off-budget enterprises "subvert the wishes of the electorate whenever the voters express a demand for fiscal restraint by local political decision-makers . . . " (Bennett and DiLorenzo 1982: 14).[6]

Beginning in the late 1970s, the popular press found the activities of public authorities to be perfect subjects for investigative reporting.[7] Sometimes real corruption was uncovered. More often the press found someone who claimed that authority activities were not in the public interest and out of control. Robert Caro's best-selling biography of public authority empire-builder Robert Moses, *The Power Broker*, dramatically spelled out for the general public the potential for abuse in these organizations.

States such as New York and New Jersey are now investigating ways to make public authorities more accountable to elected officials, and the federal government has also considered recommendations to control more carefully its governmental corporations. Even British government officials are concerned with their equivalent of public authorities. In 1979 the Thatcher government took extensive action to control British quangos, quasi non-governmental organizations.

Although the Supply System's problems have been different from those usually associated with public authorities, WPPSS was indeed out of control, but that characterization is usually applied to authorities that are not under outside control. There is typically very little public participation of any kind in the decisionmaking processes of public authorities, and elected officials as well as community groups often become frustrated with what they see as a lack of accountability or responsiveness. In other words, "out of control" in this sense means too much control in the hands of too few. WPPSS, on the other hand, was truly beyond the control of any one group or individual, including its own management, its board, the project participants, Washington State, BPA, and ratepayers.

Part of the difference between WPPSS and other authorities stems from the attitudes, beliefs and, values behind their creation and operation. Other authorities had ideological underpinnings that facilitated the assumption and exercise of power by individuals within the organizational structure. WPPSS did not.

When the Port Authority of New York and New Jersey became the nation's first modern authority in 1921, the ideological impulse behind it was an odd and sometimes contradictory combination of views with roots in the Progressive reform movement and a renewal of faith in laissez-faire capitalism.[8] The Progressive movement, powerful in the United States during the first two decades of this century, promoted such views as the rationality and perfectibility of human nature, the viability of direct, participatory democracy, and the need to weed corruption out of business and government.

During roughly the same period, the corporate successes of American business fueled new appreciation for what were considered the virtues of American business leadership. What the Progressives and the lionizers of big business had in common was their contempt for the kind of corruption that muckraking journalists frequently identified with professional politicians during those years. The Port Authority was conceived and created by the New York Chamber of

Commerce, and politicians were carefully excluded from the PA's operation in favor of the businesslike management considered necessary to accomplish large jobs quickly and efficiently. Businesslike management was promoted by granting the Port Authority freedom from politics and normal governmental regulations. The PA's board of commissioners was and is to this day made up predominantly of businesspeople appointed by the governors of the two states.

This anti-politics, pro-business theme became dominant in the folklore of the U.S. public authority. The Progressives' distrust of big business faded quickly, as did their faith in direct democracy and the perfectibility of man. The great expansion of governmental corporations at the federal level during the period of the New Deal and war helped to preserve the theme and protect it against the great business failures of the Depression. FDR's administration promoted public authorities at the state and local level and used the Port Authority of New York and New Jersey as a model for government corporations at the federal level.

For the sake of businesslike speed and flexibility, public authorities have generally been designed as concentrations of the kind of public power that is usually distributed among elected officials and checked and balanced throughout a state or city government. In a public authority a very few hands typically control planning, financing, management—in short, all decisionmaking. The president, managing director, or chief executive, as he or she is variously titled, naturally becomes the most important person in such organizations. This figure resembles a corporate president of a private sector firm, but because of the characteristics of the typical public authority board of directors, a president or managing director can—and often must—be even more responsible for the direction of his organization than his or her private sector counterpart.

Most public authority boards do not manage or oversee their enterprises to a great extent. They are usually part-time and poorly informed entities. The fact that their members are usually appointed for fixed terms and are not responsible to stockholders relieves them of much of the pressure to perform that private sector directors must bear. Public authority boards rarely carry out planning functions and usually approve programs and policies formulated by the top management and the management staff. Dissident board members—those who come to the board critical of existing policies or determined to spur tighter board control over the organization—are easily socialized in the ways and attitudes of the existing board. In many of the largest and most successful authorities, board members use their often considerable power and influence in the political and financial communities to support the policies formulated by the managing directors and their staffs. In this sense, public authority boards enhance rather than check or oversee the power of top management. The result is a further concentration of public power. It is not surprising that arrogant and talented public authority leaders such as Moses can carve out for themselves immense empires of power and influence.

No one ever accused Moses of not doing anything he set out to do. Of course, he did not always end up doing what was in the minds of those who wrote and approved the enabling legislation for his authorities, and his projects were often not the most efficient in terms of financial or social cost. But his record is one of vast accomplishment.

Moses was able to step into a kind of power vacuum that organizational realities make possible in public authorities. No one outside such an organization has real control over a public authority. The board of directors lacks the time, the resources, and the interest to control the organization, but it is usually willing and capable of hiring a managing director who has the kind of executive experience with which most of the members are familiar and comfortable. An enterprising manager, operating like the chief executive of a private sector corporation, can transform his or her limited formal authority into extensive power simply by taking advantage of the situation and by exploiting the kinds of informal influence that charismatic and politically minded individuals such as Moses, and so many other authority managers, have an instinct for finding.

Origins of WPPSS Management Style

WPPSS was an organization with the concentrated power and the vast potential for accomplishment or failure of a typical public authority. But WPPSS leadership was never equipped with the managerial and political skills necessary to exploit this power. This was partly because the managerial values, beliefs, and habits—the managerial style—of the organization's leaders helped to preclude the assumption and effective exercise of that power. The discussion in the first part of this chapter describes *how* management style contributed to the problems of WPPSS; a look at the origins of that style in a corporate culture specific to the public power industry in the Pacific Northwest will shed some light on *why*.

As a public authority, WPPSS drew its ideological underpinnings more directly from ideals like those embraced by the Progressives than from faith in business management and laissez-faire capitalism. In many respects the joint-action agency legislation in Washington State was explicitly based on legislation that had set up the state's public utility districts. Nineteen of the twenty-three members of WPPSS were PUDs. By the same token, nineteen of the twenty-three WPPSS board members were representatives of PUDs. Until 1977 the managing directors of WPPSS had been former PUD managers. The frame of mind that created and managed PUDs was always strongly in evidence at WPPSS.

That frame of mind, however, was not necessarily conducive to effective management. The PUDs were the products of an agrarian reform movement in Washington State during the late 1920s. As such, they brought together their own variety of sometimes conflicting ideologies. Progressivism was an urban-based reform movement that drew much of its strength from a widespread popular reaction against the changes brought on by industrialization. What the Progressives and agrarian reformers had in common was an antipathy toward large corporations, railroads, and all of the other Eastern bankers and business executives that they considered as dangerous to the interests of the common man as any corrupt politician. Farmers' alliances, formed in the 1880s during the height of the Populist era, fought for currency reforms that were expected to protect farmers from the greed of bankers and industrialists.

In the first two decades of this century, the Progressives and agrarian reformers fought side by side, first to regulate private, investor-owned utilities, then to place the sale of electric power under public control. By 1920 financial conglomerates controlled many of the investor-owned electric companies across the nation. These holding companies set their own rates, usually with more concern for the interest of stockholders than for ratepayers. The alternatives to these private businesses were the municipal power agencies and the public utility districts (or public power districts, or people's utility districts). These were typically countywide taxing districts that were allowed to generate and/or distribute electricity in cases where local municipalities were too small or lacked legal power to provide power to people outside city limits. Farmers who needed abundant power for irrigation and flood control often fought with private companies over rates and extension policies.

The PUDs in Washington State were created before 1933, when such districts across the country typically began to fall more directly under the supervision of the parent states. The PUDs were created at a time of renewed faith in participatory democracy. They were provided with sweeping powers to tax, to issue debt, and to set electric rates. It was thought that there was no need to protect people from enterprises that were created and operated by democratically elected representatives of those same people.

This frame of mind, which mixed ideas from the Progressives, agrarian reformers, and other sources, never became a systematic philosophy, and the identification of it with specific names like Progressivism and populism was quickly lost. But it has been as powerful and enduring as the slightly different set of attitudes used to help rationalize and organize most of the nation's other public authorities. In fact, it always existed to some degree in the PUDs and their creation, WPPSS.

What we have referred to as a frame of mind is an example of what organization theorists and management consultants call corporate culture—the amalgam of beliefs, values, and even mythology that helps define a person's relationship with the organization that employs him or her and often, that person's own management style. Corporate culture is more extensive than the managerial attitudes, values, and habits that make up managerial style. Corporate culture, in so far as it affects middle- and lower level employees, is perpetuated largely by the organization itself, through its everyday routines, as well as through the personalities and actions of its chief operating officers. An organization's corporate culture can have profound influence on the firm's productivity and may take years or even decades to change. If change occurs, it is usually carried out by a leader in the organization who creates a new management style that successfully revises existing myths, values, and rituals. Of course, today the manipulation of corporate culture has become a conscious aim of management in many corporations, involving everything from extensive revisions in corporate management, personnel, and marketing policies to office parties and company songs.

In the successes of the most powerful and profitable public authorities, especially those led by legendary figures such as Robert Moses and Austin Tobin, corporate culture usually plays a very tangible and significant role. In fact, those charismatic power brokers themselves often defined distinct corporate cultures that helped them to justify their control of internal organizational affairs and manipulation of relationships with their external environments. In these cases, the general nature of the culture, particularly its pro-business elements, greatly assisted the organization's leader in gaining and keeping power and influence. But just as important is the fact that men like Moses and Tobin recognized the value of these ideas and were willing to manipulate them to serve the interests of their organization—even if at the public interest's expense.

The situation at WPPSS was quite different. The reigning corporate culture, inherited from the PUDs, was counterproductive to the effective accumulation and use of power. It was also a set of values and attitudes that was taken quite seriously, at least by the WPPSS board.

The frame of mind developed by association with the PUDs was anti-political and anti-big business as well. Public power was supposed to be a truly public enterprise. There was no need for politicians or big businesspeople to tell people of normal human intelligence and common decency what to do, or how to do it. The public authority device, with its broad freedoms from outside governmental control, was the perfect organizational vehicle for these people.

Moreover, these were honorable people, who would live up to their commitments and pay their debts. There was no need, for example, to detail legally the oversight responsibilities of BPA when everyone involved was honest and fair and committed to finishing the projects as quickly and efficiently as possible. There was no need to impose excessive discipline on the participating utilities—interest costs and all other costs could be capitalized without fear that a significant number of participants would refuse to pay what would ultimately be a huge debt. There was no need to name one utility as WPPSS manager—all of the member utilities would select a managing director and set management policies. Normal, reasonable people could quickly and easily come to agreement on such matters.

The WPPSS directors did not want to hire a proven executive to manage WPPSS. Such executives combine the qualities of politicians and big business executives. Until 1980 the board selected managing directors with whom it was familiar and comfortable. Until 1977 former PUD managers were hired for the job. From 1977 to 1980 the job was held by a long-time WPPSS employee who had worked his way up through the organization.

In addition to the fact that they were familiar faces, these managing directors were especially appropriate, from the board's point of view, in that they all had engineering backgrounds. They were straight-talking, honest "doers," not merely "talkers"; their accomplishments could be measured in terms of specific, existing projects. These managing directors were control oriented. They made rules and expected all to follow them. They, rather than managers, directed management and made decisions without negotiation or other kinds of interference. This approach to management was familiar to the board members, who considered it rational and orderly.

With the recognition of the importance of informal organization structures (what later became known as corporate culture) in the 1940s, the rigid, scientific approach to public management began to lose its credibility. Even though this approach was a distinct and, as we have seen in the case of WPPSS, highly inappropriate management style, the WPPSS managing directors were simply unaware that there were other, equally rational, and more appropriate styles. They had no appreciation of what corporate culture was or of its role in their organization. Ironically, the board of directors must have instinctively recognized this ignorance as proof of the appropriateness of these men for the job. It ensured that these managing directors would not play politics, would not use the informal tools available to them to usurp power that was not formally theirs. As makers and followers of specific rules, these managing directors would spend less time with policies and rationales. They would also be unable to fill the cavernous leadership void that existed at WPPSS.

If the board were prepared and capable of exercising leadership, these kinds of managing directors would have made appropriate employees. But the limits on the time and interest of WPPSS board members severely restricted the board's ability to exercise real control over the organization.

NOTES TO CHAPTER 2

1. An additional control over some WPPSS activities was exercised by participant committees established for both net-billed and take-or-pay projects. These committees had the responsibility to approve Supply System budgets, but not until the late 1970s did they do more than follow the lead of the WPPSS board. This was especially true of the Participants' Review Board for Projects 1, 2, and 3, the membership of which was not restricted to participants without representation on the board.

2. See William R. Boulton, "The Evolving Board: A Look at the Board's Changing Roles and Information Needs," *Academy of Management Review* 3 (1978): 827-36.
3. See, for example, U.S. Department of Energy, *Nuclear Plant Cancellations: Causes, Costs and Consequences* (Washington, D.C.: U.S. Government Printing Office, April 1983).
4. See Richard D. Conner, "Contracting for Construction Management Services," *Law and Contemporary Problems* 46 (1983): 5-23.
5. See, for example, New York State Assembly Committee on Corporations, Authorities and Commissions, *Agency Out of Control: A Critical Assessment of the Finances and Mission of the Port Authority of New York and New Jersey* (Albany, New York: New York State Assembly Committee on Corporations, Authorities and Commissions, June 1982).
6. For a more extensive presentation of the authors' argument, see James T. Bennett and Thomas J. DiLorenzo, *Underground Government: The Off-Budget Public Sector* (Washington, D.C.: Cato Institute, 1983).
7. For a more extensive discussion of journalistic investigation of public authorities see Diana Henriques, *The Machinery of Greed: The Abuse of Public Authorities and What to Do About It* (Princeton: Princeton University Press, 1982).
8. This discussion of the history of government corporations in the United States follows the account in Annmarie H. Walsh, *The Public's Business: The Politics and Practices of Government Corporations* (Cambridge, Mass.: The MIT Press, 1978).

REFERENCES

Anderson, D. Victor. 1985. *Illusions of Power*. New York: Praeger.

Bennett, James T., and Thomas J. DeLorenzo. 1982. "How the Government Evades Taxes." *Policy Review* 19 (Winter): 71-89.

Bennett, R.R., and D.J. Kettler. 1978. *Dramatic Changes in the Costs of Nuclear and Fossil-fueled Plants*. New York: EBASCO Services, Inc.

Boeing Engineering and Construction Company. 1979. *Boeing Engineering and Construction Company Presentation to the WPPSS Board of Directors*. Seattle: Boeing Engineering and Construction Company. November 2.

Caro, Robert. 1975. *The Power Broker: Robert Moses and the Fall of New York*. New York: Random House.

Clifford, Donald K. 1973. *Managing the Threshold Company*. New York: McKinsey & Co.

Connelly, Joel. 1982. "'Mr. Public Power' Blames the Experts." *Seattle Post-Intelligencer*. March 28, D7.

Coopers and Lybrand. 1978. *Review of Contract Administration and Project Accounting*. Report submitted to F.D. McElwee, Assistant Director of Projects, Washington Public Power Supply System. New York: Coopers and Lybrand. May 17.

Cresap, McCormick and Paget Inc. 1976. *Study of Management Organization and Related Issues, Washington Public Power Supply System*. Report submitted to the WPPSS Executive Committee. San Francisco: Cresap, McCormick and Paget Inc. August.

Davis, Edward W., and Lindsay White. 1973. "How to Avoid Construction Headaches." *Harvard Business Review* 2 (March/April): 87–93.

Institute of Public Administration. 1979. *Survey of WPPSS Board*. Report to the Washington Public Power Supply System Board of Directors, Committee on Management Consultant. New York: Institute of Public Administration. July.

Komanoff, Charles. 1982. *WPPSS Costs Versus the Industry Norm*. Report to the Washington State Attorney General. New York: Komanoff Energy Associates. June.

Landau, Martin, and Russell Stout. 1979. "To Manage is Not to Control: Or the Folly of Type II Errors." *Public Administration Review* 39 (March/April): 148–56.

Management Analysis Company. 1980. Manpower Staffing Diagnostic of Projects WNP-2, WNP-1/4, and WNP-3/5. Report submitted to N.O. Strand, Managing Director of WPPSS. San Diego: Management Analysis Company. January.

Peach, J. Dexter. 1979. Letter from the director of the U.S. General Accounting Office to U.S. Representative James H. Weaver, accompanying U.S. GAO report, *Analysis of Estimated Cost for Three Pacific Northwest Nuclear Power Plants* (Washington, D.C.: U.S. Government Printing Office, July 30, 1979), July 30.

Squires, William R., and Michael Murphy. 1983. "The Impact of Fast Track Construction Management on Subcontractors." *Law and Contemporary Problems* 46 (Winter): 55-67.

Theodore Barry & Associates. 1979. *Management Study of the Roles and Relationships of Bonneville Power Administration and Washington Public Power Supply System*. Report submitted to Bonneville Power Administration. Los Angeles: Theodore Barry & Associates. January.

Vann, Harold E. 1978. *Performance Evaluation and Recommendations for Improving Future Performance on WNP-1/WNP-4*. Philadelphia: United Engineers and Constructors. August 25.

Washington Public Power Supply System. 1979. *Supply System Projects: Questions and Answers*. Richland, Wash.: Washington Public Power Supply System. February.

_____. 1980a. "Minutes of the WPPSS Regular Executive Committee Meeting." Richland, Wash.: Washington Public Power Supply System. June 27.

_____. 1980b. *Report on Implementation Status of Consultant Recommendations—Part I.* Report of the Office of Administrative Auditor. Richland, Wash.: Washington Public Power Supply System. August 8.

Washington State Senate Energy and Utilities Committee. 1981. *Causes of Cost Overruns and Schedule Delays on the Five WPPSS Nuclear Power Plants.* Volume I. Report to the Washington State Senate and the 47th Legislature. Olympia, Wash.: Washington State Senate Energy and Utilities Committee. January 12.

3 THE INVESTMENT COMMUNITY

Members of the investment community—Wall Street underwriters, dealers, institutional investors, rating firms, and bond attorneys— have played major roles in the WPPSS drama. For that reason they comprise another of the concentric circles of power and influence that surround WPPSS. But unlike the case with some of the other actors, both what the investment community actually did and what it should have done with regard to the Supply System's problems are still unclear to many observers.

The municipal bond market is a loosely organized system for issuing and selling short- and long-term securities of state and municipal agencies of all types.[1] As a method for supplying a major part of government capital expenditure resources, it is unique to the United States. The securities are in effect IOUs of cities, counties, towns, school districts, and government corporations. The interest on these securities that is paid each year to the bondholders is exempt from federal income taxes. Hence, the municipal bond market is also referred to as the tax-exempt market. The system allows public enterprise—like private business—to build now and pay later, over the life of the facilities constructed. Because the interest paid to borrowers is free of income taxes, the interest costs of the borrowing are usually lower than interest costs of corporate and federal borrowing. This is the major appeal of using municipal bonds to finance projects with high capital costs. Such financing was one distinct advantage that

WPPSS enjoyed in its competition with investor-owned utility construction consortia.

The tax-exempt market is not a fixed place or fixed activity. It includes issuers, bondholders, underwriters, fund managers, bond attorneys, and advisory services throughout the nation who are engaged in promoting, buying, selling, advising on, rating, and designing municipal bonds and notes amounting to some $50 billion annually. From the nineteenth century through the 1950s, most issuers of municipal bonds were general governments, and the security behind their bonds was their tax base and general obligation to pay interest specified in the bond certificates and to pay back capital at redemption dates.

Beginning in the 1960s the use of revenue bonds began to grow rapidly, accounting for 50 percent of all tax exempt bonds by 1975 and 73 percent by 1983. (*The Bond Buyer's Municipal Statbook 1984*: 1985). These kinds of securities are usually issued by separate public enterprises or authorities, and the security behind them is an explicit stream of revenues identified in the bond resolution and offering. Pledged revenues often include specific government subsidies or rent payments to the public corporation issuing the bond, but governments are not legally obligated to pay the debt from tax resources not earmarked in the offering. Revenue bond repayment usually depends heavily on contemplated operating revenues of the project to be built—tolls from roads and bridges; mortgage payments from housing developments; or, in the case of WPPSS, revenues from the sale of electricity when and if the plants are completed, fully tested, and operating. With the shift from general obligation bonds to revenue bonds, real credit quality hinges on the economic feasibility of the enterprise and of each individual project rather than on the full faith, credit, and tax base of governments. This is one fact, among many others, that bond analysts must take into account when researching the creditworthiness of bonds.

Bond attorneys and financial advisers devise special arrangements to strengthen the security behind revenue bonds and thereby make them more attractive to the investors to whom the bonds will be sold by underwriters. A syndicate of underwriting firms usually buys the entire bond issue from the public enterprise at a negotiated price or by competitive bid. The members of the syndicate then attempt to sell the bonds to the public at a higher price, and the difference, or spread, supplies profits to the underwriting firms. WPPSS and the utilities participating in its projects, like other public agencies, depend heavily on the advice of a relatively limited number of national bond attorney firms and investment advisory and underwriting firms both to establish their credit and to design the security arrangements behind their bond issues. The ultimate buyers of the bonds also depend on the opinions and representations of these firms.

Each bond resolution and prospectus designates a trustee, usually a bank, to represent the bondholders over the terms of the bonds for purposes of collecting and distributing interest payments and pursuing legal protection of bondholders' rights. In the case of WPPSS Project 4 and 5 bonds, the trustee is Chemical Bank. On August 5, 1983, Chemical Bank, after declaring default, initiated the first in a long list of WPPSS-related lawsuits by suing WPPSS, the participant utilities, and the Bonneville Power Administration on behalf of the bondholders. The charge was fraud in the sale and subsequent failure to pay interest on bonds.

Ironically, the two sets of natural enemies in the WPPSS default, disgruntled ratepayers in the Pacific Northwest and many bondholders, seem to assess similarly the role of the investment community in the WPPSS debacle. The core of their argument is that Wall Street had an obligation to exercise oversight of WPPSS activities—that the Supply System's problems would not have occurred if Wall Street had not encouraged WPPSS to borrow so much money and had not made that borrowing possible by underwriting and trading bond issues. Since Wall Street firms did do those things, say the ratepayers, they and the bondholders have only themselves to blame for the deterioration of the values of WPPSS securities and the consequences of any possible default.

Many bondholders, while maintaining their claim that WPPSS members and participants (and ultimately the ratepayers) have a responsibility to pay their debts no matter what, are suing, or are preparing to sue, banks and investment houses for their roles in underwriting and trading the bonds. Both ratepayers and many bondholders agree that the pursuit of short-term profit caused the investment community to lose sight of the true investment quality of WPPSS bonds. Many ratepayers and bondholders alike are now wondering if that shortsightedness was intentional.

Yet the actual responsibility of the investment community for WPPSS problems is not quite so clear as many ratepayers and bondholders believe. The members of the Wall Street investment community that participate in any underwriting-investment process all have the opportunity to identify, assess, and communicate to the issuer any problems that might lead to financial difficulties or default. Whether or not this is done by a particular firm, and how effectively it is done, depend on a variety of factors, including the nature of the role being played by the firm, its research capabilities, the size and nature of the problem, the legal liabilities involved, and the size and nature of potential profits.

This chapter's six sections will investigate investment community responsibility in the WPPSS default. The first section deals with the legal advice given WPPSS by bond counsel. That advice, particularly concerning the legal validity of the WPPSS bond issues, was the cornerstone of all other investment community activities with regard to WPPSS. The second section assesses the strengths and weaknesses of credit analysis as practiced by rating firms, investment houses, underwriters, and so on. The third discusses the quality of advice given to the Supply System by underwriters and financial advisers. Presumably that advice is based, at least in part, on an analysis of the creditworthiness of the issuer. The fourth looks at the legal liability of issuers, underwriters, dealers, and the like. The fifth section discusses some of what might be called the "standard operating procedures" of the investment community. The sixth section describes how WPPSS was described in the analyses done by investment firm analysts. It presents an examination of two credit reports on WPPSS bonds issued by a major investment house in 1979 and 1982. A short epilogue describes some aftereffects of the WPPSS default.

LEGAL ADVICE

The "opinion of counsel" is one of the most important sections of any "official statement"—the disclosure document used to market a municipal securities offering. The opinion assures potential investors that their money will be repaid and that any interest they receive will be tax free. But these are indeed only opinions. They are based on counsel's understanding of the issue; the issuer; and the federal, state, and local laws affecting the issue. The WPPSS default highlights some of the problems that can occur when bond counsel do more than simply render basic legal opinions, when bond counsel may know more about the issuer than what is included in the opinion, and when bond counsel's basic opinion turns out to be wrong—in the view of a state supreme court.

The Role of Bond Counsel

The role of the bond counsel in tax-exempt financings came into existence precisely because of the insistence by bondholders that in event of default, investors possess binding obligations to help them recover their investments. After the Civil War a number of railroad-aid bond issues defaulted because of financial difficulties faced by the railroads. But the bonds had been issued by municipalities that used payments from the railroads for the repayment of interest and principal to bondholders.

Many of the municipalities argued that they should not be held responsible for the railroads' problems, and investors were left virtually unprotected. The resulting decline in investor confidence in the municipal bond market approached crisis proportions, but municipalities moved to ease investor fears by retaining independent legal counsel to give opinions as to whether or not any given issue was a legal, valid, and binding obligation of the issuer. In giving that opinion, attorneys were expected to carefully compare the details of the financing with the requirements of state and local laws. Eventually, counsel was also asked to give opinions on the tax-exempt status of municipal issues.

The Expanded Role

Today, bond counsel can and often do perform a number of functions in addition to the aforementioned traditional ones. Bond counsel may help design and implement innovative or complicated financing arrangements. And increasingly, they are asked to help establish the legality of those kinds of arrangements by lobbying state and local officials, assisting state officials in drafting new legislation that would specifically permit innovative financing arrangements, seeking validations by state attorney generals, and trying test cases in state courts to determine whether the arrangements can withstand statutory and constitutional limitations.

The less experienced the issuer and the more complicated the required financing, the more involved bond counsel may become in these kinds of activities. A case in point was the development in 1960 of moral obligation financing for use by New York State's Housing Finance Agency. In order to sell HFA bonds at reasonable rates, New York bond lawyer John N. Mitchell (later President Nixon's attorney general) identified and adapted a financing technique that had been used for school district bond issues. Bonds were backed by the informal pledge of the New York State legislature to appropriate funds for debt service if formally designated sources of funds proved inadequate. As Mitchell has freely admitted, the technique was used primarily to bypass constitutionally required voter approvals for bond issues obligating state money for housing, mental health, and the like (Gotschall 1984).

More than twenty states have issued moral obligation revenue bonds since 1960, in spite of the central role that the technique played in New York State's mid-1970s fiscal crisis. The state's Urban Development Corporation used moral obligation bonds to expand rapidly its borrowing in the early 1970s. But at the same time, the authority plunged deeply into administrative and financial problems. UDC eventually defaulted on some of its short-term debt, and the New York State legislature suddenly found itself morally responsible for huge UDC obligations.

The Question of Responsibility

It is surprisingly difficult to determine to whom bond counsel is responsible, but the issue is critical in the WPPSS case. Bond counsel are typically retained by the issuer and paid from the proceeds of the bond issue. Theoretically, their basic role is to act as independent, legal auditors—they are not retained to act as advocates for any of the parties in the transaction. If asked to give a legal opinion on an issue that is not legal, they are obligated to say so, making them, in a sense, responsible to the ultimate purchaser of the securities being offered.

In practice, however, the issue of bond counsel responsibility becomes more difficult to sort out, especially as the duties of the bond counsel expand. Bond counsel who develop new financing techniques are, in a very real sense, retained as advocates *for* the issuer. In such a situation, presumably the legal Code of Ethics would apply, and bond counsel would owe primary loyalty to the client asking for legal advice.

The investment community uses a standard operating procedure to determine to whom bond counsel is responsible when a bond issue is found to be of questionable legality (investment community procedures are discussed in more detail later in this chapter). Bond attorneys simply report that they are unable to render an opinion. This inability is known usually only to the issuer and the financial advisers involved in setting up the issue. The issuer then either restructures the financing or finds a bond counsel willing to say that the issue is legal.

When bond counsel violate these unwritten rules, they may lose clients. In 1979 the Chicago Board of Education tried to obtain a $225 million loan from a syndicate of lenders, after being denied access to the bond market because of low credit ratings. The board voted in secret session to guarantee the loan with state educational aid payments. The board's bond counsel, Chapman & Cutler, advised the board and the potential syndicate members that the board had no legal authority to commit future state aid payments. Faced with Chapman & Cutler's inability to render an opinion, syndicate members refused to participate, and the deal collapsed. The Illinois State Legislature later solved the problem by creating the Chicago School Finance Authority to raise money for the system.

In assembly hearings, state senators criticized Chapman & Cutler for violating the confidence of their client by making syndicate members aware that the financial guarantee was not legal. Chapman & Cutler was subsequently dropped as bond counsel to the school system (Winders 1980).

The legal liability of bond counsel, like that of other parties in municipal finance transactions, is ambiguous. In cases of bond counsel knowledge of misstatement or omission of material facts in official statements, there are specific decisions of the Supreme Court that would apply (Lamb and Rappaport 1980: 277-78). But bond counsel do not opine on the creditworthiness of issuers, and attorneys usually rely on documentation presented by the issuer for their legal analysis. Bond counsel do not typically carry out thorough investigations of issuers, nor are they expected to. However, the expanded role of bond counsel may lead to changes in legal liability, as well as to efforts by bond counsel to protect themselves against liability.

The Supply System's Bond Counsel

WPPSS used two highly experienced firms for advice with regard to financing for Projects 4 and 5 (the same two firms had worked with WPPSS on earlier financings). The Seattle firm of Houghton, Cluck, Coughlin & Riley, which had long been associated with public power in the Pacific Northwest and boasted the region's most respected lawyers in that field, acted as special counsel. Wood & Dawson of New York acted as bond counsel. One of the nation's most widely known bond counsel firms, Wood & Dawson had helped design power sales agreements used by Washington State Public Utility Districts to finance the construction of mid-Columbia dams in the 1950s. The firm had a reputation as being somewhat conservative. For example, outspoken senior partner John Dawson criticized moral obligation bonds for involving an unjustified avoidance of state constitutional provisions (Walsh 1978: 75).

Working with the Supply System's financial advisor, Blyth Eastman Dillon (later Blyth Eastman Paine Webber), and lawyers from the Public Power Council, the legal counsel spent two years developing the Project 4 and 5 agreements. The Supply System kept no breakdown of legal costs over this period, but as later figures indicate, the fees were considerable. Newspaper accounts put the fees for all legal services for the period from 1979 to 1983 (including work on Project 1, 2, and 3 bond issues) at $8.7 million for Houghton, Cluck, and $2.2 million for Wood & Dawson (Gleckman 1984: 17).

For each Project 4 and 5 issue, bond counsel and special counsel rendered legal opinions concerning the authority of the participants to engage in take-or-pay financing. Each participant signed an identical hell-or-high-water pledge to pay its share of the total annual cost of the projects, including debt service on outstanding bonds

> whether or not any of the Projects are completed, operable or operating and notwithstanding the suspension, interruption, interference, reduction or curtailment of the output of either Project for any reason whatsoever in whole or in part. Such payments shall not be subject to any reduction, whether by offset or otherwise, and shall not be conditioned on the performance or nonperformance by Supply System or other Participant or entity under this or any other agreement or instrument, the remedy for any nonperformance being limited to mandamus, specific performance or other legal or equitable remedy (*Chemical Bank v. WPPSS* 1983: 778).

Take-or-pay contracts had been used in other states and on other power projects in the region. In fact, the PUDs involved in the mid-Columbia dam projects had issued municipal power revenue bonds secured by take-or-pay purchase contracts with direct service industries and investor-owned utilities. But nothing had been done in the states of Washington, Oregon, Idaho, or Montana to test the legality of these kinds of contracts or to pass laws assuring that entities such as the WPPSS participants could enter into such agreements. Nor did WPPSS legal counsel take any steps to obtain such assurances.

The attorneys working with WPPSS could not have assumed the legality of the contracts on the basis of court decisions in other states (although most credit analysts felt comfortable with the WPPSS opinions because of those other decisions). Such an assumption is inappropriate because of the wide differences in state constitutional law and the even more diverse ways in which those laws are interpreted by state courts. Most of the litigation in other states involving take-or-pay had been of the nature of test cases or bond validation proceedings, and the contracts had never been tested in federal courts. WPPSS lawyers could have recommended test cases in the Washington, Idaho, or Oregon state supreme courts, validations by state attorney generals in those states, or changes in state laws by legislators who, in the early 1970s, were more than willing to accommodate public power interests in the region. Any of these steps could have helped WPPSS avoid the Washington State Supreme Court decision voiding the contracts. None of these steps were recommended by WPPSS legal counsel, however, because those lawyers were willing to render legal opinions within the framework of existing Washington State law.

The Missing Sixteen

An issue that may eventually help clarify the question of to whom bond counsel should consider themselves responsible concerns the actual legal opinion included in WPPSS official statements. The opinion, under the letterheads of Wood & Dawson, and Houghton, Cluck, states

> We have examined into the validity of seventy-two of the Participants' Agreements, dated July 14, 1976, referred to in the Official Statement of the System. . . . In our opinion each of said seventy-two Participants' Agreements

has been duly authorized, executed and delivered by each of the parties there-
to and constitutes a valid and binding agreement enforceable in accordance
with its terms (Washington Public Power Supply System 1979: E3).

Officials of Wood & Dawson had claimed that certain minor difficulties had kept them from issuing an opinion on the legal authority
of the sixteen additional utilities, located mostly in Idaho and Oregon. However, in 1982 Wood & Dawson partner Brendan O'Brien
stated in a court deposition that those utilities were not mentioned
"Because we looked at the proceedings and we thought there was
something either wrong with their statutory authority or their proceedings that they had taken to get it, or for some reason thought
that was an insufficient basis to give the opinion" (O'Brien 1982:
68).

O'Brien had admitted in effect that things other than simple procedural problems had kept the firm from rendering an opinion regarding the missing sixteen. When asked if "an insufficient basis to
give the opinion" actually meant that the firm had arrived at an opinion that those participants could not legally enter into WPPSS take-
or-pay agreements, as this and other testimony implied, O'Brien replied, "No" (O'Brien 1982: 87). When asked if he had explained to
WPPSS officials why his firm could not render an opinion on the
missing sixteen, O'Brien replied, "I don't recall" (O'Brien 1982: 86).
Thomas L. Poscharsky, another Wood & Dawson partner, was asked
by reporters from *Business Week* to comment on O'Brien's testimony. He replied that "some of that testimony is not necessarily
correct" (*Business Week* 1983: 86). By that time the firm was being
sued for withholding information from investors.

The sixteen utilities turned out to represent only about 4 percent
of Projects 4 and 5. WPPSS officials claim to have known about the
potential problems, as do officials of Moody's and Standard & Poor's.
But no one associated with WPPSS ever made this information available to the general public. The issue of the missing sixteen raises
questions about the general performance of legal counsel, as well as
to whom they should consider themselves responsible. One wonders,
for example, how many cases of questionable authority it would
have taken for WPPSS legal counsel to be unable to render a legal
opinion on the bonds. On April 8, 1983, WPPSS hired Willkie Farr &
Gallagher to replace Wood & Dawson. The Supply System's long-
time bond counsel was let go for what a WPPSS spokesman told the

press was "certain dissatisfaction with some of its activities" (*Weekly Bond Buyer* 1983: 3).

CREDIT ANALYSIS

Credit analysis—the assessment of the ability and willingness of a debt issuer to pay back those debts in a timely fashion—is considered by nearly all the members of the investment community to be an important foundation of the work that they do. This has been especially true since the New York City/New York State financial crisis caught Wall Street by surprise in the mid-1970s. The result of that crisis was a new and generally critical look by the members of the Wall Street community at some of its most important members, the credit-rating firms.

Credit Analysis and the Rating Firms

Up to the mid-1970s the organized process of developing sophisticated, in-depth analysis of municipal creditworthiness took place for the most part only at rating firms. But both major rating firms, Moody's and Standard & Poor's, were slow to appreciate the implications of the size and nature of moral obligation financing used by the Urban Development Corporation (UDC), the New York State agency whose default on note payments plunged the state and New York City into fiscal chaos beginning in early 1975. In May 1973 both rating firms gave a UDC offering an A rating, despite dangerously high debt levels, a disclaimed opinion by an independent auditor, and concerned underwriters' insistence on an unusually detailed disclosure of UDC problems in official statements distributed prior to the bond sale.

Both rating firms also raised New York City's rating to A in 1973, despite obvious signs that the economic and fiscal condition of the city was deteriorating rapidly. In April 1975 Standard & Poor's finally suspended its rating for New York City bonds, but Moody's delayed action for another six months and then only downgraded the city's bonds. In the aftermath of the New York State/New York City crisis, many investors wondered how the rating firms, with their sophisticated credit analysis techniques, could have ignored New York City budgeting and accounting practices that quickly became classics in the history of municipal financial mismanagement. The city had been issuing tax anticipation notes for capital projects, routinely placing hundreds of millions in operating budget items in the capital budget, and continually rolling over billions in short-term debt to finance over ten years' worth of operating deficits in its operating budget. In 1975 the city's short-term debt needs amounted to roughly 30 percent of the nation's total short-term debt. The Securities and Exchange Commission eventually criticized both major rating agencies for having failed to make diligent inquiry into the New York City situation.

The SEC's criticism of the rating firms was echoed by many Wall Street firms, and since 1975 many banks, brokerage firms, and insurance companies have created or strengthened their own research departments in attempts to reduce their dependence on the rating agencies for credit analysis. A considerable number of dealer firms have become especially interested in enhancing their credit analysis capabilities because institutional investors have demanded more fundamental research. By the late 1970s, ten to twelve firms were producing various degrees of comprehensive analytical credit reports, including their own ratings.

But the WPPSS debacle once again caught Wall Street by surprise, even though the activities of investors and underwriters indicated that the rating firms no longer exercised the influence they once had over the investment community. WPPSS securities consistently traded at prices considerably below those that the ratings would suggest, especially during the late 1970s and early 1980s. Regardless of that fact, it is clear that even the enhanced credit analysis capabilities of a wide range of Wall Street firms and institutional investors were not sophisticated enough to anticipate WPPSS problems.

Analytical Techniques Applied to WPPSS

The analysis of the creditworthiness of securities such as those issued by WPPSS is often broken down into a number of factors that must be examined by analysts. In the *Standard & Poor's Ratings Guide* (1979), for example, a general approach to the analysis of revenue bond issues, such as those issued by WPPSS, is described in terms of the following factors:

1. Legal factors are important because they describe the actual security behind the bonds. In the case of WPPSS, these factors would include the nature of the power supply contracts that ultimately make revenues available for debt repayment. Other important legal factors include rate covenants, or the legal commitment that rates will be raised to sufficiently cover debt repayment costs, and other legal commitments to bondholders embodied in the bond resolution or indenture. Of course, a correct assessment of these factors depends on the opinion of bond counsel that the agreements involved are indeed legal.

2. Economic factors address the question of the strength and durability of the demand for the services produced by the facilities under construction. Without sufficient demand, revenues are not available for repayment of the debt.

3. Administrative factors involve a variety of highly qualitative characteristics of the enterprise and its operating environment. Management quality is assessed in a variety of ways, usually including an assessment of the political influences that affect a given governmental enterprise.

4. Standard & Poor's lists financial factors as a fourth category of analysis, although S & P notes that financial factors are important in all of the above categories. These factors typically include debt ratios and other quantitative indicators of financial performance.

In the case of WPPSS, the operating history of the organization was meaningful in terms of credit analysis only in so far as it showed that WPPSS had successfully undertaken the construction of two generating facilities in Washington State. Analysts have generally reacted in two ways to the Supply System's operating history. Some analysts admit privately that at first glance, the WPPSS Hanford project, which began producing power in 1966, appeared to evidence impressive nuclear power plant construction experience. After all, the Hanford project was completed under budgeted cost and represented the first significant use of nuclear power to generate commercially available electric power. Some of these analysts claim that the major rating firms, in particular, viewed the Hanford project in this light.

Analysts who were at all familiar with the Hanford project, however, were aware that the plant simply used by-product steam from an already existing federal nuclear reactor to generate power. A look at WPPSS's operating background would reveal little information about the Supply System's ability to manage or finance state-of-the-art nuclear power plants. Thus, the financial and administrative factors mentioned above were of little importance to knowledgeable analysts when WPPSS started selling bonds to finance construction of Projects 1, 2, and 3. This meant that, in the beginning at least, analysts would concentrate on legal and economic factors in order to determine the credit quality of WPPSS bonds. But the lack of a long and successful operating history did not necessarily work against WPPSS. In the WPPSS case, legal and economic factors were considered strong enough by the investment community to outweigh the lack of meaningful administrative or financial factors. However a close examination of the so-called strong credit aspects of these factors raises a number of questions that could have been asked by analysts about WPPSS in the early and middle 1970s, but evidently were not.

WPPSS Legal Factors

Traditionally, legal factors have been important in the credit analysis of revenue bond issues, in the sense that strong commitments, considered legal by consulting bond attorneys, are absolutely necessary for a strong credit rating. A facility can be built and run efficiently, and it can produce large revenues, but if those revenues are not legally committed to service debt, then there is a chance that debt service will not be paid, or will not be paid in timely fashion. Revenue bonds are usually secured by specific revenues rather than by the full faith and credit that secures general obligation bonds issued by governmental entities such as states and cities.

In certain situations there is a tendency to view the strongest possible legal commitments as almost sufficient by themselves to guarantee minimal risk to the investor. This would apply in cases where first, the debt is backed ultimately by strong secondary sources of funds in addition to the revenues to be generated by the facilities under development, and second, where those secondary sources of revenues are committed, whether or not the facilities are ever built.

WPPSS bonds—both those issued for Projects 1, 2, and 3, and those for Projects 4 and 5—possessed variations of this kind of strong secondary security backing. This backing, more than any other factor, was responsible for high credit ratings and the strong attraction of WPPSS securities for investors. Unfortunately, the opinions of bond counsel were wrong; the WPPSS take-or-pay contracts were not legal in the eyes of the Washington State Supreme Court. Credit analysts also overestimated the extent to which the contracts, even if legal, could actually secure WPPSS debt under crisis conditions.

Projects 1, 2, and 3, Net Billing Contracts. In order to reduce the cost of the money that WPPSS needed to borrow to build its projects, increased security for the borrowing was created through the use of net-billing agreements entered into by WPPSS, project participants, and the Bonneville Power Administration (BPA). WPPSS had originally used net billing in the 1963 power exchange agreement for the by-product steam generating plant at the Hanford reactor. In 1968 BPA presented the Ten-Year Hydro Power Program to Congress, and that same year Secretary of the Interior Stewart L. Udall, as well as the Bureau of the Budget, approved net billing for use in the program. In 1970 and 1971 the contract procedure was approved for use on the WPPSS projects and codified into law by the Public Works Appropriations Acts of those years. By the end of 1972 BPA had prepared the net billing agreements for the output of Plants 1, 2, and 70 percent of Plant 3.

The small utilities that made up the WPPSS participants group had little with which to secure borrowing. Most of them simply purchased power generated at federal hydroelectric plants and transmitted by BPA. BPA, on the other hand, was prohibited by its authorizing legislation from purchasing non-federal power for resale. Net billing provided a way for BPA to assist the utilities in their construction of power generating facilities.

Essentially, these agreements call for the purchase at cost by BPA of the entire power output of the shares of the three plants owned by WPPSS. Payment is to be made for this power whether or not the plants are built. In return, BPA compensates each participant by assigning credits against the amount each participant owes BPA for power transmitted or other services under separate power sales-purchase contracts. BPA is obligated to pass along its costs to its customers, many of whom are participants on the WPPSS projects.

Under these agreements, the compensation paid by BPA to the participants would cover the total annual project costs—construction costs, operating and maintenance costs, and debt service on bonds issued, as well as debt service reserve requirements. The participants, in turn, pay WPPSS the net amount set forth in BPA's billing statement, whether or not they have received cash payments from BPA. Each participant is contractually obligated to make those payments out of operating revenues by means of charges to its own customers.

If the amount that a participant owes to BPA is less than its share of annual project costs, a net-billing deficiency is said to exist. This occurs for example when project costs increase. BPA must pay for these deficiencies, and since it is required by its charter to be self-supporting, its only source of revenues to meet the costs just described is its customer base. Therefore, BPA must adjust its rate schedules to recover those costs. This means that customers of BPA who are not participants in the three WPPSS projects may be expected to help pay for project costs through the increased costs of the electricity they receive.

Because interest costs on the WPPSS debt were capitalized (or paid for out of bond proceeds) until the date on which the plants were to begin producing revenues, no payments were supposed to be made by anyone until the plants began paying for themselves. And once the intricate payment process started, BPA's involvement was intended to help decrease the ultimate costs to ratepayers because BPA planned to base its wholesale power rates on the melded cost calculated by averaging in the costs of the new nuclear power with the costs of the old hydropower generated at federal dams in the area.

As we have seen, when the date of commercial operation passed with no plants coming on line, BPA was forced to begin raising wholesale power rates to pay WPPSS debt service costs out of its hydropower revenues. Because WPPSS members and participants were customers of BPA, they and their retail ratepayers were actually paying for a large share of the debt service on WPPSS bonds. The remaining share was paid for by other BPA wholesale customers who were not parties to the WPPSS agreements, and many of whom do not reside in Washington State.

The net-billing contracts were deceptive. In all of their complexity, they appeared to invoke the security of the federal government behind WPPSS bonds. The front page of the official statement for a WPPSS debt offering in May of 1982 advertised in boldface print the connection between BPA and the United States of America, Department of Energy. But only on page thirty-one did the statement reveal that BPA does not have the authority to borrow from the federal treasury to pay for the plants. The public misperception of the nature of these contracts was propagated by repeated references by journalists, WPPSS consultants, and members of the investment community to federal guarantees behind the projects. A representative of one investment banking firm used the word guarantee to describe the net-billing agreements in a congressional hearing, and the management consulting report by Theodore Barry & Associates referred more than once to the BPA guarantee behind WPPSS bonds for Projects 1, 2, and 3.

Part of the problem with using the term guarantee is that it made the net-billing arrangements appear to be federally guaranteed debt agreements, which require the U.S. Treasury to pay back the debt if other sources of security fail. However, the Columbia River Transmission Act of 1974 established that from that date on, BPA was required to be self-supporting by means of its customer revenues. BPA had access to the U.S. Treasury for loans only, with a $1.25 billion limit on loans outstanding at any one time. But these loans could not be used for debt service or any additional payments for the net-billed projects (or for BPA's operating expenses).

Originally there had been some congressional financing of the net-billed projects, and it is possible that some analysts or investors may have misinterpreted this as a precedent for further federal involvement. In 1970 Congress had appropriated $100,000 for preliminary engineering studies on the net-billed projects, and in 1971 another $150,000 was added. But the committee reports accompanying the small appropriations make it extremely unlikely that these appropriations could be considered serious precedents for federal financial involvement.

Whether or not the rating agencies viewed net billing as a guarantee, they clearly considered the promise by BPA to pay for the plants whether or not they were ever finished as an indicator of strong credit quality. Project 1, 2, and 3 bonds received the highest possible ratings from both Moody's and Standard & Poor's until January of 1983.

Project 4 and 5 Take-or-Pay Contracts. By 1972, as a result of planning associated with Phase II of the Ten Year Hydro-Thermal Power Program, BPA had determined that by the early 1980s it would be unable to supply the power required by the region—even with the three WPPSS nuclear plants. Two additional plants, the ill-fated Plants 4 and 5, would have to be built.

BPA planned to enter into net-billing contracts with a number of its direct service customers—aluminum companies in particular—as well as with regional utilities to build the two plants. The aluminum industry used a large amount of BPA power, at rates that provided a significant competitive advantage to plants in the BPA service area, and wanted to maintain uninterrupted sources of relatively inexpensive power.

Aluminum companies, along with other direct service customers such as timber and nickel companies, would help underwrite the construction of two plants, to be built as twins of Plants 1 and 3. Bonneville, as under its previous net-billing arrangements, would have the total power output of the plants assigned to it, and the power would then be marketed to BPA customers. By 1972, however, BPA's net-billing capacity had been exhausted by high construction costs; further credits for additional plants would have exceeded the amount the customers owed BPA. BPA could not avoid the implications of that exhausted capacity because regulations were promulgated in 1972 under the Revenue and Expenditure Control Act of 1968 to prohibit the issuance of tax-exempt bonds for power resources that would be acquired by federal power marketing agencies under arrangements such as net billing. After a lawsuit, an injunction was issued to prevent BPA from proceeding on Projects 4 and 5.

With BPA's assurances that the power from the two plants would be needed by 1983 and BPA's formal notice of insufficiency issued in 1976, WPPSS and eighty-eight utilities, most of which were participants in the first three projects, decided to undertake Projects 4 and 5 themselves. In order to secure the financing necessary for the two plants the participants entered into take-or-pay, come-hell-or-high-water agreements, which obligated them to pay for the annual cost of the projects, including debt service on the bonds, whether or not the projects were ever completed or capable of operation.

The investment community has traditionally had great faith in take-or-pay contracts, which have long been used in electric revenue bond financing. Most of the forty-five joint action agencies created to develop public power projects nationwide use take-or-pay, or a variation of it. Of the eighteen joint action agencies financing major power project construction in 1982, thirteen used take-or-pay. Most experts believe that bonds could not be sold for nuclear power projects without take-or-pay backing or some other method almost as secure.[2]

The rationale behind take-or-pay agreements is similar to that behind the net-billing contracts. A strong independent source of revenue is pledged as security, in order to supplement any revenues that might be forthcoming from the facilities being constructed with the bond proceeds. The WPPSS take-or-pay arrangements rely on the ability of participants to sell electricity from sources other than Plants 4 and 5, and to sell that electricity at whatever price is necessary. Part of the reason for analysts' faith in these contracts is their strong legal history. The terms of take-or-pay contracts have been upheld in a number of court cases, including cases heard by state supreme courts in Mississippi, Louisiana, and Utah. The WPPSS Project 4 and 5 contracts were drawn up carefully so as to fully obligate the participants to pay for the plants whether or not they were completed or put into operation. And because participating utilities were not subject to regulation by federal or state utility commissions, they had unlimited authority to set rates and were fully capable of complying with the contract provisions should the plants not be completed.

But as various aforementioned court cases indicate, participants in joint action ventures are occasionally motivated to break take-or-pay contracts, and litigation can of course affect the timeliness of debt service payments. Indeed, there are grounds on which any contract can be successfully challenged. WPPSS participants might have been able to challenge their take-or-pay contracts on the grounds that bad management (failure to follow prudent utility practices) was responsible for the termination of Plants 4 and 5, or that participants were misled or coerced into signing the contracts. Other possible, but less likely, grounds for challenge included the claims that the take-or-pay contracts did not explicitly cite termination as a hell-or-high-water condition for payment of construction costs, and that the contracts constitute unconscionable, or one-sided and thus unfair, agreements that should be abrogated.

After Plants 4 and 5 were terminated on January 22, 1982, the Washington participants did indeed try to avoid honoring the take-or-pay contracts, as did participants in Idaho and Oregon. The ensuing legal battle would have led at the very least to delayed debt service payments and technical, if only short-term, default. However, the state supreme court ruled that the Washington participants never had express or implied legal authority to enter into such contracts. With that ruling, the Supply System was rapidly coursing toward the largest single tax-exempt bond default in history.

It can and will be argued that a large share of the responsibility for the consequences of the WPPSS default must be accepted by legal advisers who opined on the legality of the take-or-pay contracts. Credit analysts relied on the opinions of attorneys as the starting point for their research. Analysts do not typically challenge the opinions of legal counsel because of a lack of test cases or validations by state attorney generals. But increasingly, investment houses are turning to their own lawyers for second opinions. At the very least, in the words of one legal expert, the different state court decisions regarding WPPSS contracts "emphasize the autonomy of each state's law and the dangers of treating the doctrines of foreign states as precedent. . . . After WPPSS, practitioners rendering opinions on bond issues need to rediscover the distinctive state and local sources and limits of authority" (Falk 1985: 126).

In any case, most of the participants were not concerned with these legal issues. Indeed, most never expected to be forced to fulfill the take-or-pay provisions even in the event of hell or high water. When the contracts were signed, many of the participants expected that eventually BPA would be allowed to purchase the power output of the plants, thus spreading costs over BPA's customer base. In 1977 a bill sponsored by regional utilities was introduced to Congress, which, among other things, provided for such a purchase by BPA. But by the time a third version of the bill was passed on December 5, 1980, as the Northwest Regional Power Act, it made the purchase by BPA of power from Projects 4 and 5 difficult if not impossible. Conservation, renewable resources, and cogeneration options must be exercised before thermal power plants can be considered.

Economic Factors

A crucial area of the analysis of the creditworthiness of bonds such as those issued by WPPSS concerns the demand for the plants to be built with the bond proceeds. Since those bond proceeds will in all likelihood be paid back from the revenues of the projects, a credit analyst or investor would have to be sure that demand exists, or will exist, for the power produced by the plants and that the variability in the size of demand will not endanger the timely payments of debt service.

All five WPPSS nuclear projects were undertaken on the basis of power demand growth projections made by the Pacific Northwest Utilities Conference Committee (PNUCC), a consortium made up of BPA, 7 investor-owned utilities, and 113 public utilities in the region (most of which eventually became members or participants of WPPSS). The PNUCC forecasts were for many years the only annual series of load-resource forecasts for the Pacific Northwest. The Ten Year Hydro-Thermal Power Program was issued on the basis of PNUCC projections of a 7.5 percent annual growth in power demand to the end of the century. By February of 1976, after Projects 1, 2, and 3, were underway, the projected growth in demand had dropped to 5.5 percent annually through 1992. But that figure was still high enough for BPA to issue its notice of insufficiency a few months later, warning that the region faced a power shortage by mid-1983 unless two more nuclear plants were built. The response to the notice was the agreement by eighty-eight utilities—most of which were PNUCC members and already WPPSS 1, 2, and 3 participants—to the take-or-pay pledges that provided financing for Plants 4 and 5.

But the PNUCC forecasts, accepted as authoritative by the investment community, proved highly unreliable. Part of the problem was the lack of a scientific forecasting methodology. Up to 1977 PNUCC simply added together the individual forecasts made by its members. The methods used to arrive at those individual forecasts ranged from sophisticated econometric estimates to best guesses. The independent study of WPPSS Projects 4 and 5 commissioned by the Washington State legislature concluded that "Due to the many participating utilities and the wide variety in load forecasting techniques employed, it is difficult to assess and characterize the atrributes of the overall regional load forecast" (Washington Energy Research Center 1982: 76).

If nothing else, BPA and the individual utilities involved seem to have shared some critical assumptions about energy planning, which were in turn accepted without question by the investment community. One assumption was that resource planning should be based on worst case scenarios. This was and is a common practice among hydropower planners who must account for year-to-year fluctuation in stream flows. For example, to forecast the hydrogenerating capabilities of the region, each PNUCC member estimates its current capability under the worst or most critical stream flow conditions on record (January 1937). This estimating method seems to have combined with a common hydropower planning truism: It is more prudent to plan for demand that may grow faster than expected than to plan in a conservative fashion. Projects can always be delayed, and hydrogenerating systems are flexible enough to allow for the production of more or less power as needed.

These assumptions are not necessarily wrong, but when used in the consideration of nuclear power project development, particularly in cases where power demand growth forecasts are of questionable reliability, they may not always be appropriate. Nuclear power plants are considered base-load plants because they are not well suited to rapid adjustments in their power output. In other words, they are not flexible instruments of power production; if they are built and used, they must be used in base-load fashion, in spite of other power resources available. And, of course, large nuclear power plant construction projects are almost impossible to delay without incurring monumental costs.

The most crucial and damaging PNUCC forecasting assumption was that the increased cost of power produced by nuclear power plants would not reduce demand. The failure to carefully estimate possible price-demand relationships plagued PNUCC even after a computerized electric sales forecast model was adopted in 1977 to supplement the combined estimates of the PNUCC members. The independent study commissioned by the Washington State Legislature concluded in 1982 that "The extent to which the PNUCC procedure accounts for the demand dampening effect of increasing electricity rates caused by the addition of relatively expensive new thermal resources has not been explicitly detailed and is difficult to determine" (Washington Energy Research Center 1972: 76).

The basis for PNUCC reasoning was the fact that ratepayers in the Pacific Northwest paid less for electricity than those in any other region. In 1980 electric rates in Washington were by far the lowest in the nation, despite WPPSS-related BPA rate increases in the late 1970s. In addition, Northwest ratepayers used substantially more electricity per capita than ratepayers elsewhere in the country during the late 1970s. Thus it seemed possible that rate increases, even large ones, might not cut retail demand. Other assumptions fortified this conclusion. Electricity was supposed to be an essential commodity for which there is no substitute, and electricity costs were considered relatively small proportions of ratepayer incomes. The wholesale demand for electricity by regional industries such as aerospace, forest products, and aluminum was also expected to continue growing steadily as it had done in the 1950s and 1960s, in spite of rate increases.

But by 1970 academics were already exploring the tendency of rising prices to dampen energy demand in the Northwest. And far from being simply a sign of unlimited ratepayer willingness to purchase cheap power, the power-use statistics of the region represented a great capability for reducing demand—a larger capability than in any other region of the country. Recession, inflation, and the 1973 oil embargo hurt wholesale power users in the Pacific Northwest and made rate increases of the late 1970s even more painful to retail ratepayers. In fact, the size of rate increases relative to old rates has been a far greater influence on retail usage than any arguments about the absolute size of new rates. Some Pacific Northwest utility districts had not increased rates in over twenty-five years, until BPA began raising rates in the late 1970s. Ratepayers in such districts have not been moved by claims that their electricity is still much cheaper than that in other states. "Rate shock" is a term now used, especially in northeastern states, to describe ratepayer resistance to large, construction-related rate increases. No better term describes the reaction of ratepayers in the Pacific Northwest as WPPSS-related costs began to affect their electric bills.

The PNUCC forecasts were far from actual demand figures. The overestimation made in 1969 of the average FY 1979–80 load is higher than the output of three 1200 megawatt nuclear power plants. In 1977 the PNUCC nineteen-year forecast for annual average compound rate of growth in the demand for electricity was 4.5 percent. By 1981 the PNUCC nineteen-year forecast had dropped to 2.9 percent, and in 1982 to 2.6 percent. However, by 1982 the PNUCC forecasts had been largely discredited even in the eyes of many PNUCC members. In 1982 BPA made its own prediction of a 1.7 percent annual growth rate through the year 2000 and tried to withhold an independent study it had commissioned that showed an annual rate of growth of 1.2 percent through the early 1990s. The independent review commissioned by the state legislature and published in March 1982 predicted an annual 1.5 percent growth rate from 1980 to 2000.

The inaccuracy of the PNUCC estimates would not seem so great were it not for the existence of independent studies, completed as early as 1975, that offered more sophisticated and more accurate predictions about future changes in the regional energy environment.[3] In 1975 the Environmental Research Center at Washington State University estimated that the annual average compound rate of growth in the demand for electricity in the Pacific Northwest would be between 1.4 and 2.5 percent for the period from 1975 to 2000 (Hinman, Swamidass, and Butcher 1975).

In 1976 BPA commissioned the consulting firm of Skidmore, Owings & Merrill to undertake an independent study of the area's future energy needs. The study concluded that conservation would significantly dampen the demand for power from the five WPPSS nuclear plants and, if carried far enough, could even make the plants unnecessary (Skidmore, Owings, & Merrill 1976). The study was withheld by BPA until internal studies were prepared to show that such conservation was impossible in the area.

Also in 1976 Seattle City Light completed an internal study showing that increased costs of electricity in the region would stimulate conservation activities and severely cut the demand for power (Northwest Environmental Technology Laboratories 1976). Seattle City Light was a participant in WPPSS Projects 1, 2, and 3, but based in large part on this study the utility decided not to become involved in Projects 4 and 5.

In 1977 the U.S. Energy Research and Development Administration funded a study by the Natural Resources Defense Council Inc. that explored ways in which conservation and renewable resources could be used to meet the area's energy needs. The study results indicated much less need for new thermal generating plants than did the PNUCC analysis (Beers and Lash 1977).

Also in 1977 the state of Oregon decided to establish its own procedures for estimating future power demand rather than to continue relying solely on PNUCC projections. The state's first estimate was for a 3.1 percent annual average compound rate of growth for the period from 1976 to 1996 (Oregon Department of Energy 1977: 33).

In May 1978 energy demand estimates were published by the Northwest Energy Policy Project, under sponsorship of the federal government and the states of Washington, Oregon, and Idaho. The mid-range or most likely average annual compound rate of growth in demand was judged to be 2.93 percent from 1974 to 2000 (Northwest Energy Policy Project 1978: 56). In August 1978 the U.S. General Accounting Office reviewed PNUCC and NEPP estimates of annual growth for the period from 1977 to 2000 and concluded that the NEPP mid-range forecast—almost 2 percent lower than PNUCC's—appeared to be more accurate (U.S. General Accounting Office 1978: Chapter 5).

Shortcomings of Credit Research

Credit analyses prepared by major Wall Street firms routinely fell into the above-mentioned traps with regard to the legal and economic factors. Authors of credit reports took for granted the opinions of bond attorneys who assumed the legal validity of take-or-pay contracts without considering how state judges might view those contracts under the politically charged conditions of WPPSS project failure. Analysts routinely ignored the fact that bond counsel provided opinions on the legal validity of only seventy-two of the eighty-eight participant agreements. Analysts also failed to correctly estimate the chances of delayed debt service payments resulting from court challenges of those contracts. Typically, analysts expected that the Northwest Regional Power Bill would allow BPA to purchase the output of Plants 4 and 5, even after the bill was passed and such a purchase was made highly unlikely. Net billing was often described as invoking federal guarantees. PNUCC projections of future demand growth were taken at face value, and the conflicting demand growth studies of other groups or public agencies were almost never mentioned. The Supply System's own explanations for administrative problems were also unquestioned, as were the assurances that those difficulties had been solved. The many management consulting studies commissioned by WPPSS and BPA were never examined by most credit analysts, even though those studies were available to the general public. Perhaps most embarrassing of all, many analysts assumed that WPPSS had a successful history of managing the construction of hydropower and nuclear power projects. Of course that history included no more than the construction of two small generating facilities in Washington State—one of which merely involved the attachment of a generator that converted the waste steam from the Hanford nuclear reactor to electricity.

What almost every credit report missed or ignored was the growing public antipathy toward the projects and the importance of that antipathy. Before the summer of 1982 almost everyone believed that WPPSS participants had legal obligations to pay for terminated plants. But in a situation where those participants believed that the negligence of others was really to blame for WPPSS difficulties, those legal obligations became vulnerable to court tests or even repudiation. Evidence that others were to blame was readily available in the form of alternative power demand forecasts, state Senate reports, and the great amount of material leaked to local newspapers. Ratepayers may be forced to pay higher rates for electricity, but in the climate of public opinion marked by Proposition 14, enraged ratepayers are likely to find ways to communicate their displeasure to officials involved—especially elected officials. What credit analysts tended to ignore completely was the high level of antipathy toward WPPSS expressed by everyone from the ratepayers to Congress.

FINANCIAL ADVICE

The mistakes and omissions of credit analysis, as practiced by Wall Street firms, were reflected in the financial advice given by many of those firms to WPPSS. It might be even more accurate to say that the advice given WPPSS actually had very little to do with strengthening WPPSS creditworthiness. The outside advice WPPSS received was overwhelmingly marketing advice. These advisers saw as their role helping WPPSS to sell more bonds.

WPPSS Financial Advice

The myth of financial advice to an institution like WPPSS is that it is given objectively. Ideally, an issuer would look to its financial adviser for important assistance on a variety of matters. The adviser would make recommendations about debt management from a long-term perspective, for example, including advice about the determination of capital requirements (the financial feasibility of projects, the determination of debt repayment capacity, debt limits, debt mix, the timing and nature of debt issues, etc.). The ideal adviser would also provide a two-way channel of communication between the issuer and the investment community and suggest changes that would improve the marketability of a client's debt issue. And since credit worthiness is an important determinant of marketability, the adviser would have an obligation to bring to the issuer's attention any credit problems it uncovers, either through its own analysis or through its ongoing communication with underwriters and investors.

The Supply System's Financial Advisers

In February 1980 WPPSS financial adviser Blyth Eastman Paine Webber noted that the dismissal of WPPSS Managing Director Neil O. Strand had hurt the image of WPPSS among underwriters and investors because it suggested that the board lacked confidence in WPPSS management (Patterson 1980). Blyth Eastman also noted that the Washington State Senate proposal calling for outside members on the WPPSS board would probably do more harm than good in terms of costs, delays, and investor confidence. The implication was that Wall Street was willing to accept a certain number of managerial problems but no publicizing of those problems that would weaken investor confidence—even if that publicity was the result of attempts to correct the problems. Blyth Eastman warned against the "straw that broke the camel's back"; once investor confidence was seriously weakened for whatever reason, it would be impossible to market WPPSS bonds, even if they were secure from a credit perspective. But what the financial adviser failed to acknowledge was that questionable creditworthiness was the real weakness of the securities. Management shortcomings and other problems were already contributing to construction cost increases and schedule delays. These, in turn, were eroding the loyalty of BPA and the project participants to the WPPSS organization and shaking investor confidence. The marketing problems that WPPSS was beginning to face were symptoms, not the cause, of organizational disease. Treating the symptoms was not the answer.

Blyth Eastman, however, seems to have been concerned primarily with marketing problems. In April 1980 it reported that the portfolios of institutional investors, traditionally the largest purchasers

of WPPSS bonds, were saturated with those securities (Blyth Eastman Paine Webber Public Power Finance Group 1980). The spaces
typically reserved in those portfolios for securities of the type issued
by WPPSS—public power revenue bonds issued by a joint action
agency—were largely filled. This had happened for two reasons. First,
by 1980 WPPSS had become the largest issuer of tax-exempt revenue
bonds, with $4.47 billion outstanding. WPPSS had marketed a major
long-term bond issue about every six or seven weeks.

Second, in cases where WPPSS bonds had not actually saturated
portfolios, other similar kinds of securities were competing for the
same space. Between 1970 and 1979 the dollar volume of revenue
bond financing had grown from $6 billion to $34 billion. Many new
public power issues had entered the market over this same period,
and by 1980 dozens of joint action agencies were preparing to issue
debt; in 1973 WPPSS had been the only joint action agency to do so.

Along with saturation, the Supply System faced the problem of
raising an additional $5.34 billion before 1985. Thus, investors could
expect a rapid succession of WPPSS issues from which they could
select those with the most attractive interest rates.

Managerial problems were not mentioned in the Blyth Eastman
report. Nor were pessimistic power-use growth forecasts, growing
ratepayer resistance, or the disintegrating relationships with BPA
and the state legislature. The report also asserted, based on a survey
of thirty portfolio managers, that "Three Mile Island has not resulted
in any significant limitations on purchases of nuclear construction
bonds (Blyth Eastman Paine Webber Public Power Finance Group
1980: Appendix 1, p. 1). Yet an accompanying chart indicates that
eight of the thirty portfolio managers surveyed (27 percent) said that
limitations had indeed been placed on their ability to buy Supply
System securities because of that incident.

The authors of the report concluded that the Supply System
should simply tailor its offerings to occupy some new "space" in
investor portfolios. Apparently one way to do this was to emphasize
the "attractive" qualities of WPPSS in disclosure to potential investors. Based on the survey of portfolio managers, the report notes that
"Perceptions of Supply System credit have become more hydro-
oriented as a result of emphasis in recent official statements" (Blyth
Eastman Paine Webber Public Power Finance Group 1980: Appendix 1, p. 1). The accompanying statistics indicate that of the managers of the largest seven portfolios in the sample (the seven ranging in

size from $2.3 to $7.7 billion in assets), four considered WPPSS bonds to be "Hydro-Generated" rather than "Nuclear-Based Securities." This change in perception reflected WPPSS changes in its official statements describing new bond issues to emphasize the role of BPA in the construction of Projects 1, 2, and 3. The money to pay for those plants would come in part from revenues produced by the power generated at the region's federally owned and operated dams — power marketed and transmitted by BPA. (Of course, BPA had no involvement in Projects 4 and 5.) But to perceive the bonds for all five projects to be hydro-backed rather than nuclear-backed securities clearly involves, at best, a fundamental overstatement of the role of BPA in WPPSS activities.

The primary method recommended for avoiding portfolio saturation was to issue short-term debt instruments (in this case, bond anticipation notes or BANs) rather than long-term bonds: "Long-term debt should be deferred to the longest extent possible until a time when the projects are operational and revenues are being generated" (Blyth Eastman Paine Webber Public Power Finance Group 1980: 1-3). This recommendation was made partly on the basis of a survey finding that "A significant percentage of institutions expressed a willingness to purchase short-term paper" (Blyth Eastman Paine Webber Public Power Finance Group 1980: Appendix 1, p. 1). However, the accompanying statistics show that only eight of the thirty portfolio managers expressed an unqualified willingness to purchase WPPSS paper. Nine managers said they were unwilling, and the rest said they would be willing under certain (but unspecified) circumstances, a routine answer for any manager not expressly prohibited from buying.

Note that the percentage of portfolios expressing an unqualified willingness to purchase WPPSS short-term paper was "significant," while the percentage of portfolios restricted after Three Mile Island was "not significant" — but the percentages were exactly the same. The ambiguity of this research renders its conclusions almost meaningless, but the message of the report is clear: Sell more bonds.

Issuing short-term debt was an obvious way to continue raising money, but many experts considered it to be a dangerous financing alternative for WPPSS at that time. In a memorandum to the WPPSS board of directors three months later in 1980, consultants from the Institute of Public Administration pointed out what should have been obvious to everyone — that the inability to refinance or roll over short-term debt had been one important cause of New York City's fiscal crisis in 1975. The report also questioned the ease with which the Supply System's financial consultant compared WPPSS financing needs with those of other, much smaller entities for whom short-term debt financing was an appropriate option:

> The comparative short and intermediate-term financing programs which the financial community can turn to for precedent in advising the Supply System are of an altogether different scale from that of Supply System capital needs. Therefore, a realistic approach to risk estimation is needed on the part of the Supply System and its project participants (Institute of Public Administration 1980: 2).

By the late 1970s many public-finance specialists expected problems with short-term debt to be among the most serious facing municipalities during the 1980s. If interest rates go up significantly after short-term debt is issued, or if credit quality goes down, the issuing entity may have serious problems refinancing its short-term obligations. If the issuer's access to the credit market is interrupted for any reason, the issuer could quickly face a default situation. If interest is capitalized and short-term debt rolled over a number of times, which would have been the case with WPPSS, the size of the debt can increase more quickly than often is anticipated.

In 1981 the Washington State Legislature commissioned an independent review of WPPSS Projects 4 and 5, which among other things surveyed rating agencies, underwriters, and others in the financial community about the feasibility of short-term debt financing for WPPSS. The review found that "most of the people surveyed were strongly against the Supply System entering the short-term market" (Washington Energy Research Center 1982: 60).

The Underwriting Process

When competitive bidding is used to sell debt, as WPPSS was required by law to do until 1980, investment bankers join together in groups or syndicates that bid for the right to purchase the entire issue of securities and sell them again at a slightly higher price. Prior to officially bidding for the issue, members of each competing syndicate canvass potential buyers to get an idea of what they will offer for the bonds. In syndicate meetings the members discuss possible bids based on information from potential buyers, credit ratings, general market and economic conditions, and so on. They agree on specific interest rates considered attractive to investors and on a reoffering price for all of the bonds in the issue. Syndicate members are free to drop out at any time before the final bid is made, and if enough drop out, the interest rate may be raised or the syndicate may decide not to bid.

The winning syndicate begins selling the securities immediately at the reoffering price, in the hopes of unloading them all within a few days. Occasionally, the interest of buyers is much lower than anticipated, and after a designated period members of the syndicate are allowed to offer the securities at whatever price the market will accept. Some members may choose to keep the securities until a later date when they can be sold at a more favorable price. Either way, because each member must still pay for its share of the issue at the agreed-upon price, the syndicate members usually experience financial losses.

Thus there are a number of ways for underwriters and investors to communicate their opinions of a bond issue to the issuer. If an issue is unattractive, high interest rates may be established to attract investors, few bids may be received, and underwriters may have difficulty reselling the securities. But it should also be remembered that these signals are not unambiguous. Many factors affect the establishment of interest rates in the underwriting process, and factors having nothing to do with the credit risk of bonds often influence investor enthusiasm.

Nor are underwriters, for example, particularly interested in credit quality. Their major focus is on buying the bonds and then reselling them for a profit in as short a time as possible. Credit worthiness is considered only to the extent that it enhances or diminishes the attractiveness of the bonds in the eyes of customers to whom the underwriter tries to resell. And weak credit often can be offset by high interest offered to investors.

But a great deal of formal and informal communication takes place in the underwriting process, and underwriters and other investment firms seem quick to reach a general consensus about the investment quality of certain issues. When negative assessments of credit quality begin to appear, the news spreads rapidly through the investment community.

Advice from WPPSS Underwriters

The advice given directly to WPPSS by underwriters was somewhat different from that of the WPPSS financial adviser. The financial adviser's report in April 1980 had warned that because of market conditions and portfolio saturation, the issuance of more long-term debt would be very costly if not impossible—even if laws requiring competitive bids were changed to allow negotiated placement. Later that month the Supply System received only one, extremely high bid on a $130 million long-term bond offering. After interviewing a number of underwriting firms, WPPSS executives became convinced that instead of cancelling the sale or selling short-term securities the issue could be sold through a negotiated offering. (State law allowed WPPSS to use negotiated sales only after a competitive bid was rejected.) A month later WPPSS successfully negotiated a sale of the offering at a net interest cost significantly lower than that proposed earlier in the competitive bid (9.23 percent versus 10.07 percent). The success of this negotiated offering along with unease about relying exclusively on short-term debt for funding led the Supply System to appeal to the state legislature for a permanent change in the law requiring competitive bidding.

The managing underwriter of that first negotiated sale, Merrill Lynch White Weld Capital Markets Group, assisted WPPSS executives in their consideration of the merits of negotiated bond sales by preparing a 100-page study that argued for the superiority of the negotiated sale method over competitive bidding under conditions such as those faced by WPPSS (Marion and Quinn 1980). The study also highlighted Merrill Lynch's qualifications for the job of managing underwriter on negotiated offerings. What the study did not highlight were the factors other than portfolio saturation that were contributing to the underwriters' difficulties in placing WPPSS bonds. Nowhere does the report mention the growing concern about WPPSS creditworthiness. Rather, the WPPSS situation is presented as a marketing problem to be solved with marketing techniques. The report includes excerpts from a *Bond Buyer* article noting the Supply System's interest in negotiated sales (Marion and Quinn 1980: 100). Edited out of the reprint are two paragraphs describing WPPSS cost increases and schedule delays, labor difficulties, efforts to strengthen project management, criticism of WPPSS quality control by the

Nuclear Regulatory Commission, and public and press criticism of WPPSS executive salaries and hiring practices.

In proposing itself as the best qualified underwriter to manage WPPSS negotiated offerings, Merrill Lynch was in an awkward position. Merrill Lynch had been co-lead underwriter of the syndicate that submitted the single bid on April 29, 1980. That bid was so high that the Supply System rejected it—the first time in its history that WPPSS had done so—and began considering negotiated sales. But now the authors of the report felt compelled to argue that the April 1980 competitive bid did not reflect the true value of the WPPSS bonds, that WPPSS was right to reject that bid and consider negotiated sales, and that Merrill Lynch was still somehow capable of negotiating a fair market price for a bond issue, despite its involvement in the April bid.

As might be expected, the authors of the report are sometimes at odds among themselves. The report argues that "In rejecting the sole competitive bid, the Supply System very clearly and, we think, properly, served notice to the Wall Street that the bid did not reflect the true value of the bonds" (Marion and Quinn 1980: 78). As for Merrill Lynch's role in the bid, the report notes that because Merrill Lynch was only co-managing underwriter, it did not have the influence to convince other syndicate members of its own perception that the bid was significantly higher than the true value of the bonds (Marion and Quinn 1980: 83). But elsewhere in the report, the argument is made for the general superiority of negotiated sales over competitive bidding. It is pointed out that in competitive situations with only one bidder, as was the case with the rejected bid, true value is typically not on the minds of participating underwriters:

> . . . in negotiated offerings the underwriter might refrain from exploiting any bargaining position, believing that to do so would lead to the loss of future negotiated business, while in the case of a single bidder, concern for the future would be absent and the desire to maximize current return can be fully indulged (Marion and Quinn 1980: i).

Regardless of whether Merrill Lynch's role in the April bid was that of champion of fair market price or maximizer of current return, the firm was indeed highly qualified to be managing underwriter on negotiated WPPSS bond sales because of its size, experience, and resources. And negotiation was clearly at least a short-run palliative for WPPSS bond marketing problems. In 1981 the Washington State Legislature passed a law allowing the negotiated sale of WPPSS securities, and in September 1981 WPPSS initiated its negotiated bond program with a $750 million issue for the net-billed plants. Merrill Lynch served as managing underwriter on the sale. Among the other underwriters in the syndicate was Blyth Eastman, the former WPPSS financial advisor that in April 1980 had advised that portfolio saturation would mean excessive interest rates on sales of long-term bond issues of over $175 million.

The negotiated offering procedure did not decrease the risks associated with WPPSS bonds; it only facilitated the underwriters' job of passing the securities along to the ultimate customers, which in turn was supposed to help underwriters lower the cost to WPPSS. The risks associated with the bonds were clearly increasing and were apparent to most sophisticated investors. Knowledgeable institutional investors had begun to shy away from WPPSS, so bonds had to be sold in smaller than usual lots to individuals. The increasing degree of credit risk associated with WPPSS bonds increased underwriters' capital losses as a result of rapid price changes. But Merrill Lynch, known as the biggest of the wire houses and possessing an unmatched capacity to retail securities to individual investors across the country, was able to profitably market WPPSS securities. Its techniques for marketing the bonds included extensive pre-sale surveys and public relations efforts. For the negotiated issue in September, Merrill Lynch promoted sales by distributing blue campaign buttons reading "I'm bullish on the Supply System." The underwriter's promotional activities apparently worked. Because of investor demand, the issue was increased to $750 million from the $450 million originally proposed by the Supply System. The record 15 percent tax-free yield also helped attract investors, about 70 percent of whom were individuals.

Pre-sale promotion of WPPSS securities was especially necessary in 1981 as critical research reports were beginning to appear on Wall Street. During the spring prior to the first in the series of WPPSS negotiated bond sales, analysts at Wertheim & Company argued that WPPSS borrowing requirements had grown too large to be adequately supported by the investment community. Based on this analysis, Wertheim may have become the first prominent Wall Street brokerage firm to recommend termination of Plants 4 and 5. In June, Drexel Burnham Lambert issued a report arguing that the Supply

System probably could not raise the funds to complete Plants 4 and 5 because of portfolio saturation.

Ironically, Merrill Lynch's own fixed-income research department issued a critical report in July 1981 entitled *Washington Public Power Supply System: At the Crossroads* (Sitzer and Karvelis 1981). The report discussed portfolio saturation; the likelihood that Plants 4 and 5 would be terminated; the serious difficulties involved in financing such a termination; the improbability of a state or federal bailout of the projects; new, much lower regional power-use growth forecasts; and the increasingly inhospitable political climate in Washington State. The report was probably the most thorough and critical of all Wall Street analyses to that time. But it came at an inopportune time for the firm's sales staff, who were preparing for their upcoming role as managing underwriter on what would prove to be one of the largest municipal bond sales in history (at least until Merrill Lynch managed an $850 million negotiated sale five months later). The authors of the *Crossroads* report were told not to speak to the press, and Seattle newspapers reported rumors of growing internal conflict between Merrill Lynch research and sales staffs. Shortly after the bond sale, both authors of the report left Merrill Lynch for jobs at other firms.

LEGAL LIABILITY

The question is often asked, particularly in the Pacific Northwest, "If the WPPSS plants were not needed, or if the Supply System's management was so inept, why did Wall Street continue to loan WPPSS money?" The investment community is often portrayed as partly responsible, even legally responsible, for the WPPSS disaster.

Legally, however, the issue is unclear. There are few precise definitions of the legal liabilities of municipal bond issuers, underwriters, dealers, traders, brokers, and so on. Legislation exists, but much of it is vague or ambiguous and must be interpreted by the courts.

In the 1930s, when most of the federal legislation regulating the activities of the securities markets was written, municipal securities were considered to be immune to many of the problems that were associated with private corporate securities. The municipal market was relatively small, and municipal securities were relatively secure and free from problems of misrepresentation. Thus, they were exempted from many of the requirements set forth in the two primary pieces of legislation regulating securities, the Securities Act of 1933 (which was directed primarily at underwriting activities) and the Securities and Exchange Act of 1934 (which was directed primarily at buying, selling, and trading). Municipal securities were also exempt from most of the regulatory powers of the newly formed Securities and Exchange Commission. The only part of the Securities Act that directly applies to municipal securities is Section 17. This section deals with the fraudulent omission or misstatement of facts in an official document provided to potential investors.

Sections 17(a) and 10(b)(5) of the Securities and Exchange Act of 1934 have been applied in fraud cases involving municipal securities. The latter section sets forth the responsibilities of those who market municipal securities, including what constitutes due diligence investigations of municipal issuers.

The liability associated with any of these acts is defined in broad terms and requires definition and specification by the courts as to the actual degree of negligence in any given case. In the last major case of the 1970s, *Ernst & Ernst v. Hochfelder* (1976), the Supreme Court narrowed the scope of negligence liability. The court ruled that a securities firm is not liable for damage suffered by an investor in a case of fraud or misstatement of fact if the firm did not investigate because it had no reason to suspect fraud. In other words, if the firm did not investigate, but acted in good faith, it was not liable.

In 1975, after a series of fraud cases involving municipal brokers and dealers, Congress amended the Securities and Exchange Act of 1934. Brokers and dealers were forced to register with the SEC, and the Municipal Securities Rulemaking Board was created as an independent body to register and regulate the activities of municipal brokers and dealers, who were now required to provide certain information about the securities involved. But the continuing exemption of issuers and underwriters from disclosure regulation has created confusion.

Also in 1975 the SEC investigated issues associated with the financial crisis of New York State and New York City. The SEC concluded that standardized accounting and disclosure regulations were required to help prevent a recurrence of that kind of financial emergency. Bills proposed in Congress during the late 1970s were opposed by the municipal securities industry and never passed.

If nothing else, the many lawsuits and investigations that arise from the WPPSS disaster may help to clarify the legal responsibility of Wall Street investment and rating firms for adequate disclosure and financial advice.

STANDARD OPERATING PROCEDURES

While the lawsuits and investigations proceed, and until court decisions or legislation clarifies the legal responsibilities of the investment community, members of that community will continue to use what might be called their standard operating procedures. Most analysts, traders, underwriters, and so forth admit that these procedures can be reduced to a single maxim: Whatever is profitable, and legal, will be done. This is the essence of street ethics, the code of behavior that governs Wall Street more as a fact of life than as a moral imperative.

In other words, the individuals and organizations that make up the Wall Street community are not always motivated to fulfill the kinds of textbook role requirements described in this chapter. Street ethics considers it a mistake to assume that underwriters will question the need for a public debt financed project if the bonds can be sold at a profit and bond counsel declares the sale to be legal. Investment banking is a highly lucrative and highly competitive business.

Street ethics has also established that the traditional role of an analyst at an investment banking firm is to help market bonds. Most credit reports produced by these firms simply describe the issue, and reports seldom conflict with the marketing efforts of an investment firm's sell side. Street ethics also allow most major financial advisory firms to act at one time or another as underwriters for their advisees. When Blyth Eastman ended its relationship with WPPSS as the Supply System's financial adviser, it became an underwriter of WPPSS bonds. This potential for serving as an underwriter for their client's bonds contributes to limiting the financial advice given to marketing strategy.

How the Bonds Were Sold

In marketing bonds, especially when they are sold to individual purchasers, the rule that governs behavior is an even more freewheeling variation of the maxim mentioned above: Whatever is profitable, and not illegal, will be used to retail bonds. In other words, no attorney stands by and approves the legality of marketing techniques in the way that bond counsel give opinions on the legality of bond issues. This maxim manifested itself in three ways as the WPPSS crisis took shape and billions of dollars' worth of bonds were sold.

On the Basis of Ratings.   Above all, the bonds were sold on the basis of ratings that, by the 1980s, many salespeople knew to be unrealistically high. Until January 1983 both Standard & Poor's and Moody's gave bonds for WPPSS Projects 1, 2, and 3 a rating of AAA—the firms' highest rating. Roughly $6 billion in bonds were sold with the benefit of that rating. In June 1981 Standard and Poor's lowered its rating for Project 4 and 5 bonds from A-plus to A, shortly after Moody's downgraded 4 and 5 to Baa 1. These actions resulted from the Supply System's announcement that the total completion price for Projects 4 and 5 would be $12 billion, not the $8 billion estimate cited by the Supply System just months before. WPPSS 4 and 5 never came to market again. But $2.25 billion worth of Project 4 and 5 bonds had been sold with the benefit of Moody's A-1 and S & P's A-plus ratings. The downgradings came too late to benefit the bondbuying public. By June 1983 Moody's had suspended ratings for all projects, and Standard & Poor's had suspended ratings for Projects 1, 2, and 3. Project 4 and 5 bonds received Standard & Poor's highly speculative CC rating, the lowest possible rating for an issue that has not yet missed an interest payment.

Throughout this period the real significance of municipal ratings was obvious to anyone familiar with recent municipal defaults or near-defaults. Since the New York State crisis in 1975, all of the major municipal debt issues that eventually went into default were initially given investment grade ratings. This includes the Urban Development Corporation, as we have seen, and the bonds and notes of the Chicago Board of Education, which were rated investment grade in 1980 when the board was clearly in danger of default. When the Oklahoma Housing Finance Agency went into default in 1982, its construction bonds and notes were rated AAA and MIG-1 by Standard & Poor's and Moody's.[4]

As we have indicated, by 1975 Wall Street firms had already begun relying less on Moody's and Standard & Poor's credit ratings as indicators of credit quality. Even though in-house credit analyses still tended to support the activities of each firm's sell side, by the late 1970s these analyses were questioning the credit ratings assigned by the major rating agencies. For example, in February 1979 almost two and a half years before the major rating firms downgraded Project 4 and 5 bonds, Susan Linden, an analyst at Merrill Lynch Fixed Income Research, published a report on WPPSS 4 and 5 that openly questioned the existing A+ ratings. Linden cited the Theodore Barry management consulting report to emphasize the importance of construction cost-overruns and construction delays and show evidence of inadequate management capability. The Merrill Lynch report described Projects 4 and 5 as " . . . equivalent to a conditional low-range 'A'. The conditional nature of the rating will be removed and a higher credit level justifiable only upon successful operation of the project. Downward revision may be necessary unless timely financing and completion of the Projects occur" (Linden and Karvelis 1979: 1).

But the growing lack of faith in the major rating agencies evidenced in Linden's reports and those by analysts at other firms had little effect on the behavior of salespeople, especially when Moody's or S & P ratings could be used to sell bonds. In fact, Linden's approach to in-house analysis exemplifies very well the already growing tension between analysts and salespeople. After issuing a similarly negative opinion of ratings for the North Carolina Municipal Power Agency No. 1, a major underwriting client for the public finance department at Merrill, Linden left the Merrill Lynch staff. She was replaced by Howard Sitzer, who left Merrill under similar circumstances two years later.

Through UITs.[5]   Not only did ratings allow bond salesmen to retail billions of dollars of WPPSS bonds to individuals directly, but they also made possible indirect sales to sometimes unknowing investors. This second method of retailing involves unit investment trusts (UITs). UITs represent one of the three ways in which individuals buy municipal bonds—direct purchases can be made of individual bonds (which are typically in $5,000 denominations) or of shares of managed municipal bond funds.

Participation in a UIT involves the purchase of a unit, or share, in a large portfolio of bonds maintained by an investment house. UITs are especially convenient for small investors who simply do not have enough money to put together a defensive portfolio of municipal bonds. Unit investment trusts, usually offered in $1,000 shares, consist of portfolios that generally limit single-issue concentration in a range of 7.5 to 10 percent.

The UITs bought WPPSS 4 and 5 early and often and stayed with the issues until 1981. When they stopped buying, the denial to WPPSS of market access was inevitable. Unlike bond funds, UITs do not involve actively managed portfolios; instead, UITs are supposed to contain reasonably safe collections of bonds that have the highest possible yield. The major UITs, such as the Nuveen Trust and the Municipal Investment Trust (sponsored by Merrill Lynch, Bache, and Shearson, among others) have requirements specifying that only bonds with A ratings or better can be purchased for the trusts. It is possible that UITs purchased as much as 25 percent of all the WPPSS 4 and 5 bonds; they certainly combined to form the single largest category of institutional purchasing.

It is sometimes charged that the major brokerage firms, which were members of the WPPSS underwriting syndicates, simply used their UITs as a convenient place to dump a portion of their WPPSS underwritings. This may have been a consideration in some cases, but it pales beside the short-term competitive disadvantage a UIT would have created for itself had it not used WPPSS bonds in its portfolio as other, competing UITs did. UITs are marketed to people who are assumed to know almost nothing about municipal bonds, and if all the bonds in all the competing UITs are rated A or better, the only apparent difference to the buyer is the portfolio yield. WPPSS provided tremendous extra yield, and if a UIT decided to eliminate WPPSS from the portfolio, the yield became non-competitive with the other trusts.

Not only did UITs buy a lot of WPPSS bonds, but they continued to buy and hold WPPSS bonds. In other words, they helped support the market for those bonds long after the denial of market access should have occurred, and they also helped deny individual investors the danger signal that an institutional dumping of WPPSS securities would have provided. If interest rates steadily rise during the purchase period, the current market value of the total holding will decline substantially below the original purchase price. A decision to sell holdings (for reasons of declining credit quality) results in a direct loss. An insurance company (a casualty company that buys municipal bonds) can write off the loss against taxes. A bank can do this also, but when a UIT sells a holding, the portfolio loss is directly passed on to the unit holder, whose individual tax status is unknown to the trust sponsor. UIT portfolio managers do not like to sell and pass through losses because, historically, most UITs have found it more in their interests to sit through a workout in default, or a near miss, than to sell bonds at sharply discounted prices. If a portfolio manager sells a major holding at a substantial loss and the issue later works out to par value, it will not reflect well on the manager's performance. Most institutions, especially UITs, held on as long as possible to WPPSS bonds.

Through Misinformation. A third technique for selling bonds to individual investors took advantage of the fact that most individuals—even those making direct purchases of bonds—know very little about municipal securities. This did not necessarily involve any misrepresentation of fact, it simply meant allowing potential investors to believe something that was not necessarily true. As we have already seen, by the late 1970s the WPPSS staff was working closely with its financial adviser to tailor official statements to attract individual investors to its bonds. Whatever the actual intent of this tailoring, the effect was to make the careless reader or unsophisticated investor think the bonds were somehow backed by the federal government. Many investors in WPPSS bonds now consider this tailoring to be misrepresentation.

Widespread misuse of the term federal guarantee had a similar, if less profound effect. So too did other inaccuracies in the press. A late 1981 *New York Times* article reported the high yields associated with bonds for WPPSS Projects 1, 2, and 3, which were then "trading to yield 14 percent—equivalent to 28 percent for a taxpayer in the 50 percent bracket." Moreover, the article reported that all three plants "steadily produce power."[6]

Perhaps the best-known example of a mistatement contributing to what may have been millions of dollars in sales of WPPSS bonds is the letter from Comptroller of the Currency James E. Smith to a vice president of a New York City bank. The August 27, 1975, letter was a response to a question about whether or not banks, prohibited from underwriting most revenue bond issues by the Glass-Steagall Banking Reform Act of 1933, could underwrite WPPSS Project 1, 2, and 3 bonds. After describing the net billing arrangements, Mr. Smith went on to conclude that

> Through these arrangements the United States acting through Bonneville has undertaken an obligation to make available to the System amounts sufficient

to meet annual interest and principal payments on these bonds as well as all other costs of operating the Projects.

It is our conclusion that the $175,000 Washington Public Power Supply System, Nuclear Project No. 1, 1975 Revenue Bonds are obligations of the United States under paragraph Seven of 12 U.S.C. 24 and are eligible for purchase, dealing in, underwriting and unlimited holding by national banks (Smith 1975: 2).

In the process of upholding what has been a longstanding if informal policy of the comptroller's office to extend the area of national bank activity, Mr. Smith unwittingly helped brokers all over the country sell WPPSS bonds. Copies of the letter quickly circulated throughout Wall Street, and potential investors were soon being told that WPPSS Project 1, 2, and 3 bonds were "obligations of the United States."

Let the Buyer Beware

One reality confirmed by the WPPSS disaster is that whether selling bonds to investors or advice to public borrowers, the investment community cannot be relied on to consider all of the issues of interest to its clients. But neither does the financial community actually claim to cover that full range. Issuers of tax-exempt securities, like purchasers of tax-exempt bonds, are responsible for recognizing what the investment community can and cannot do for them, given the standard operating procedures discussed above. The alliance of public entities, private financial institutions, and investors is a powerful one, but it works to benefit all only when the roles and responsibilities of each are clearly understood by all.

A CASE STUDY IN WPPSS CREDIT ANALYSIS

To conclude this chapter on the role of the investment community in the WPPSS drama we will examine a case study of the kinds of research that promotional materials of investment firms claim to be the basis of their recommendations to buy and sell. The following example is actually a pair of credit analyses published by the investment firm of John Nuveen & Co. in the late 1970s and early 1980s. These analyses do not include every error or misrepresentation mentioned

in the above discussion, but they do present a cross section of interpretations of the WPPSS situation.

Nuveen advertises itself as the only major investment banking firm
specializing in the underwriting of municipal bonds: "Nobody knows
municipal bonds like Nuveen." Presumably to better understand and
market bonds such as those issued by WPPSS, Nuveen hired Sterling
Munro as a vice president after he left his position as administrator
of the Bonneville Power Administration in 1981. Nuveen was a co-
underwriter on a number of WPPSS bond issues and also purchased
over $100 million in Project 4 and 5 bonds for unit investment trusts
that the firm has marketed. (Nuveen sold off its portfolio of WPPSS
Project 4 and 5 bonds in August 1983, shortly after default.)

One extensive analysis of the general credit quality of all WPPSS
bonds was issued by Nuveen on June 29, 1979, in a twenty-seven-
page report entitled "Washington Public Power Supply System: Its
Role and Its Credit" (Lepinski 1979). The report was written while
Nuveen was preparing to act as co-managing underwriter of a syndicate bidding for $150 million in WPPSS Project 1 bonds. That bid
was unsuccessful, but Nuveen's activities as buyer and seller of
WPPSS bonds would continue, and presumably a positive credit
report could only help Nuveen in its selling efforts.

Neither Nuveen's activities as underwriter for WPPSS bonds (or
any other securities) nor its own purchases of WPPSS bonds were
acknowledged in the June 29 report. Like all credit reports of this
kind, however, it does include a disclaimer about possible misstate-
ments of fact or conflicts of interest: "Statements herein contained
are based upon information furnished us from official or other
sources. While we do not guarantee their correctness we believe them
to be reliable and have ourselves relied upon them" (Lepinski 1979:
cover sheet).

The report discusses the traditional areas of credit analysis, but
some of its conclusions, at least in retrospect, seem to reflect shortcomings of the standard approach.

Legal Factors

The report carefully points out that both net-billing contracts and
take-or-pay contracts in effect commit the revenue streams of the
WPPSS participants to the payment of WPPSS bonds, whether or not

power is ever generated. The report correctly notes that net-billing does not involve federal guarantees and that BPA does not have access to the U.S. Treasury for funds to pay for the net-billed plants.

But it does not conclude from this that bonds for the net-billed Projects 1, 2, and 3 should be considered of lower credit quality than their Aaa/AAA credit ratings would indicate. Those ratings are accepted without question. It is the lower ratings for Project 4 and 5 bonds that are questioned. The conclusion is that the take-or-pay Project 4 and 5 bonds are just as creditworthy as the net-billed project bonds and should be purchased when yield spreads are high enough to outweigh the loss of marketability caused by lower credit ratings. The report implies that the bonds differ in terms of marketability rather than credit quality and that the marketability difference results primarily from an unrealistic spread in ratings.

> Is the credit differential between the WPPSS Aaa/AAA bonds and the A 1/A+ bonds as great as indicated by the ratings? In other words, does Bonneville's involvement make WNP-1, 2 and 3 bonds substantially superior to the others? ... We believe that, ultimately, payment of principal and interest on all WPPSS securities will be derived from sales of continuing reasonably priced power to residents and industries of the Pacific Northwest—whether "Participants" or other customers of Bonneville Power Administration. We consider both types of WPPSS bonds appropriate for continued inclusion in revenue bond portfolios (Lepinski 1979: 18).

The report also adds a measure of optimism concerning the possibility that BPA might be allowed to purchase the output of Plants 4 and 5. The Northwest Regional Power Bill had already undergone two years of revisions without gaining passage by the time the Nuveen report was issued. But the report fails to mention the continuing legislative battle over the bill, and asserts that

> If the Regional Power Bill is passed, Bonneville would be authorized to continue supplying the major portion of power to the Pacific Northwest. BPA then, in the short-run, would have to purchase additional power from utilites with excess capacity and could purchase the output of any new WPPSS projects (Lepinski 1979: 14).

However, as the Nuveen report notes in another context, pending versions of the bill required BPA to try to meet its power needs through conservation and renewable resources *before* nuclear power could be considered.

Economic Factors

The report's analysis of economic factors simply assumes that the PNUCC projections of future demand growth were correct, even though a host of conflicting studies were available. The Natural Resources Defense Council report on the probability that conservation would drastically reduce the demand for electricity in the region was published a month before WPPSS began selling bonds for Projects 4 and 5 in February 1977 (Beers and Lash 1977).

The Nuveen report does note the possibility that conservation, rate increases, and other developments could dampen demand. But the report dismisses these possibilities with short opinions about their unlikelihood. It simply asserts that although conservation will be necessary in other parts of the country, "in the Pacific Northwest, hydro-facilities, together with thermal (nuclear or coal) generators, should not be drastically affected by the necessity of conservation" (Lepinski 1979: 8). And although the report describes rate increases as imminent, it quickly discounts their effects on demand:

> ... the presence of hydro-power should never let them [electric rates] approach rates necessary in other parts of the country. Although demand for electricity does decrease as rates increase in some parts of the country, these effects should not be significant in the Pacific Northwest (Lepinski 1979: 8).

The report never mentions the interaction of these possibilities, for example, to what degree rate increases might act as incentives for more conservation. The extremely high electricity usage levels in the Northwest are cited only as evidence that power costs are extremely low, not as evidence that tremendous potential existed in the late 1970s for conservation.

In sections that read more like a sales pitch than analysis, the report recites arguments why ratepayers should accept rate hikes, and why they should recognize that the risks of nuclear accidents, nuclear waste disposal problems, and damage to the environment are very low. The report notes that "Even if the average rate is tripled, the typical Pacific Northwest customer would still be paying less per KWH in 1990 than the residential customer of Consolidated Edison of New York paid in 1977 (96 mills)" (Lepinski 1979: 11). And to bolster its claim that the general public (and presumably investors) should not be fearful or critical of nuclear power, the report reprints U.S. Nuclear Regulatory Commission reactor safety statistics and includes an encouraging report on the aftermath of the Three Mile Island nuclear power plant accident. The report also points out that ratepayers have little choice but to accept the problems associated with WPPSS projects—the participating utilities were free from rate-making regulation and had the power to raise rates as high as necessary to cover their legal obligations.

Administrative Factors

The Nuveen report simply accepts the explanation of WPPSS management regarding the causes of already serious construction cost increases and schedule delays. The report states that "Information provided by the Supply System reveals that the cost increases can largely be attributed as follows: " and then shows a pie chart distributing cost increases among five categories of factors (Lepinski 1979: 12). Inflation and estimating and design refinements are shown to account for 40 percent of the increases; regulatory requirements and licensing delays account for 30 percent; nuclear fuel costs account for 15 percent; strikes, adverse weather conditions, contractor disagreements, etc. account for 12 percent; and special financing accounts for 7 percent. The Supply System's arguments are also given in the Nuveen report to explain away most of the apparent differences in costs between WPPSS projects and other similar projects across the nation.

The Nuveen report notes that the management of WPPSS "has suffered growing pains" (Lepinski 1979: 12). The report by Theodore Barry & Associates is mentioned, as is the fact that the WPPSS board had recently engaged the Institute of Public Administration to further study management problems. But the Nuveen report clearly states its view of the importance of problems that apparently had administrative causes:

> There will be additional cost escalations and, perhaps, more state control over WPPSS' operations. Bonneville's oversight role in the three net billed projects will be increased. Other factors will also surface. It is our opinion that, given the facts as in Benton County [a county in which electric rates increased in 1975 for the first time in twenty-eight years] , the area *will* accept these cost increases and *will* pay for these projects (Lepinski 1979: 14).

Financial Factors

Since no plants were in commercial operation in 1979, the Nuveen report could not include a debt ratio analysis to assess the actual operating performance of a governmental enterprise such as WPPSS. There were other financial factors that could have been mentioned, but were not. Chief among these was the fact that with over $4 billion in WPPSS bonds outstanding, and revised estimates showing a need for almost another $6 billion, WPPSS would soon face the problem of portfolio saturation. In fact, less than a year after the Nuveen report, WPPSS financial adviser Blyth Eastman reported that saturation had occurred in the portfolios of institutional investors. At that point, as noted earlier, the Supply System began to consider the possibility that it could lose access to the long-term bond market. But the Nuveen report simply reproduced without comment a table showing WPPSS debt outstanding and estimated future financing required.

A Follow-up Report

On January 27, 1982, shortly after the decision to terminate WPPSS Projects 4 and 5, Nuveen issued another research report, this time entitled "Termination is Good News for WPPSS and its Bondholders" (Daniels 1982). This report precedes by less than a week a negotiated sale of $500 million in WPPSS bonds. John Nuveen & Company was a member of the syndicate that underwrote the issue, and although the fact of such involvement is again not mentioned in the report, the standard disclaimer is included.

This report explicitly reaffirms Nuveen's June 1979 conclusion about the credit quality of all WPPSS bonds (Daniels 1982: 13). Termination was called "good news for bondholders" because it ended uncertainty concerning WPPSS plans; it refocused the energies of the WPPSS management team on Projects 1, 2, and 3; it reduced total costs and lowered total financing requirements; and it required the project participants to begin paying debt service payments after one year.

Legal factors are again important in the analysis. The report notes that all legal counsel associated with WPPSS and BPA were of the opinion that the take-or-pay contracts are legal and binding on the participants. The report does raise the possibility that participants might go into default or declare bankruptcy in spite of their legal obligations, but it notes that such action would probably have "long lasting effects on the ability of municipalities and PUDs to obtain credit" (Daniels 1982: 11). The report does not mention the extent to which most participants were aware of, or cared about, the possibility of limited access to credit markets in the future. By 1982 board members of most small utilities involved realized that their constituents would not let them borrow again in the near future, even if they wanted to.

Although BPA had no involvement with the take-or-pay projects, the Nuveen report seems to imply otherwise. In a summary of conclusions "from the perspective of a holder of 4-5 Project bonds," the report claims that "The Pacific Northwest's Federal hydro-electric and transmission system is a significant indirect credit strength" (Daniels 1982: cover sheet). The precise meaning of this statement is not clear.

In terms of economic analysis, the report refers to the now obvious overestimation of regional power needs by the PNUCC and the existence of new studies commissioned by the state legislature and authorized by the Regional Power Act. Earlier independent studies that had much more accurately forecast regional power needs are not mentioned. The necessity for rate increases is noted, as is the possibility that conservation might dampen demand. But since the absolute size of electric rates would still be low relative to those in other parts of the country, the report concludes that "it is our opinion that the average retail costs of power to the customers of a vast majority of Participants are affordable" (Daniels 1982: 8). The report fails to mention the fact that regional ratepayers viewed the rate increases in terms of their size relative to existing rates rather than relative to rates in New York or New Jersey. By the time the Nuveen report was issued, activist ratepayer groups were already exerting unexpectedly forceful pressure on the participants to hold down rate increases.

With regard to administrative analysis, this report fails to mention any of the management consultant studies commissioned by BPA or by WPPSS. Nor does it mention the conclusion of the Washington State Senate Energy and Utilities Committee in January 1981 that "WPPSS management has been the most significant cause of cost overruns and schedule delays on the WPPSS projects"—a fact that was routinely disclosed in the official statements for WPPSS bond offerings (Washington State Senate Energy and Utilities Committee 1981: 40).

The resignation of three outside members of the WPPSS board in January 1982 is mentioned as an attempt on their part to highlight organizational deficiencies of WPPSS. "Insofar as their resignation does, in fact, call attention to such deficiencies and results in constructive measures to improve the Supply System's management capabilities, the resignation may be regarded as a positive event" (Daniels 1982: 4). The termination of Projects 4 and 5 is seen as allowing WPPSS management to refocus their energies on the three remaining projects. But whatever the problems with the administration of WPPSS projects, either in terms of construction or financing, the Nuveen report claims that they should be distinguished from true credit problems: "We believe that part of the recent price deterioration in certain of the bonds is due to bond market participants not properly distinguishing between underlying credit issues and publicized construction-financing issues" (Daniels 1982: cover sheet).

In connection with financial issues, the report mentions problems of portfolio saturation but notes that with the termination of Projects 4 and 5, WPPSS "should be able to proceed with the orderly marketing of bonds to complete Projects 1, 2, and 3" (Daniels 1982: 7). The high costs of termination are noted, but the report assumes that the financial details would be worked out when WPPSS adopted its next budget and that participants would raise rates to cover costs (Daniels 1982: 7).

As this Nuveen report was being issued, WPPSS was already very clearly in a dangerous situation. The Project 4 and 5 participants were unhappily contemplating the rate increases that the report so quickly assumed would be affordable. Those increases would have had to cover termination costs, debt service costs, and wholesale power rates that already were being increased because BPA was forced to begin paying debt service on Project 2 bonds in 1977.

Moreover, rate increases would have to be borne by ratepayers who refused to accept abstract arguments about the absolute size of electric rates. And ratepayers were increasingly pressuring elected PUD directors. The fact that WPPSS management and BPA were widely held responsible for most of the cost escalations and inaccurate predictions of growth in the demand for power led many participants to believe that they were being made to pay for the mistakes of others.

The participants refused to settle on a budget in June 1982, and many decided to test in court the provisions of the take-or-pay contracts. By 1984 Nuveen had joined Merrill Lynch and other investment houses who were sued for their sales of WPPSS bonds as part of their unit investment trusts. Nuveen was charged with having "failed to disclose information concerning WPPSS available to it because of its expertise" (*Credit Markets* 1984: 4).

EPILOGUE

On June 15, 1983, the day of the state supreme court ruling voiding the take-or-pay contracts, trading in WPPSS 4 and 5 bonds came to a halt, although bonds issued in support of construction for the other three WPPSS plants continued to be traded, with declining values. On that same day, other municipal bond issues fell a half a point across the board. The reason, one trader reported, was that 15 to 18 percent of all municipal debt at that time was backed by agreements similar to those declared invalid by the court (Hale 1983: 5).

By the next day, trading on 4 and 5 bonds resumed, with the value of the bonds down by about $6 per $100 in face value. Speculators began actively seeking the bonds as their values continued to drop. On June 16 Moody's withdrew its Caa rating on the 4 and 5 bonds (Standard & Poor's had suspended its ratings on the bonds earlier). On July 22 WPPSS admitted it could not pay back interest or principal on the bonds.

The state of Washington was thought by many to be vulnerable to investor hostility after the state supreme court decision. One study sponsored by Washington State in 1981 speculated that the default would eventually cost the region $15 billion. A more recent study commissioned by Washington's governor concluded that "business will be unwilling to locate, and perhaps expand in the Northwest" (Knight/Bonniwell 1983: 3).

But in mid-August, two months after the court decision and just days before the default became official, the state successfully marketed a $150 million general obligation bond issue in the municipal bond market. Shortly thereafter Snohomish County PUD, the largest participant-owner of WPPSS 4 and 5, marketed a revenue bond issue to finance hydroelectric project construction. Both the state of

Washington and the Snohomish issues met some investor resistance, but both sold with only a slight penalty/premium, proving that Washington State and WPPSS participants could continue to obtain credit in the national market if their issues were otherwise well secured.

To some extent this reflects history. Major revenue bonds defaulted in the 1950s and 1960s without causing significant difficulties for the states and cities that issued them. For example, the West Virginia Turnpike, the Chesepeake Bay Bridge and Tunnel Authority, and the City of Chicago Calumet Skyway all defaulted, and these defaults had negligible impact on the overlapping jurisdictions.

However, these were defaults in which (1) the sponsored facility had been completed, (2) the pledged revenues (tolls) were being collected, (3) the pledged rate covenants were being enforced, and (4) the states or cities involved were not interfering with the administration or contracts of the defaulted operation. None of these previous defaults involved contract invalidation. The circumstances that led to the WPPSS 4 and 5 default were different from the toll-road and bridge defaults of the 1950s. Yet, despite an actual occurrence of what many investors, analysts, investment bankers, and so on considered a clear-cut case of state repudiation of debt, the municipal bond market continued to accommodate Pacific Northwest borrowers as though nothing particularly significant had happened.

A large number of institutional investors had expected that if the WPPSS 4 and 5 contracts were not upheld and enforced, or if the participants refused to pay their obligations by raising their rates, these actions would be followed by an institutional investor boycott of Pacific Northwest bonds, and possibly even the denial of access by Washington State to the bond markets.

Indeed, such a reaction seemed to be taking shape just prior to the $150 million bond sale by Washington State. Two weeks before the sale Oppenheimer & Company published a credit report recommending that investors avoid the issue. The report was prepared by Edward Hosinger, vice president and manager of Oppenheimer's Municipal Credit Analysis Department. Hosinger questioned the willingness of the state to pay back such loans because of the clear unwillingness of the states' residents to assume responsibility for WPPSS debt:

> Given the environment under which the residents have clearly voiced an unwillingness to pay a debt and given the inability to weigh the possibility that this same rate paying group may choose to do likewise on G.O. debt, we do not recommend the purchase, regardless of the interest rate (Hosinger 1983: 1).

Many investors and investment analysts agreed with Hosinger's conclusion. But officials of Washington State and Oppenheimer, a member of the syndicate that would price and sell the bonds, did not agree. After Washington State Treasurer Robert O'Brien threatened to sue the firm over alleged inaccuracies in the report, the firm withdrew it and replaced it with one written by John J. Bingham, senior vice president and national manager of Oppenheimer's Municipal Bond Department. Bingham's report reversed Oppenheimer's stand on the bonds and represented a major victory in Washington State's battle to escape punishment for the default:

> Contrary to an earlier report sent to some of Oppenheimer's clients in July 1983, Oppenheimer believes that the full faith and credit commitment and the unconditional pledge of the State's taxing power backing this proposed issue is sufficient to recommend purchase by Oppenheimer clients (Bingham 1983: 1).

Outraged members of the Municipal Analysts Group of New York met to consider issuing a statement on Hosinger's behalf, but after long debate the group voted not to speak out.

Washington State and some of its municipalities have paid higher interest rates on bond issues as a result of default. But none of these entities, with the exception of WPPSS itself, have been denied access to the capital markets because of the default, as so many investment bankers predicted. Nor is such denial of access likely as long as the market in municipal bonds continues to expand and there is money to be made selling the tax-exempt bonds of the state and its localities.

NOTES TO CHAPTER 3

1. This introductory section follows the discussion in Annmarie H. Walsh, *The Public's Business: The Politics and Practices of Government Corporations* (Cambridge: MIT Press, 1978), Chapter 3.
2. See Robert B. Nolan, " 'Take-Or-Pay' Contracts: Are They Necessary for Municipal Project Financing?" *Municipal Finance Journal* 4 (1983): 111-15.
3. For a discussion and comparison of most of the studies mentioned in this section, see the Washington Energy Research Center's *Independent Review*, pp. 75-82. See also George Hinman et al., *Energy Projections for the Pacific Northwest* (Pullman, Wash.: Environmental Research Center, Washington State University, 1975).
4. These observations about the quality of ratings by the major credit rating firms have moved some Wall Street analysts to publish their own frame-

works for analyzing the creditworthiness of municipal bonds. See the Preface to Sylvan G. Feldstein, Frank Fabozzi, and Irving Pollack (eds.), *The Municipal Bond Handbook*, Volume II (Homewood, Ill.: Dow Jones Irwin, 1983).

5. Special assistance in writing this section about unit investment trusts was provided by investment analyst "Sidney Smith."

6. Robert Metz, "Power Bonds in Northwest," *The New York Times*, December 7, 1981, pp. IV-8. A correction appeared the next day, but considerable damage probably had already been done. Potential bondholders who missed the correction could not help but be impressed with Metz's description of the bonds. Worse yet, unscrupulous bond salesmen had one more weapon to add to their marketing arsenals.

REFERENCES

Austen, Eileen Titmuss. 1981. *Washington Public Power Supply System.* New York: Drexel Burnham Lambert Inc., June 3.

Beers, Roger, and Terry R. Lash. 1977. *Choosing an Electrical Energy Future for the Pacific Northwest: An Alternative Scenario.* Palo Alto, Calif.: Natural Resources Defense Council, Inc. January.

Bingham, John J. 1983. *State of Washington, General Obligation Bonds.* New York: Oppenheimer & Co., Inc. July.

Blyth Eastman Paine Webber Public Power Finance Group. 1980. *Presentation to Washington Public Power Supply System: A Balanced Financing Program.* New York: Blyth Eastman Paine Webber Inc. April.

The Bond Buyer's Municipal Statbook 1984. 1985. New York: The Bond Buyer.

Business Week. 1983. "The Fallout From 'Whoops.'" (July 11): 80–87.

Chemical Bank v. WPPSS. 1983. 99 Wn.2d 772. June.

Credit Markets. 1984. "Nuveen Sued for Fraud Over Sales of Unit Trusts with WPPSS Bonds." (July 23): 3.

Daniels, Paul R. 1982. *Termination Is Good News for WPPSS and Its Bondholders.* Nuveen Research Comment. Chicago: John Nuveen & Co., January 27.

Falk, Theodore C. 1985. "Comparing the State WPPSS Cases: The Municipal Constitution." *Municipal Finance Journal* 6 (Spring): 111–36.

Gleckman, Howard. 1984. *WPPSS: From Dream to Default.* New York: Credit Markets.

Gotschall, Mary G. 1984. "John Mitchell, Dean of Bond Counsel, Discusses the Old Power Elite. *Credit Markets* (November 19): 13.

Hale, Jeannie. 1983. "Chemical Bank Decision–Liability of Washington PUDs and Municipal Participants." Memorandum to the Washington State Senate Energy and Utilities Committee from Staff Attorney. June 20.

Hinman, George; Paul Swanidass; and Walter Butcher. 1975. *Energy Projections for the Pacific Northwest.* Pullman, Wash.: Environmental Research Center, Washington State University.

Hosinger, Edward. 1983. *State of Washington, General Obligation Bonds.* New York: Oppenheimer & Co., Inc. July.

Institute of Public Administration. 1980. "Memorandum to Committee on Management Consultant, WPPSS Board of Directors." New York: Institute of Public Administration. July 16.

Knight/Bonniwell. 1983. *What Would Be the Potential Financial and Economic Impacts on the Northwest Should WPPSS Default on Plants 4 and 5?* Final report to the Office of the Governor, State of Washington. Chicago: Knight/Bonniwell. March 29.

Lamb, Robert, and Stephen P. Rappaport. 1980. *Municipal Bonds: The Comprehensive Review of Tax-Exempt Securities and Public Finance.* New York: McGraw-Hill.

Lepinski, Jerry. 1979. *Washington Public Power Supply System: Its Role and Its Credit.* Nuveen Research Comment. Chicago: John Nuveen & Co. June 29.

Linden, Susan M., and Leon J. Karvelis. 1981. *Washington Public Power Supply System: State of Washington (Nuclear Projects Nos. 4 and 5).* New York: Merrill Lynch Pierce Fenner & Smith Inc., Fixed Income Research Department, February 12.

Marion, Joseph, and Francis J. Quinn. 1980. *Competitive and Negotiated Offering: The Relative Merits of the Negotiated Method.* A report prepared for the Washington Public Power Supply System by Merrill Lynch White Weld Capital Markets Group. New York: Merrill Lynch Pierce Fenner & Smith Inc. November 24.

Northwest Energy Policy Project. 1978. *Energy Futures Northwest.* Portland, Ore.: Northwest Energy Policy Project. May.

Northwest Environmental Technology Laboratories. 1976. *Energy 1990 Consultants' Report.* Bellevue, Wash.: Northwest Environmental Technology Laboratories.

O'Brien, Brendan. 1982. Deposition given in *DeFazio et al. v. Washington Public Power Supply System et al.* September 29, 1982. Transcript on file in the staff office of the Washington State Senate Energy and Utilities Committee, Olympia, Wash.

Oregon Department of Energy. 1977. *Oregon's Energy Future.* Salem, Ore.: Oregon Department of Energy. January 1.

Patterson, Donald C. 1980. Letter from Senior Vice President of Blyth Eastman Paine Webber Inc. to James Perko, Assistant Director of Finance and Treasurer of the Washington Public Power Supply System. February 27.

Sitzer, Howard, and Leon J. Karvelis. 1981. *Washington Public Power Supply System: At the Crossroads.* New York: Merrill Lynch Pierce Fenner & Smith Inc., Fixed Income Research Department. July 24.

Skidmore, Owings, and Merrill. 1976. *Electric Energy Conservation Study.* Report prepared for the Bonneville Power Administration. Portland: Skidmore, Owings, and Merrill. July.

Smith, James E. 1975. Letter from Comptroller of the Currency, to Paul S. Tracy, Jr., Vice President of First National City Bank of New York. August 27.

Standard & Poor's. 1979. *Standard & Poor's Ratings Guide.* New York: McGraw-Hill.

U.S. General Accounting Office. 1978. *Region at the Crossroads—the Pacific Northwest Search for New Sources of Electric Energy.* Washington, D.C.: U.S. Government Printing Office. August 10.

Walsh, Annmarie Hauck. 1978. *The Public's Business: The Politics and Practices of Government Corporations.* Cambridge, Mass.: MIT Press.

Washington Energy Research Center, Office of Applied Energy Studies. 1982. *Independent Review of Washington Public Power Supply System Nuclear Plants 4 and 5: Final Report to the Washington State Legislature.* Seattle: Washington Energy Research Center, Washington State University/University of Washington. March 15.

Washington Public Power Supply System. 1979. *Official Statement of Washington Public Power Supply System.* Relating to its $175,000,000 Generating Facilities Revenue Bonds, Series 1979A (Nuclear Projects Nos. 4 and 5). Richland, Wash.: Washington Public Power Supply System. January 29.

Weekly Bond Buyer. 1983. "WPPSS Looks to Curb Escalating Legal Costs" (June 6): 3.

Winders, John J. 1980. "Are Bond Counsel Obliged to Serve Others in Addition to Their Clients?" *Weekly Bond Buyer* (August 25): 1.

4 FORMAL OVERSIGHT

In terms often used in private business, the ongoing, day-to-day management of an organization such as WPPSS is the responsibility of its full-time executive officers. The board of directors is responsible for the direction of the organization—the establishment of its goals and major policies. The WPPSS board has ultimate legal responsibility for the organization.

Oversight is not a term that is generally used in business management. The most common use of the term is a legislative one, referring to the monitoring of federal government bureaus by the committees of the U.S. House or Senate that brought them into existence and remain responsible for their conduct. This kind of oversight is undertaken to judge the efficacy of existing legislation and to generate recommendations for new legislation. But this use of the term is not accurate in the WPPSS case since there are no inherent federal oversight prerogatives over state and regional agencies, even when those agencies depend upon federal loans and grants (which the Supply System did not).

In connection with public agencies of various sorts, including WPPSS, oversight refers to existing, legally based power and responsibility to act as a line of defense—beyond managers and directors—against violations of the public interest. In the case of WPPSS, a number of groups shared formal and informal oversight functions; these

135

groups constitute the outer concentric rings of power and influence that shared in the responsibility for the problems of WPPSS.

The relative position of these oversight rings has corresponded with their influence on WPPSS. The innermost rings, such as BPA, have more formalized and direct responsibility for day-to-day oversight than do the more distant rings such as the ratepayers, courts, or Congress, whose responsibilities are less clear-cut and whose actual oversight activities may be infrequent. Project co-owners and participants (as opposed to Supply System members) have agreements with WPPSS that allow for certain review and approval-granting powers. Because the creation of WPPSS was made possible by state law WPPSS is, in a sense, a state agency subject to Washington State law. BPA's oversight powers are based on contractual provisions of the project agreements, subsequent laws, and agreements with WPPSS. State courts may be asked to rule on the legality of WPPSS activities. The U.S. Nuclear Regulatory Commission has oversight power because of its charge to inspect, regulate, and enforce standards with respect to the construction and operation of nuclear power plants. All of these bodies have legal responsibility of one kind or another to exercise formal oversight powers in the interest of their respective constituencies.

Another variety of formal oversight power is exercised by those constituencies that possess limited rights and responsibilities to protect their own interests. Ratepayers in Washington State public utility districts (PUDs) have the right to elect or recall members of PUD boards. Voters in Washington State have the right to pass referenda limiting the activities of state corporations there. And any citizen can bring questions of law before the courts.

In the case of WPPSS, little effective oversight was exercised. Although a number of actors in the WPPSS drama had formal rights and responsibilities for overseeing WPPSS activities, few practical, constructive avenues for exercising that oversight had ever been built. Under these conditions, rights and responsibilities may conflict or be used simply to protect the overseer from blame. Most destructive is the case in which the inner rings simply fail to provide adequate oversight. Too much responsibility may be pushed outward to groups and individuals such as the courts and ratepayers, whose oversight methods are more strictly punitive than constructive.

Any effort to explain the difficulties facing WPPSS must take into account the roles played by all of these oversight groups. This chapter discusses four of the most important ones: Washington State, the Bonneville Power Administration, the region's ratepayers, and the Washington State courts.

WASHINGTON STATE OVERSIGHT

Washington State's governmental apparatus and tradition is characterized by many features that tend to work against both strong state oversight with regard to entities like WPPSS and decisive action to resolve problems once they occur:

- A weak governor, with inadequate staff and no tradition of strong, independent leadership. On public power issues (a vital state interest), both the governor and legislature have been virtually frozen out of meaningful decisionmaking.

- Washington has no income tax. It operates on a biannual budget in which massive revenue-to-expenditure shortfalls can (and do) occur in periods of economic downturn.

- The Washington legislature has no tradition of managing a crisis or reaching negotiated settlements involving hard political choices.

- Washington, like the rest of the Pacific Coast, is an initiative-referendum state. The state code can be amended by a direct vote of the people.

- Washington, like Oregon, has a history of agrarian populism that has been reinforced by physical isolation from other large U.S. population centers. Both states are "swing states" that may vote heavily Republican or Democrat in national elections. In both states there is a major east-west (of the Cascades) division pitting rural (irrigated farming) interests against the population centers on Puget Sound and the Willamet Valley.

Without a tradition of strong state government and a strong governor, and a West Coast penchant for direct democratic populism, the odds were greatly reduced that any single actor or group in the Washington State government would ever be in a position to provide either strong oversight with regard to WPPSS activities during the 1970s or the leadership to initiate a negotiated resolution of WPPSS problems when they began to become apparent in 1979. But the Washington State government further complicated its relationship with WPPSS in two ways. First, the state legislature passed laws enabling WPPSS to be constituted as a municipal corporation of the state, with all of the freedoms from outside control that such organizations typically enjoy. Second, state legislation also made possible the Supply System's status as a joint action agency. As such, WPPSS shares some unique powers and freedoms with the governmental bodies that comprise it.

WPPSS—The Public Authority

As pointed out in Chapter 2's analysis of WPPSS management problems, WPPSS is a public authority or municipal corporation of Washington State. This little-understood form of American government is a mystery to many state and local legislators, as well as to most of the general public. Known across the country as corporations, authorities, banks, services, agencies, commissions, and so forth—but usually referred to as public authorities—these authorities build and run bridges, tunnels, parkways, dams, ports, airports, public buildings, railroads, and industrial and recreational parks. They provide essential services, including water, gas, electric power, transportation, training, and insurance. And they increasingly administer a wide array of loans and subsidies to private business and other governmental agencies. By the late 1970s probably at least 6,000 local or regional authorities and 1,000 state and interstate authorities were in operation (Walsh and Mammen 1983: 5).

Authorities such as WPPSS are bodies authorized by legislative action to function outside of the regular executive structure of state government. They function outside in that they are independent legal entities with purposes and powers defined in a statute or charter granted under law. They do not have powers to tax, but because of their legal identity they can use and reuse revenues, borrow, and own assets. They also can sue or be sued, enter into contracts in their own names, and have liability distinct from that of the government that chartered them. Their independent character allows them to act almost as if they were not governmental at all, and that is precisely the point of their existence. Public authorities are designed to have the independence and flexibility to act in a businesslike fashion.

Specifically, this separate legal nature provides two kinds of flexibility, both of which were enjoyed by WPPSS. First, authorities are usually permitted a great deal of administrative flexibility by being exempted from many of the procedures and regulations that apply to executive line agencies, including civil service and personnel rules, procurement procedures, and internal operating rules. They are typically allowed to determine their own auditing, accounting, and budgeting procedures.

Second, authorities are capable of independent borrowing. In fact, this is probably their most distinctive single characteristic. In many states, constitutions or legislatures have instituted strict limits on the amount of general obligation debt the state can issue. Such debt is backed primarily by the taxing powers of the state. Many states also require popular referenda in advance of state borrowing and prohibit executive line agencies from selling revenue bonds. Most public authorities can circumvent these constraints and gain access to the bond market by issuing revenue bonds, which are backed by the revenues of their projects rather than by the taxing powers of a specific city or state.

Both kinds of flexibility can have negative consequences. Administrative flexibility makes it difficult for oversight bodies to guard against mismanagement. Financial flexibility, in the form of independent borrowing capacity, makes it difficult for legislative bodies to influence policy priorities of authorities or to ensure prudent issuance of debt.

It is typical, however, for authorities to operate within some kind of minimal regulatory framework. The Port Authority of New York and New Jersey is usually credited with being the first authority established in the United States, and it has become a model for many later ones. It has grown into one of the richest and most powerful, even though it is theoretically subject to a wide range of administrative regulations and procedural rules. Resolutions of its board of commissioners (the functional equivalent of the WPPSS board of directors) are subject to veto by the two governors. All requests for new projects or powers must be authorized by the two state legislatures. And the taking over of property requires the consent of the landowning municipality. As is the case with many other state authorities, the two governors appoint the Port Authority board members, and legislative committees and state auditors are empowered by law to conduct investigations and audits whenever they choose.

WPPSS—The Joint Action Agency

As a public authority, WPPSS enjoyed all of the aforementioned kinds of administrative and financial flexibility. But because WPPSS was also a joint action agency the state assumed few of even the most minimal oversight powers. Based on state legislation enacted in 1953 any two or more public utility districts or municipalities were allowed to form a municipal corporation for the purposes of purchasing, building, owning, and operating electrical generation and transmission facilities. Washington was only the second state to pass such legislation (California was the first in 1949), and it was not until 1972 that more states followed suit.

The Washington State Public Utility District Association played a major part in getting the legislation passed, and in some respects the curious character of Washington's PUDs was responsible for the curious character of the state's oversight relationship with WPPSS. From 1933, when Grand Coulee Dam was built on the Columbia River, to the mid-1950s, public power development in the Pacific Northwest was largely in the hands of the federal government. When direct federal sponsorship of public hydropower development began to taper off, area PUDs increased their involvement. These were a unique variety of what the Federal Census of Governments calls a special district. Special districts are distinguished from public authorities in that they tax residents and often have a closer legal relationship to their parent governmental bodies than do public authorities. If these special districts issue debt at all, it tends to be general obligation (GO) bonds rather than revenue bonds.

But in Washington State the PUDs enjoy a wide range of governmental powers, virtually combining the legal autonomy and revenue debt issuing capacity of public authorities with the taxing powers of special districts. PUDs even have the power to create, at their discretion, local assessment districts (*Washington Revised Code* 1981c). Perhaps most important was the fact that the electric rates set by PUDs and municipal utilities were not subject to regulation by any federal or state utility commission or similar agency. Because Washington State's PUDs had democratically elected boards and because the PUDs had inherited a highly successful legacy of hydropower expansion, they became the focus of regional public power development and a source of pride for the region. But because many of them were small, they considered legislation enabling the formation of joint ventures a necessary part of their role in developing the area's power resources.

The desire to help PUDs develop the hydroelectric potential of the area was the motive behind the state law, and it explains to some extent why the legislation describes joint action agencies as though they were public utility districts writ large. The powers of joint action agencies were described in terms of PUDs: "Except as otherwise provided in this section, a joint operating agency shall have all powers now or hereafter granted public utility districts under the laws of the state" (*Washington Revised Code* 1981a). The duties of the board officers are described similarly: "The president and secretary shall perform the same duties with respect to the operating agency as are provided by law for the president and secretary, respectively, of public utility districts. . . . " (*Washington Revised Code* 1981b).

Most important of all, the locally based democratic control over PUDs was to be used to control joint action agencies as well. After initial certification was granted by the state, the chief form of joint action agency oversight was to be exercised by its members, all of whom were to be represented on the board of directors. All policy decisions, including what new projects would be taken on and who would be accepted as new members and project participants, were left to the discretion of the board. Because WPPSS was a municipal corporation, its board was required to appoint an independent financial auditor whose report was to be filed with the state auditor. Also, approval for the initiation of certain projects required permits, licenses, and approvals from state agencies. But any kind of ongoing, institutionalized oversight activities by the state legislature were essentially nonexistent.

Legislative Action

It would be inaccurate to suggest that many more controls would have been available to legislators had WPPSS not been a joint action agency. Municipal corporations in Washington State, as in most other states, have almost complete freedom from outside interference. But it appears that because WPPSS was an offspring of the highly respected PUDs, state legislators considered WPPSS and its problems to be the responsibility of WPPSS members, if any consideration was paid at all. Through the 1970s state officials were certainly far less critical of Supply System problems than they would have been if WPPSS were a traditional state authority. The state legislature paid very little attention to WPPSS problems until the release of the first drafts of the Theodore Barry report in 1978. This coincided with the first public awareness of BPA rate increases and with the local news media's closer coverage of WPPSS. In 1979 a number of legislative proposals were made to institute ongoing oversight activities by the state legislature or by interstate bodies. The response to such proposals from influential regional public power lobbyist Ken Billington typifies the attitude of state legislators who voted down most of these bills:

> What would be the purpose of legislative oversight? There's a board of duly elected public utility district commissioners doing that job right now. And they are tough. Can a legislator give a better judgment on nuclear plant construction than the supervisor of Seattle City Light? (Scates 1982a: D9)

In May of 1979, as the first wave of WPPSS problems was cresting, the state legislature added a new section to the state joint operating agency law, requiring that the Supply System appoint an independent consultant to provide administrative audits of WPPSS efforts to control costs, schedules, productivity, contract amendments, project design, and other areas specified by the board. The bill also set up a legislative review procedure. The reports of the consultant were to be furnished to the Legislative Budget Committee, which was charged with evaluating these management audits as to adequacy and effectiveness of procedure. That committee was also required to file its report and recommendations with each committee chairman. The Supply System was required to file copies of the consultant's reports with the chairmen of the Senate and House Energy Committees. And if requested by those committees, WPPSS was to report to each on a quarterly basis.

The WPPSS board objected to the idea of even this kind of minimal state scrutiny of its activities. In a letter to Governor Dixy Lee Ray, dated May 18, 1979, board President Glen Walkley criticized the proposed oversight bill because it

> ... does not establish any effective way to control project cost escalation, schedule slippage, internal project control, and the change order process. Thus, there are no benefits to the ratepayer provided by the bill. We would welcome such a bill if it could accomplish such ends (Walkley 1979).

Of course, accomplishing such ends was precisely and exclusively the responsibility of the WPPSS board. These legislative review procedures represented the first meaningful attempt by the Washington State government to carry out its own responsibilities with regard to what was, in effect, a subsidiary governmental corporation. The state government was finally setting up the kind of oversight framework that, in the WPPSS case at least, should have been in existence eight years earlier.

On February 7, 1980, the State Senate Energy and Utilities Committee sent a resolution to the Senate Committee on Rules requesting subpoena power to conduct an in-depth investigation of WPPSS problems. On January 12, 1981, the report was issued. It blamed mismanagement as the primary cause of cost overruns and called for an independent study of whether or not Plants 4 and 5 were needed.

In an attempt to improve WPPSS management, the legislature next passed a law requiring that the WPPSS executive committee be reconstituted as an eleven-member executive board with four outside directors. This was to be done by October 26, 1981, and the new executive board was to assume all of the old powers of the full board, with the exception of budget approval, decisions about termination and sale of projects, and some powers of appointment. Four outside directors were appointed on October 23, but one resigned a few weeks later. The other three resigned on January 15, 1982, when it became clear that Projects 4 and 5 would be terminated and a plan simply to delay construction on the plants would not be supported by the project participants. The outside directors claimed that when they assumed their directorships they had believed that the plans for a construction slowdown would be implemented. They also felt that the decision to terminate the plants would take most of the decisions with respect to those plants out of the hands of the Executive Board.

On January 22, 1982, WPPSS officially terminated Projects 4 and 5. In March the legislature again passed legislation reconstituting the WPPSS executive board. The new eleven-member executive board was to have six outside members—three appointed by the governor and three by the full board. The other five members were to come from the existing board.

On March 18, 1982, a bipartisan group of eighteen Washington State legislators called on WPPSS to mothball another plant because of new, low power forecasts; huge additional financing requirements; and ratepayer protests. They suggested a work stoppage at Plant 3, which, at only 50 percent complete, would be the last plant to become operational. In April BPA requested that WPPSS mothball Plant 1 for up to five years because some of the participants in Plant 3 were investor-owned utilities who were likely to create legal problems if the construction of their plant were delayed. The board of directors complied. Work was later stopped on Plant 3 as well.

Since 1982, the governor and state legislature have called for investigations and study commissions, held hearings, asked for assistance from federal officials, and tried to reassure members of the investment community. The one thing that Washington State officials have not done, and will not, is to voluntarily take responsibility for the actions of their subsidiary corporation. In early November 1984 the National WPPSS 4 and 5 Bondholders Committee filed a $7.25 billion lawsuit against Washington State to recover principal and interest on the defaulted bonds. Among other things, the suit charged that the state had a moral obligation to bondholders and that the state auditor was negligent in certifying that WPPSS bonds were issued in accordance with state law—the auditor's opinion had appeared in offering statements for WPPSS bond sales. At the time this suit was filed in King County Superior Court, Washington State securities law stipulated that charges of fraud could be proven if negligence could be shown. In other words, unlike federal securities law, state law did not require investors to prove that state officials deliberately intended to defraud in order to win their claims.

But although WPPSS is indeed a public corporation of the state, as the lawsuit contends, the legal independence afforded WPPSS precisely because of that status will make it difficult to prove that the state has obligations, moral or otherwise, associated with Supply System actions. In the spring of 1985 the Washington State Legislature tried to ensure that bondholders and others could not recover damages even if state officials, such as the state auditor, WPPSS executives, or public utility officials, could be shown to be negligent in carrying out their duties. In an amendment to the Washington State Securities Act, legislators required that deliberate intention to defraud be proven before damages could be awarded. An aide to the governor told the press that the law was "designed to be retroactive" (Gleckman and Gresock 1985: 57). A federal judge ruled in January 1986 that such a law could not apply to events occurring prior to its enactment, but the state legislature has vowed to find other ways to protect state officials from lawsuits.

BPA OVERSIGHT

Through the 1970s the formal oversight responsibilities of BPA with regard to WPPSS activities were defined in project and net-billing agreements with WPPSS, as well as in WPPSS bond covenants. If we were concerned only with legal liability for the WPPSS disaster, these would be the places where we would look for formal description of the WPPSS-BPA relationship. But in terms of responsibility in a cause and effect sense, we must look also at BPA informal influence over WPPSS activities and its role in the design and implementation of the region's nuclear power development efforts.

Background

From the late 1960s to the late 1970s, BPA was without doubt the most influential body in regional power planning for the Pacific Northwest. Its influence was the result of its responsibility for the acquisition, marketing, and transmission of electricity produced by federally owned dams in the region, and the fact that it dealt regularly with about 150 utility, industrial, and government customers in eight western states.

BPA initiated discussions of area power needs by the Joint Power Planning Council in the late 1960s, took the lead in formulating the Ten Year Hydro-Thermal Power Program, and presented the program to Congress that same year. Net-billing agreements allowed BPA to provide an indirect security behind Projects 1, 2, and 3. And BPA's charter helped to determine who would make use of that security and manage the actual construction—a public body such as WPPSS.

In 1976 BPA notified its customers that by the early 1980s it would be unable to supply the amount of power required by the region, and it made plans to build two more plants, again with the help of net-billing agreements. But because BPA's net-billing capacity was exhausted (and because net billing had since been disallowed by federal law), WPPSS and eighty-eight participants decided to build the two plants themselves. In order to provide adequate security for bond issues, they entered into take-or-pay, come-hell-or-high-water agreements to guarantee repayment of the bonds whether or not the projects were ever completed or capable of operation.

However as we have already noted, many, if not all, of the participants expected that eventually BPA would be allowed to purchase the power output of the plants, thus spreading costs throughout BPA's customer base. Most participants expected that the Northwest Regional Power Act, which their planning organization introduced before Congress in 1977, would provide BPA with the authority to make such a purchase. Nevertheless, in spite of the BPA role in urging the construction of Projects 4 and 5, BPA had no legal involvement in the projects and no oversight responsibilities. Its formal, legal oversight role was limited to WPPSS Projects 1, 2, and 3.

Formal Oversight

BPA's active involvement in WPPSS activities was determined by its original mission, further specified by Congress in 1974, to encourage "the widest possible diversified use of electric power at the lowest possible rates to consumers consistent with sound business principles" (Columbia River Transmission Act 1974: Sect. 9). This mission also required that BPA exercise certain oversight functions with regard to WPPSS activities, and these functions were included in project and net-billing agreements and bond covenants. But most of the problems that would eventually confront WPPSS were not even contemplated at the time those documents were drawn up. As a result, the actual descriptions of oversight responsibilities reflected the informality and lack of attention to detail that plagued most aspects of WPPSS contracting procedures during the early 1970s.

BPA's past involvement in WPPSS projects also played a part in its relaxed attitude toward formal provisions for oversight on the three net-billed nuclear plants. In the early 1960s BPA had exercised an oversight role in the construction of the Richland project because of power-exchange contracts that allowed BPA to acquire power from that plant. As federal auditors noted years later, the level of BPA involvement in WPPSS construction of the Richland plant was very high compared to that in the three net-billed plants. When questioned about this, BPA officials reported that BPA involvement on the Richland project was eventually judged to be unnecessary and even excessive, and when contracts were signed for the later projects BPA willingly accepted a much less active role (U.S. General Accounting Office 1979: 8).

Most BPA responsibilities relating to the net-billed projects were defined in general terms. BPA had the right of budget approval, but the level of detail for this approval was not specified. BPA also had the right to approve line-item changes exceeding $500,000, the selection of architect-engineer firms, the selection of major plant systems, and financing issues. In extreme cases, BPA could demand that WPPSS make use of alternative business practices if WPPSS were judged by an independent consultant to be violating prudent utility practices.

In actual practice, at least until 1977, BPA took the Supply System's word on the vast majority of questions that arose between the two organizations. Budgets were reviewed and approved in the most general way, and the extreme measures available to BPA were never used because they were highly impractical. Prudent utility practices were very difficult to define, especially in an industry as dynamic as nuclear power plant construction. By themselves such extreme measures would increase costs and interfere with schedules, not to mention damage the Supply System's reputation in the investment community.

Nor did BPA have personnel able to make informed judgments about WPPSS construction activities. A report by the U.S. Comptroller General, issued in late 1979, noted that although BPA had originally set up a Thermal Projects Office to oversee the WPPSS construction program, the office had never been staffed adequately. In 1979 only 6 of BPA's 800 professional positions were assigned to the office; at the time of the comptroller's study, only 5 of these positions were filled, and none of the individuals had previous experience with nuclear construction projects (U.S. General Accounting Office 1979: 8). As the Theodore Barry & Associates report pointed out in 1978 (pp. III-23, 24), BPA simply did not know what information to request from WPPSS and did not have the staff to review it even if WPPSS was willing to supply it.

Through 1978, according to the Theodore Barry report, BPA was not even represented at the WPPSS board meetings, much less at staff meetings, and had no regular interaction with top management. Most of the BPA involvement in WPPSS activities was through project engineers at each of the net-billed sites. But these engineers were also inexperienced in nuclear power plant construction, their review work at the three plants was not coordinated, and they did not interact with WPPSS project personnel above the project level. Because

WPPSS project personnel were delegated little decisionmaking authority, the BPA engineers were able to react to major decisions only after the fact. Nor were the evaluations of BPA engineers routinely communicated to higher level WPPSS executives.

Attempts to Strengthen Oversight

BPA was forced to heed its oversight role as it became clear that Project 2 would not be completed as of June 1977, when the plant was originally scheduled to begin commercial operation. Until that time WPPSS was able to meet debt service requirements with continued borrowing. But under the project agreements, as of "date certain" BPA was required to begin making debt service payments out of its own revenues. Because the plant was not yet in operation, BPA was forced to increase rates to its customers. And because of provisions in its contracts with customers, BPA was unable to schedule rate increases between 1974 and 1979. There was no way to gradually introduce customers to higher rates. BPA first projected the 1979 rate increase to be 40 percent. But with continued WPPSS cost increases and schedule delays, BPA was forced to begin revising upward the projected rate figure. In 1976, it was projected at 60 percent, and in 1978 it was raised to 90 percent. BPA also announced changes in customer contracts to allow for annual rate increases and indicated that rates would be raised annually at least through 1985. The large rate increases caught the attention of the press, and BPA came under fire for exposing ratepayers to the dangers of the WPPSS situation.

In September 1977 the Department of the Interior's Office of Audit and Investigation reported that BPA had been ineffective in dealing with WPPSS and its problems. In the auditors' view, the major BPA oversight weakness was the lack of any mechanisms for influencing WPPSS decisions. The report suggested working toward "mutually agreeable" means for BPA participation in critical decisionmaking, the definition of BPA oversight activities in "functional and organizational terms," and language in any future agreements between the two agencies to enable BPA to "effectively influence the management decision-making process (U.S. Department of the Interior 1977: 7).

The spring of 1978 was a pivotal time for the WPPSS-BPA relationship. It may have been the last time that BPA could have created some kind of constructive oversight role for itself. Instead, the relationship began to deteriorate badly, and never recovered. In 1978 Sterling Munro was appointed to head BPA, taking over from Donald Hodel, who had held the position from 1972 to 1978. Munro had come from Senator Henry Jackson's staff, and in the minds of many WPPSS directors Munro was being groomed for higher political office, possibly that held by Washington State's other long-time U.S. Senator, Warren Magnusen. Munro did little to dispel that suspicion, and he quickly made many enemies at WPPSS by launching a highly aggressive and visible campaign of criticism against the Supply System. WPPSS board members and top executives were already growing more and more defensive and, if anything, Munro's attacks encouraged the Supply System to be even less cooperative both with BPA and the press.

One of the first telling blows in the BPA-WPPSS conflict came in the spring of 1978 when BPA explained its price increases primarily in terms of WPPSS cost overruns. WPPSS director Neil O. Strand responded that the figures were somewhat inflated and the explanation unfair because BPA costs also depended on other projects.

Next, in response to the Department of the Interior's audit, BPA announced the hiring of a management consultant Theodore Barry & Associates to investigate cost increases on the net-billed projects. In its statements to the press announcing the new study, BPA spokesmen used the preliminary WPPSS cost estimate figures, which WPPSS had always disowned, to underscore the huge construction cost increases experienced by the Supply System. According to press accounts, the BPA spokesmen emphasized that the target of the investigation was WPPSS and its problems. Theodore Barry's actual objective was to

> make an overall assessment of the roles of BPA and WPPSS in the net-billed projects with the ideal of improving the effectiveness of this relationship as it contributes to the timely and economic construction of these facilities (Washington Public Power Supply System 1980: 4).

WPPSS management responded by announcing the assignment of monitors to all WPPSS employees to be interviewed by the BPA consultants. In the fall, the local press acquired a copy of a letter sent by Munro to Strand noting that in effect BPA had the power to halt all of the projects by disapproving budgets. Munro assured the press that this measure would never be taken but added that BPA was very concerned with WPPSS shortcomings. In December the first drafts of the Theodore Barry report were sent to WPPSS board members and simultaneously made available to the press by BPA. The president of the WPPSS board agreed with a reporter's suggestion that the report could be seen as "a hatchet job," but the board refused to discuss the report in open meeting (members of the press were expelled from the board room).

In late 1978 Munro acknowledged the growing public awareness of his adversarial relationship with WPPSS, telling a U.S. House subcommittee that Bonneville had pursued in news releases, speeches, newsletters, and direct communication a "policy of openness" with regard to WPPSS construction cost increases and schedule delays. Munro admitted that it was a policy "that has bruised some feelings but which I think was absolutely necessary" (Munro 1979: 6). Because of the vagueness of the project and net-billing agreements, and because BPA had made almost no attempt to establish a formal oversight relationship with WPPSS before 1978, there was very little, besides bruising feelings, that Munro or his staff could do to force WPPSS to change its ways.

But WPPSS was woefully unprepared for public relations warfare. Because the Supply System had not operated in the public eye during the early and middle 1970s, WPPSS' public relations capabilities were almost nonexistent. It was not until the spring of 1979 that WPPSS took the first steps in establishing a formal, high-level public relations office to serve as a primary point of liaison with the outside (Institute of Public Administration 1979b). WPPSS was an open and inviting target for embarrassing attacks in the press, yet this very fact probably meant that such abrasive tactics could only be counterproductive. With their centralized management style and increasingly defensive attitudes, WPPSS administrators were not about to take the patronizing advice of outsiders, especially when it was communicated in local newspapers.

TBA Oversight Recommendations

The Theodore Barry & Associates report documents the problems facing BPA as it attempted to create and apply oversight authority, with very little legal precedent, and after ten years of allowing WPPSS a free rein in its affairs. The Theodore Barry consultants had been asked to suggest ways of improving an oversight relationship that, in reality, did not exist. There was obviously an urgent need for someone to take control of the growing WPPSS problems. As noted earlier at length, the consultants identified many of the same fundamental management problems that the Cresap consultants had cited two years earlier: the basic inexperience and lack of direction provided by the WPPSS board; BPA shortcomings such as not knowing what kind of information to request from WPPSS and a shortage of experienced staff to handle data once it was transferred; and problems with press release coordination and "some deterioration in confidence between the two agencies" (Theodore Barry & Associates 1979: III-14).

But the Theodore Barry consultants also recognized that, at this point, BPA oversight was not in itself the answer to the Supply System's problems. In fact, meaningful oversight was not even possible given the chaotic nature of the situation. There first had to be someone in control of WPPSS before BPA could use whatever influence it might acquire to review and recommend changes in the nature of that control. It was clear that major changes in personnel and management practices were required. The Supply System's top management had failed to make the kinds of necessary changes discussed earlier in connection with the requirements of a rapidly growing organization. Those kinds of changes had become the responsibility of the board of directors, and many of the Theodore Barry recommendations were simply ways of prodding the board into taking a more active role.

One way of doing that was to document the urgent need for that role by highlighting some of the broad inadequacies of WPPSS management, and most of the report was devoted to that purpose. Unfortunately, this tactic proved counterproductive. When BPA first announced the study as primarily an investigation of WPPSS rather than of the oversight relationship, the WPPSS board and management became highly defensive. Not surprisingly, when the report was finally issued many board members initially viewed it as a hunt for a scapegoat.

Another way of alerting the board that it needed to assume more direction was to suggest that past BPA oversight efforts had gone much less smoothly than many board members apparently assumed.

Members of the board relied on BPA for some kinds of advice and may have felt that BPA's presence guaranteed against serious problems. The Theodore Barry report points out that this was not true and that the WPPSS staff was being uncooperative in dealing with BPA. The report argues that the board and the staff had fundamentally different attitudes about oversight: "The WPPSS staff generally believes that a meaningful BPA oversight role cannot be structured. . . . However, a majority of the WPPSS Board members seem to feel that BPA can and should play a very significant oversight role" (Theodore Barry & Associates 1979: III-12). The report also noted that WPPSS management kept to itself any disagreements with BPA personnel performing oversight functions: " . . . it appears that these differences are rarely highlighted to the WPPSS Executive Committee or the Board" (p. III-13).

The board was now being called upon to take control of an organization that had grown in size and complexity without developing adequate formal administrative control mechanisms. But even if the board could be convinced that a serious problem existed, it still needed the means to solve that problem. The board had never developed any managerial expertise. Beyond the executive committee it did not even make use of special committees. And management had developed a pattern of trying to keep the board's work as uncomplicated as possible, resulting in a flood of trivial information and only a small stream of important sources of WPPSS data. For example, although the board appointed the internal auditor, it did not receive the internal audit reports. The Theodore Barry report frames the problem with a touch of understatement: "The Board does not now have any process by which it can effectively gain clear insights into WPPSS operations except through the WPPSS staff" (Theodore Barry & Associates 1979: IV-8). It goes without saying that the staff of any organization should be the primary source of information about internal operations. The consultants' point was that the WPPSS staff was not doing a very effective job.

To solve this difficult problem, the Theodore Barry report suggested a number of steps. First, the executive committee was urged to strengthen its role in overseeing the activities of the management staff. Aside from the many specific problems and recommendations already mentioned above, a major suggestion of the report was for WPPSS to have a consultant conduct a comprehensive review of staffing levels to determine how many employees WPPSS actually needed to complete its projects.

Second, the report suggested that the committee hire its own staff, independent of WPPSS management, to assist in carrying out these activities. The nucleus of this staff would be two to four management analysts who would review and analyze managerial performance information, monitor the implementation of the executive committee's recommendations, and generally provide the expertise that the board now needed to take control of its own organization. This new staff would also help improve BPA oversight by acting as a liaison between BPA and WPPSS.

Finally, the report suggested that BPA's oversight role be formalized in an agreement between the two agencies. The exact form of the agreement was not specified. There was no precedent for such an agreement; it was entirely in the interests of BPA. The very elusive proposed agreement became known as the "memorandum of understanding."

Implementation of Theodore Barry Recommendations

The Theodore Barry report became the focal point of BPA efforts to improve and formalize its oversight responsibilities. But, as might be expected, the actual implementation of the report's recommendations was a very difficult matter. The report had been preceded by a war of accusations and threats waged by Munro in the local press. The announcement that the study would be conducted at all put the WPPSS board on the defensive even before the report was issued. In a move that surprised and embarrassed the board, BPA made the first draft of the report available to members of the local press, who quickly demanded explanations. All of this contributed to the growing distrust between the two agencies and made unlikely any immediate WPPSS acceptance of the report's findings.

In addition, the board was far from able to digest and evaluate the findings of a highly technical 200-page management consulting study of this kind. There was growing awareness that the board needed to strengthen its directorship of the organization, but no one was certain how that should be done. Although the Theodore Barry report reserved most of its criticism for WPPSS management and clearly placed most of its hopes for change with the board, the board members were hesitant to take any kind of immediate action that would antagonize the managing director or his staff. The management staff, whatever its drawbacks, was still the board's only source of information about internal operations. In a memo to the board that preceded the final draft of the Theodore Barry report by three months, Managing Director Strand had already unequivocally warned the board about the kinds of problems caused by a permanent, independent staff. Such an idea, he said, "suffers from the very severe disadvantage of setting up the BOD and outside agencies in an adversary role to the staff. . . . If the BOD could hire a consultant staff more capable than the CEO and his staff to manage the firm, that staff should be placed in charge of managing the firm" (Strand 1978: 3-4).

Finally, the board was also likely to delay immediate action on the Theodore Barry recommendations until Congress passed some version of the proposed Northwest Regional Power Act, which promised to redefine BPA's role in regional power planning and development. The bill had originally been introduced in 1977, and although it had already gone through two versions by the time the Theodore Barry report was issued, its passage in some form seemed likely in the near future. Any of the proposed versions of the bill could alter the BPA-WPPSS relationship and supersede any existing memorandum of understanding between the two agencies.

A special committee assembled by the board to review the Theodore Barry recommendations did accept one of them immediately: "The Barry Report suggested that the Board may need outside assistance to implement some of the recommendations. The Committee agrees that this help is needed . . ." (Washington Public Power Supply System, Board of Directors 1979: 3). The board agreed to hire the Institute of Public Administration (IPA) for this purpose, but IPA's formal mission was not actually to implement specific Theodore Barry recommendations or even to review them. Rather, it was to review the general issues raised by the Theodore Barry report. Thus, just as BPA had responded to the criticisms of the Department of the Interior's audit by commissioning its own management consulting study, WPPSS responded to the Theodore Barry report by seeking advice from IPA.

In a series of four reports issued from October 1979 to January 1980, IPA indicated that many of the problems noted by earlier consultants had never been addressed. Foremost among these were those related to management style. Too much decisionmaking authority remained centralized in the hands of the managing director, but his attention to day-to-day details—including all varieties of public relations—meant that decisions relating to policy and strategy were not made and WPPSS relations with external groups were handled badly. IPA suggested hiring two new deputy directors to whom decisionmaking and public relations duties could be delegated. (One of the IPA reports was devoted to ways in which the Supply System could expand and professionalize its community relations program.) The establishment of a new executive staff office was also recommended as a means of increasing management capacity.

IPA recommended strengthening the board through the creation of special board committees that would be supported by services of the proposed new executive staff office. IPA rejected the idea of an independent staff for the board because of the factionalism that would result. Board meeting agendas were to be improved and specific management information reports and strategic policy reports were to be prepared for the board on a regular basis.

With regard to BPA oversight, another IPA report agreed with the Theodore Barry consultants who pointed out that oversight responsibility should not be translated into tight control. To do so would violate the basic requirement of any large organization to have a unified authority structure. Prior approval of budget line items or change orders would be time-consuming and counterproductive. In situations where oversight responsibility is not precisely detailed, voluntary cooperation between the agencies involved is necessary. IPA consultants noted that meaningful oversight could not be exercised in an atmosphere of political maneuvering and adversarial statements. They assisted the WPPSS board in concluding the memorandum of understanding with BPA that was originally recommended in the Theodore Barry study. IPA also recommended a complete budget and construction schedule review.

In February 1980 the WPPSS executive committee requested Neil O. Strand's resignation as managing director. During the six months the Supply System spent looking for a replacement, Strand served as acting director but was denied permission to make any changes in top management. Most of the recommended changes called for by IPA were made subsequently by the new management.

The move to force Strand's resignation, which came as the Washington State Senate was beginning its full-scale inquiry into WPPSS problems, was engineered by a small coalition of the largest and most politically conscious utilities on the board. Nevertheless, the move caught many board members by surprise. A majority of them eventually concurred in the decision, but all realized it was a calculated gamble. As noted many times, the board was heavily dependent on the managing director, so was cautious about antagonizing him or his staff. Moreover, firing Strand would necessitate finding a replacement and assembling a new management team. More delays and cost increases would undoubtedly result. One director estimated that total costs would increase by as much as $1 billion.

But all of these factors had to be weighed against strong new external pressures on the board, in the form of intense new legislative involvement and declining public confidence. If nothing else, the board, and particularly the larger utilities represented on it, realized that in order to maintain the Supply System's independence, as well as investor confidence in its projects, the WPPSS organization had to appear to be under decisive control. Even if Strand's resignation meant $1 billion in increased costs, in early 1980 it still seemed as if WPPSS could afford it. At that time, the total projected cost for the five plants was under $12 billion—WPPSS was still 15 months away from Ferguson's $24 billion revised total cost estimate.

The Struggle for Budget Control

The attempts by BPA to pressure WPPSS into accepting the recommendations of the Theodore Barry report and WPPSS' attempts to move at its own deliberate speed heightened the intensity of the quarrel between the two agencies in 1979. The war in the press continued and indicated the growing hostility.[1] In February Munro suggested that WPPSS officials "had not known a high standard of candor" in a presentation before a congressional subcommittee (Gomena 1979: 1). WPPSS Managing Director Strand had announced a percentage completion figure for Plant 2, without realizing that the figure had already been revised downward. In April Munro released to the press a letter he sent to Strand and other WPPSS officials citing incidents in which BPA aides had been excluded from WPPSS meetings, denied information, or offered incomplete data regarding project costs and schedules. Munro's implication was that WPPSS officials were delaying implementation of the Theodore Barry study recommendations. WPPSS President Goldsbury in turn told reporters that Munro was simply preparing to run for Senator and that BPA officials were using oversight as an excuse to control WPPSS without actually taking responsibility for it. Goldsbury also said that Munro had been opposed to the involvement of the Institute of Public Administration because IPA could give WPPSS advice on how to deal with the federal government. In May a Seattle newspaper learned that BPA possessed a series of embarrassing internal WPPSS documents. The documents were acquired under the Freedom of Information Act and given extensive coverage in the newspaper.

BPA was concerned that all of the Theodore Barry recommendations—especially the memorandum of understanding—be implemented immediately, but beyond that it was concerned with achieving some kind of direct control over WPPSS—an action that Theodore Barry consultants had not recommended.

The focus of BPA concern was the construction budget process for the three net-billed plants, which as we have already noted at some length, was largely beyond the control of WPPSS management. After the 1979 construction budget was first submitted in October 1978, it was revised upward by $824 million in January, and again by $623 million in June. After the June increase BPA demanded an explanation, including a detailed breakdown of cost increases, why they occurred, why costs were not correctly estimated initially, and specific capital cost comparisons with other utilities. WPPSS officials attempted to comply, but their explanations did little to satisfy BPA.

BPA's dissatisfaction was not based on any insight into the actual problems involved in the WPPSS budget process. Instead, BPA Administrator Sterling Munro reacted in the same way that WPPSS top management had reacted to most problems—by insisting on tighter control of details. Munro demanded approval on every construction-related expenditure made by WPPSS, as if this would somehow reduce costs. Munro was called to testify before the Subcommittee on Energy of the House Commerce Committee on October 19, where he unilaterally announced new procedures for BPA approval of WPPSS construction budgets. Essentially, Munro demanded that WPPSS present its budgets with a complete breakdown of detailed information and that BPA approval be required on all details. He also demanded that specific written approval from BPA be secured prior to the expenditure of any amount in excess of the approved budget item and for any expenditure not specifically detailed in the budget.

The WPPSS board assembled a committee to study Munro's demands. The committee concluded that BPA's demands amounted to a move to take over the day-to-day management of the net-billed projects. Munro's demands were rejected, leaving him with no recourse but the unrealistic one of calling in an independent consultant to judge prudent utility practice.

Whether Munro was aware of the difficult and impractical nature of many of his demands is unclear. He may have been unaware that the project agreements did not provide for BPA approval of expenditures in excess of budgeted amounts. This fact alone ensured that WPPSS would not accept his demands. Nor did he seem aware that construction budgets were supposed to be general estimates of construction expenditures rather than documents authorizing expenditures. Experience in business and government indicates that attempts to break down such estimates so as to increase line-item precision often diminish the accuracy of aggregate budget estimates. As we have already noted, the construction budget process required many improvements, some of which could conceivably have resulted from constructive advice by BPA and its consultants. But Munro's demands for line-item approval simply confused the situation and contributed to the adversary atmosphere between the two agencies that precluded a constructive relationship.

The Northwest Regional Power Bill

Federal legislation was proposed in 1977 that could have considerably clarified the relationship between WPPSS and BPA. But by the time Congress finally passed the bill in late 1980, it had undergone three major revisions and was a very different document from the one originally favored by BPA. The transformation of the bill reflects the breakdown of faith in the region's existing public power planning establishment that had eagerly promoted the WPPSS nuclear projects in the early 1970s.

As the region began expanding past its hydropower base in the 1960s, confusion developed about how much new power would be required, who would get how much of it, how it would be priced and generated, and who would develop it. The PUDs, the municipal utilities, BPA, investor-owned utilities, and the major industrial users of electricity—especially the aluminum companies in the region—all wanted answers to those questions. Everyone agreed that some kind of regional power planning authority had to be set up and that federal legislation to do so would probably be necessary.

BPA was already in many ways the leader in the region's power planning because it was marketing and transmitting such a high proportion of the region's power produced in the federal generating system. But because BPA did not have the authority to build additional generating capacity, or even purchase generating capacity, changes in federal law were required.

The first major legislative proposal came from the Pacific Northwest Utilities Conference Committee (PNUCC), which included in its membership nearly all WPPSS members, as well as WPPSS itself. BPA was not technically a member but was represented on the committee and probably had more influence than any individual member. The PNUCC bill placed responsibility for regional power planning and distribution with the regional utilities and BPA, and it allowed BPA to purchase power output. Most WPPSS members viewed this bill as a way to allow BPA to guarantee its purchase of the power from WPPSS Plants 4 and 5—a situation that many believed was an eventual certainty when they entered into their take-or-pay, come-hell-or-high-water contracts.

But support for this form of the bill was fragmented. Public utilities felt that investor-owned utilities were being promised an unfair share of the power, environmental groups felt that conservation was not emphasized enough, good-government groups objected to a lack of public participation, and so forth.

A second major version of the bill was proposed by Washington's Senator Henry Jackson. This version greatly expanded the regional role played by BPA and its administrator (and co-author of the bill), former Jackson aide Sterling Munro. BPA would assume overall regional energy planning and decisionmaking authority, advised by a citizen and utilities' council. The bill provided for BPA purchase of power output and the development of renewable energy sources. This bill also gave authority to BPA for considerable control of WPPSS activities. But this bill also met stiff opposition from a variety of groups. Regional governors believed they were not given enough influence. Environmentalists believed that BPA would have too large a discretionary role in assessing the need and viability of conservation measures. Regional utilities believed that the bill might be interpreted so as to allow BPA authority to undertake its own construction.

The third major version of the bill was passed in December 1980, after intense lobbying from all sides. It established a new regional power planning body, the Northwest Power Planning Council, composed of two members each from the four Northwest states (Idaho, Washington, Montana, and Oregon). The council's duties include the formulation of a regional plan, estimating regional demand for power over the next twenty years, and outlining ways in which the demand can be met. The bill also allows BPA to purchase power-generating capability. But tight power development priorities are outlined in a four-step scale. Conservation is given first priority, and nuclear and coal power are last.

On January 26, 1983, the council issued its first twenty-year plan for the region's energy future. Provisions of the plan were based on forecasts that power demand would grow at an annual rate of between 0.8 and 2.8 percent per year, as opposed to growth forecasts in 1970 of 7.5 percent per year, and in 1980 of 3.9 percent per year. The council concluded that the region would need no additional nuclear or coal-fired power plants beyond the three WPPSS plants still technically had under construction at that time.

BPA's New Role

On April 5, 1982, BPA issued its own report on the future power needs of the region. Preliminary figures, already released, forecasted a 1.7 percent annual increase in electricity demand in the region over the next twenty years, indicating that the output from Projects 1 and 3 would not be needed in 1986, at the time they were scheduled for completion. In April BPA requested that WPPSS mothball Plant 1 for up to five years, and the board of directors reluctantly complied. BPA's recommendation to halt construction on Plant 1 represented a new, more direct involvement by the federal authority in the financial activities of the Supply System—at least when compared with BPA's role since 1976. BPA hoped that the mothballing would speed and ensure the completion of Plant 2 and thus increase the credibility of WPPSS with investors. It was also hoped that ratepayers would be partially placated by a somewhat reduced wholesale rate increase scheduled for September (a 60 percent increase instead of a 73 percent increase).

In addition to the recommendation, BPA began work on a financial plan that would ensure completion of the remaining plants, even if Washington residents voted down further Supply System funding, a possibility that had increased with the passage in late 1981 of Initiative 394, which required voter approval of WPPSS bond issues after July 1, 1982. BPA announced that it would finance the completion of Project 2 if necessary. BPA also began quiet efforts to have the U.S. Department of Justice sue to overturn Initiative 394 and prevent Washington State from holding the referendum. The Justice Department was joined in the suit by three large banks acting as trustees for WPPSS bondholders, and the initiative was subsequently overturned by the Washington State Supreme Court.

The possibility that BPA might be able to carry out its plans to assist in the construction of the remaining two plants seemed stronger in late 1982 with the nomination of former BPA Administrator Donald Hodel as Secretary of Energy. Hodel had headed BPA from 1972 to 1978 and had played a prominent role in persuading utilities to participate in the WPPSS projects. In November of 1982 he was confirmed and immediately began making statements that implied the possibility of special federal aid, provided through BPA, to assist in the completion of the first three WPPSS plants. In letters to two senators he also left open the possibility of a future federal bailout of Plants 4 and 5.

But BPA's ability to implement its plans remained in question. Hodel and Department of Energy spokesmen eventually acknowledged that any special federal help for WPPSS would come far in the future. And BPA may never have enough money in its treasury to help WPPSS, even if Congress were willing to seriously consider such assistance. By the end of 1982 it was clear that for a variety of reasons BPA's own revenues were sharply down from budgeted estimates. BPA also had obligations to repay the U.S. Treasury for money borrowed to finance construction of a Colorado dam and was burdened with debt service payments for the first three WPPSS projects.

In 1984 the General Accounting Office issued a report claiming that BPA oversight activities with regard to WPPSS were still inadequate. The report charged that BPA was not adequately reviewing WPPSS budgets or personnel decisions and had not even settled on a definition of what its oversight responsibilities were or should be. Among other things, the report claimed that in one instance poor communications among BPA officials had prevented WPPSS from saving $60 million in construction costs (U.S. General Accounting Office 1984: 37).

ORGANIZED RATEPAYER RESISTANCE

Individual ratepayers in the Pacific Northwest—those families and businesses that pay local utilities for electricity—have limited formal powers of oversight with regard to the activities of governmental entities such as WPPSS. The participating utilities have the power to raise electric rates without regulation in order to cover their financial commitments, and ratepayers have no formal review powers in connection with lending or construction plans of the local PUDs or of WPPSS. But PUD commissioners are elected officials, and when electric rates began to rise precipitously many ratepayers felt as though a trust had been violated. They looked to their PUD commissioners for explanations.

Battle Lines are Drawn

Organized anti-WPPSS ratepayer groups did not begin concerted action in Washington until 1981. The various groups were not particularly large in terms of the number of active members, they were not always successful in rallying popular support for specific acts of protest, and they maintained high levels of activity for relatively short periods of time. Many of the most active of these groups came from rural counties of the state where unemployment was soaring to record highs in the early 1980s.[2] Their understanding of why WPPSS faced problems and what could be done about those problems was rather simplistic, and the dollar increases in electric rates, or absolute rate levels, that most of these ratepayers faced would not have been considered unbearable or even surprising by ratepayers in the rest of the country.

But as the news media in the Pacific Northwest began to recognize WPPSS as an attractive target for investigative journalism, activist groups became centers of media attention. The media christened these groups the leaders of the growing ill-will toward WPPSS that was crystallizing throughout the region. But, owing largely to this attention given by the news media, it would be hard to overestimate the influence of the activist ratepayer groups. A bipartisan group of Washington State legislators that called on WPPSS to mothball a third plant in March 1982 cited ratepayer protests as a reason to stop construction. Ratepayer pressure was also behind the failure of many WPPSS participants to begin paying their share of debt service on the terminated projects in 1983. A small number of ratepayers made it clear that they would sue individual PUD directors to recover payments made to WPPSS if the courts eventually ruled that take-or-pay contracts were invalid.

The influence of activist ratepayers was partly due to the fact that they were gradually perceived by the general public as being respectable, middle-class citizens not otherwise given to protest. It was also fueled by the public's increasing perception of WPPSS as badly mismanaged, too often willing to ignore waste and fraud in its construction operations, insensitive to the plight of ratepayers, and absolutely unwilling to be made accountable to anyone.

The local news media, fed by information leaks created by the public relations war between WPPSS and BPA, helped to reinforce these opinions. Especially prominent in so-called investigative reports published in newspapers were suggestions of fraudulent or near-fraudulent behavior that resulted in profits for various contractors. Newspaper accounts in 1981 and 1982 reported that WPPSS auditors found that some contractors were charging WPPSS for entertainment expenses for executives, their spouses, and their friends. Money was paid by WPPSS for liquor, cigars, dance bands, hunting trips, and gifts. WPPSS paid commuting expenses to contractor employees who traveled up to 330 miles round-trip a day rather than relocate near their work. Other employees relocated at WPPSS expense and then either quit or continued to charge the commuting fees.

Suggestions of bid-rigging and sweetheart contracting sometimes appeared in local papers. In May of 1983 the *Seattle Times* published a long investigative account of the 215 contract, the largest construction job done on Project 2, and eventually the largest of all WPPSS construction contracts (Whitely 1983). By the spring of 1983 the costs to WPPSS of the contract were already expected to exceed $600 million, roughly ten times the original 1974 bid and more than the original estimated cost of the entire plant. The newspaper raised questions about the cost overruns and change orders submitted by contractors. The paper based its story in part on its review of what it claimed were "more than a thousand pages of BPA documents dealing with the 215 contract and others." A month after the newspaper account of the 215 contract was published, local papers noted that six major electrical contractors were indicted by a grand jury on federal charges of rigging bids on four of the WPPSS projects.

Although fraudulent practices may have contributed to WPPSS cost increases, investigative news accounts helped to convince ratepayers that contractors, lawyers, and underwriters were unfairly and possibly illegally profiting at their expense. When debt service payments to bondholders were required to begin, many ratepayers concluded that bondholders should bear the financial burden of WPPSS mismanagement and fraud. Very few ratepayers were also bondholders. Marshall & Meyer, one of Seattle's largest dealers in WPPSS bonds, has reported that few Project 4 and 5 bonds were sold to residents of the Pacific Northwest (Connelly 1983). Many ratepayers perceive WPPSS bondholders as wealthy individuals or large corporations who must expect to assume some of the risks of investing. And many ratepayers believe rightly or wrongly that nonpayment of debt service is an investment risk that bondholders must pay for, given the unusual nature of WPPSS' problems.

The first important beachhead in the ratepayer war against WPPSS was established in November 1981, when Washington State voters passed Initiative 394. The initiative required voter approval of WPPSS bond issues after July 1, 1982. It was championed by the Don't Bankrupt Washington Committee, a group led by veterans of Ralph Nader-inspired consumer groups in the region. After the initiative passed by a 58 to 42 percent margin the committee led the legal fight to have the measure upheld in the courts.

In February 1982 the Irate Ratepayer movement was born in a town meeting attended by Grays Harbor County PUD commissioners and other local and state officials. Newspapers estimated that 3,200 people filled a local high school gymnasium to demand explanations for a doubling of electric rates over the previous three years. Electric rates in the Grays Harbor PUD were expected to double again in two years, largely as a result of the $315 million owed over the next thirty years for the PUD's 4.5 percent share of Projects 4 and 5, terminated a month earlier. PUD commissioners had further enraged local residents by voting a $2.5 million loan to help WPPSS with termination costs. One of the attending commissioners reportedly admitted that the turnout at the meeting convinced him that Grays Harbor should investigate all legal means for avoiding payment of the debt. But already in February, utilities were willing to go further to accede to ratepayer demands. On February 18 a small electric utility serving the San Juan Islands cited its sole responsibility to its ratepayers and became the first Project 4 and 5 participant to unilaterally abort its hell-or-high-water financial commitments to WPPSS.

The attorney for that utility provided one of many local interpretations of the ethical and legal questions raised by WPPSS difficulties. He noted that if WPPSS defaulted, it would be the biggest default in the history of Wall Street. "But you guys have been brainwashed," he told reporters. "There's no default where there's no obligation. And there's no obligation to pay off those bonds unless the two projects are completed" (Scates 1982b: A-10). The utility board president scoffed at suggestions that the repudiation of debt would hurt the utility's credit standing. "New York City was supposed to not be able to sell another bond, but they seem to be getting along pretty good. Any bond issue will be judged on its own merits, not WPPSS' reputation" (Connelly 1982: 2).

Owners of a small motel in Ellensburg, Washington, explained in moral terms their refusal to pay WPPSS-related electric surcharges. "It's a little embarrassing, but we have to do this. It isn't the amount of $50, it's the principle of the thing. It's a moral issue. I don't pay for services and goods I don't receive" (*Seattle Post-Intelligencer* 1982: A-5). Many other ratepayers were not so reflective or hesitant to take action. A pamphlet distributed by the Ellensburg, Washington, Irate Ratepayers argued that "There is no better solution than to kill the WPPSS organization as quickly as possible by whatever means possible" (Zonana 1982: 29).

According to a Seattle newspaper, within six weeks of the Grays Harbor town meeting Irate Ratepayers and related groups had spread to every county in western Washington served by a public utility. Their tactics included town meetings, demands that utilities refuse to pay their shares of Project 4 and 5 costs, and recall campaigns directed against PUD commissioners and WPPSS board members.

One of the most successful actions of the Irate Ratepayers and other activist groups was Draw Day, which took place on April 2, 1982, as a protest against the participation of Seattle-First National Bank in the bond trustee lawsuit opposing Initiative 394. Customers of the bank were encouraged to withdraw their money from the bank, and Sea-First reported that on the day of the protest 341 customers had withdrawn $640,000. As the movement spread, the bank reported that 804 customers, including three PUDs, had withdrawn $2.5 million (Carter 1983: B5).

One prominent group associated with the Irate Ratepayers was Progress Under Democracy ("P.U.D."). Formed in 1981 in Wenatchee, Washington, this group focused on recruiting candidates to run for PUD commissioners, especially those on the WPPSS board. The group's leader took credit for the fact that of the twenty-four PUD commissioners up for re-election in the fall of 1982, two resigned before the election, twelve others decided not to run for reelection, and four were voted out of office. One of the commissioners who resigned in the spring of 1982 was replaced by wood stove salesman Robert Olsen, who became the first ratepayer activist to be named to the WPPSS board.

Other activist groups include the Seattle-Tacoma Light Brigade, which used the confrontationist tactics of Chicago community organizer Saul Alinsky, and the Northwest Conservation Act Coalition, which sponsored planning efforts to increase the region's reliance on conservation and renewable resources.

Ratepayers vs. Bondholders

The reactions of some ratepayers to the problems of WPPSS and the associated increases in the cost of electricity have startled observers in other parts of the country, especially in places where electric power is still twice as expensive as it is in Washington State and where public disclosure of local political ineptitude and corruption is not uncommon. The investment community in particular has been surprised at the straightforward refusal of a significant number of ratepayers to take any responsibility for the debts incurred by their WPPSS representatives.

But this development is not so surprising if one keeps in mind first, that most ratepayers did not participate in organized activity, and second, that many of the ratepayers serviced by Washington PUDs (most of the activists) share to some degree the mix of values that comprised the corporate culture of WPPSS. An anti-big business, anti-politics attitude is clearly evident in the statements and activities of many of the activist ratepayer organizations. When WPPSS began to experience problems, when electric power began to increase in cost beyond what had been promised, ratepayers began to suspect that their representatives had been co-opted or deceived by politicians, and particularly by big business. This was especially true in the rural areas of the state, where unemployment was high. Plentiful, inexpensive electric power had long been a symbol of the victory of the private citizen over the selfishness of private business interests in the Northwest, and the disappearance of that symbol threatened the disappearance of a way of life.

In August 1983 longtime critic of WPPSS, Representative Jim Weaver of Oregon, responded to a charge that populist attitudes played a role in the problems of WPPSS. In a letter to the editor of the *Wall Street Journal*, Weaver offered a classic, if unintentional, example of populist rhetoric:

> You claim that WPPSS represents a Populist fiasco. The opposite is the truth. Whoops was perpetrated by a tightly knit band of oligopolists, without public involvement. In their rush to create an energy empire, these private utility and aluminum company officials gave WPPSS a blank check drawn on the accounts of the Northwest ratepayer (Weaver 1983: 33).

Many activist ratepayers had no qualms about shifting the burden of WPPSS debts to the bondholders because the latter were identified as either large businesses or wealthy individuals. Individual investors were generally perceived to live outside the Pacific Northwest and to be wealthy enough to withstand a loss on their investments. Most important of course is the fact that individual bondholders are easily associated with the kind of greed that the neopopulism of the region has traditionally seen at the root of corruption in business and politics. Activist ratepayers have accused bondholders of wanting something for nothing and of being unwilling to accept the risks associated with investing.

THE COURT DECISIONS

On July 15, 1983, the Washington State Supreme Court ruled that the Project 4 and 5 take-or-pay agreements were void and that the utilities involved did not have to pay for their shares of the plants. The decision shocked virtually everyone connected with the investment community. Harold E. Rogers, Jr., head of the Municipal Finance Department of Manatt, Phelps, Rothenberg & Tunney, reported that

> In holding against the bondholders of WNP 4 and 5, the court rendered what many considered to be a political decision, siding with the Washington State and Northwest ratepayers whose votes would return them to judicial office, and against the New York bankers. Presumably the bankers had talked the relatively unsophisticated local utilities and others into borrowings that they could not afford and that were otherwise ill-advised (Rogers 1984: 82).

The seven to two decision by elected justices was handed down in the midst of an intense climate of anger and uncertainty surrounding the activities of WPPSS in 1983. The activist ratepayers and the crusading news media contributed to that climate, as did the general economic misfortunes of the area, against which the justices could not help but measure the magnitude of the damage done by Supply System to Washington State. The state was coming out of its worst economic downturn since the mid-1930s. Its major industries—lumber-paper-forest products, aircraft, and nonferrous metals—were distressed, and some localities had unemployment rates of well over 20 percent. The state has no income tax; sales tax collections were flat and state outlays for basic entitlements were very high. Localities were operating under recently enacted tax limitations. The state had borrowed heavily in 1981 in the short-term debt market for budget requirements, and with the Supply System's problems, there was speculation in local newspapers that the state's credit line had become questionable.

While some assume that the decision was an outright act of politically motivated debt repudiation, many others outside the investment community contend that the decision was an objective one. The ratepayers and local public officials who make up this second group argue that Washington State's constitution made the court's decision inescapable, and they charge that WPPSS legal counsel are to blame for not recognizing that fact.

Of course, there is no easily discoverable answer. The answer, like the supreme court decision itself, seems to be a matter of interpretation. The following section examines the various decisions regarding the authority of participants to enter into the take-or-pay contracts.

A Summary of Major Cases and Findings

1. *King County Superior Court.* In 1982, Chemical Bank, the trustee for the bondholders of the terminated Projects 4 and 5, filed an action in King County Superior Court asking for a declaratory judgment to the effect that the WPPSS take-or-pay agreements with Washington State municipalities and PUDs were valid, enforceable, and within the statutory authority of the participants to enter into. In other words, Chemical Bank and WPPSS wanted the court to tell the participants they had to pay for their shares of the plants— exactly what those participants were refusing to do. Twenty-eight participants were involved, representing about two-thirds of the Project 4 and 5 shares. On October 15, 1982, Superior Court Judge H. Joseph Coleman held the agreements enforceable, as Chemical Bank fully expected him to do.

2. *Washington State Supreme Court I.* In the first appeal of the King County Superior Court case, the Washington supreme court, in a seven to two decision, reversed the judgment and held that the twenty-eight Washington utilities lacked the authority to enter into the contracts. This was the now famous June 15, 1983 decision that, in effect, made the WPPSS default inevitable. The supreme court also ruled that because the participants involved in this decision represented such a large share of the projects, the agreements of the remaining eighty-eight participants were unenforceable as well.

3. *Washington State Supreme Court II.* In 1984 a second decision of the supreme court upheld both parts of its earlier decision and added two additional grounds for the second part of the previous decision, involving the sixty utilities not included in the original suit.

4. *The DeFazio Case.* In late 1981 three Oregon consumers brought suit against WPPSS over the enforceability of the contracts. The case was expanded to include all eleven Oregon participants in Projects 4 and 5. At the end of September 1982, just two weeks before the King County Superior Court decision, the Oregon court held that the contracts were void because the utilities did not have the authority to enter into such agreements. This was the famous *DeFazio v. Washington Public Power Supply System* case. It produced the embar-

rassing admissions by Brenden O'Brien concerning Wood & Dawson's role as WPPSS bond counsel and, until the Washington State Supreme Court ruling, helped to encourage opposition to WPPSS by ratepayers and others.

5. *Oregon State Supreme Court.* WPPSS appealed this case to the Oregon State Supreme Court in 1984. The court reversed the earlier decision, holding that the eleven participants' agreements were indeed enforceable. Although this decision came between the two appeals to the Washington State Supreme Court mentioned above, it had no influence on the final Washington court decision.

6. *Idaho State Supreme Court.* In 1984 the Idaho State Supreme Court prohibited five Idaho utilities from raising rates to make payments to WPPSS.

Washington Supreme Court I: The July 15, 1983 Decision[3]

The reversal of the King County Superior Court decision regarding the authority of the twenty-eight Washington utilities was the key court decision in the long and troubled legal history of the Supply System. That decision was upheld virtually without change when the Washington State Supreme Court reconsidered its judgment, and it led to the supreme court's related decision that the other eighty contracts were not enforceable. Even though the Oregon State Supreme Court had held valid the contracts between Oregon participants and WPPSS, those contracts could never have been fulfilled since two-thirds of the money for the plants had disappeared. As one Northwest legal expert puts it, "In a practical sense, the Washington court declared the agreements of the Oregon and Idaho participants unenforceable" (Falk 1985: 112).

Specifically, the state supreme court ruled that the Washington PUDs and municipal participants in the two terminated nuclear plants had no express or implied authority (1) to enter into financial agreements with WPPSS that required them to guarantee bond payments regardless of whether the plants were ever completed; (2) to surrender ownership interest and considerable control to WPPSS; or (3) to assume the obligations of defaulting participants.

This absence of authority rendered the contracts void and unenforceable under a doctrine known as *ultra vires*. As applied to governmental entities, this doctrine invalidates unauthorized contracts to protect citizens and taxpayers from unjust, ill-considered, or extortionate contracts entered into by the entity representing them.

Legal Sources of the Judgment.   In coming to its decision, the supreme court claims to have consulted a wide range of legal sources. The list indicates the complexity of the issue and the opportunities for judicial discretion in the interpretation of existing law:

1. *Existing statutes* that authorize PUDs and municipalities to purchase electricity; to acquire or construct electric generating facilities; to enter into joint operating agreements for the purchase of electricity; and to enter into agreements for the joint development of nuclear, thermal, or electric generating facilities;

2. *Constitutional provisions* governing the authority of home rule cities; and

3. *Case law* interpreting the express and implied powers of PUDs and municipalities.

Reasons for the Decision.   The supreme court's arguments can be summarized in terms of its conclusions concerning different sorts of specific legal authority that might have allowed the Washington participants to enter into the take-or-pay contracts.

1. *Authority to purchase capability.*   Washington PUDs and municipalities are authorized by statute law to purchase electricity. However, those statutes do not authorize the purchase of project capability in cases where participants' payments must be made even if the project is not completed—and there is a possibility of noncompletion.

In reaching this conclusion the court reasoned that the purchase of a share of project capability under these conditions is not actually a purchase of electricity, and thus not authorized by statute. Washington State WPPSS participants were committing themselves to buy what might turn out to be a share of no power, and they were guaranteeing payment even if they got no electricity in return. The court stated that "The unconditional obligation to pay for no electricity is hardly the purchase of electricity" (*Chemical Bank v. WPPSS* 1983: 784).

2. *Authority to build and operate.* Washington PUDs and municipalities are authorized by statute to construct, acquire, and operate electric generating facilities. But they cannot do so when they do not have an ownership interest in the projects.

The court reasoned that earlier cases interpreting these same statutes required that, in order to maintain their authority to build, buy, or operate such project, Washington participants had to retain either an ownership interest in the project or significant control or active participation in the management of the facilities. The court noted that the bond resolutions for Project 4 and 5 bonds clearly stated that only WPPSS and Pacific Power and Light Company owned the projects—the participants agreed only to pay for, and thus retain, a share of project capability. But the Washington participants could not retain a share of project capability because, as pointed out above, they had no authority to guarantee payment for project capability that might turn out to be nonexistent.

The court noted that if the participants had enough control over the projects, then this would constitute the equivalent of ownership. The participant agreements did indeed require that participants establish a participants' committee with authority to approve or disapprove major management decisions. But the court concluded that the procedures that had to be followed by the participants' committee in disapproving a WPPSS decision were too rigid to allow meaningful participation by the committee in WPPSS management. In this regard, the court stated:

> [W]e are not prepared to sanction a virtual abdication of all management functions and policy decisions to an operating agency such as WPPSS. Here, the participants' committee apparently served as a rubber stamp for WPPSS' decisions, resulting in two terminated projects, less than 25 percent complete, at a cost of $2.25 billion, or almost $7 billion over the 30-year repayment period. As a matter of public policy, the enormous risk to ratepayers must be balanced by either the benefit of ownership or substantial management control (*Chemical Bank v. WPPSS* 1983: 788).

3. *General authority to provide services.* Statutes expressly authorize Washington PUDs and municipalities to purchase services for their citizens, but this does not imply that they are free to guar-

antee payment in cases where there is no assurance that the services will be provided. Even though there was a practical necessity for participants to sign the take-or-pay contracts (they could not have sold the bonds otherwise), specific legal authorization rather than implied authority was required to allow participants to make what the state supreme court considered to be such an extraordinary kind of payment guarantee.

Here the court was addressing the possibility that a general grant of authority to provide services might somehow effectively imply rather than expressly permit the authority to incur indebtedness in this particular case. The court stated:

> [A] municipal corporation's powers are limited to those conferred in express terms or those necessarily implied. . . . The test for necessary or implied municipal powers is legal necessity rather than practical necessity (*Chemical Bank v. WPPSS* 1983: 792).

In other words, the court is noting that certain kinds of authority can be implied in statutes because that authority is necessary to carry out the intent of the statutes. But the court is also stating that although the guaranty of payment for project capability by Washington PUDs and municipalities may be necessary in a practical sense (e.g., to help WPPSS sell the bonds in the investment market), it is not necessary in a legal sense—statutes do not permit it, and the Washington legislature never authorized the public participants to enter into such agreements. In short, those participants are not legally obligated to make payments for project capability.

4. *Joint operating authority.* The enabling statutes under which WPPSS was created authorize Washington participants to enter into a joint operating agreement with WPPSS for the purchase of electric energy. But no matter what these statutes authorize WPPSS to do, they do not authorize Washington PUDs and municipalities to purchase project capability.

The court noted the distinction between the grants of authority to the participants and to WPPSS. While the participants' authority is limited to the purchase of electricity (rather than capability), WPPSS is authorized to contract for any term relating to the purchase, sale, interchange, or wheeling of power. Like the other statutes mentioned above, the enabling statutes under which WPPSS was created do not authorize PUDs and municipalities to guarantee payment for something that may never exist.

Dissent and Disagreement. The dissent in the second Washington State Supreme Court decision cited a flood of critical comment published in 1984 in the wake of the first decision. Some of the titles indicate the reactions of legal experts to the court's decision: "Chemical Bank v. WPPSS: A Case of Judicial Meltdown," *Journal of Energy Law and Policy*; "Chemical Bank v. Washington Public Power Supply System: An Aberration in Washington's Application of the Ultra Vires Doctrine," *University of Puget Sound Law Review*; "A Cry for Reform in Construing Washington Municipal Corporation Statutes," *Washington Law Review*; "Chemical Bank v. Washington Public Power Supply System: The Questionable Use of Ultra Vires Doctrine to Invalidate Governmental Take-or-Pay Obligations," *Cornell Law Review.*

As these legal observers and others began to analyze the decision, a number of significant questions arose about the nature of the court's reasoning. The cry from Wall Street that the decision was indeed political was strengthened by the following kinds of questions and comments:

- Dissenting Justice Robert F. Utter, a twelve-year veteran of the court, viewed the contractual arrangement as a form of purchase falling within the statutory authority of the participants to enter into agreements. He found support for this conclusion in the legislature's failure to react to the well-publicized contract. He reasoned, "Legislative acquiescence in such an entity's interpretation of the statutes under which it operates is a significant indication of legislative intent" (*Chemical Bank v. WPPSS* 1983: 813).

- WPPSS argued that participants did have a measure of control through their Participants' Committee, and in fact exercised that control when the projects were terminated. By 1980 that committee was indeed meeting often to discuss WPPSS problems.

- The issue of that committee's effectiveness was not considered in the Oregon and Idaho Supreme Court decisions. In those cases the legal structure of participation was of paramount importance.

- Membership in WPPSS and representation on the board was another way in which some participants exercised control, according to WPPSS. Most of the board members were in fact participants on the 4 and 5 Projects. The majority decision in the supreme court case did not address this issue.

- The dissent pointed out that the majority's contention that the Washington participants had no authority to purchase project capability would rule out option contracts or in fact any municipal participation in capital ventures involving risk.

- In the Oregon Supreme Court case the majority opinion held that the Oregon participants could engage in take-or-pay contracts because there was no distinction between purchase of electricity at an expensive price (which is authorized), and purchase that involves risk that the product might never be delivered (i.e., in the case of a municipality paying someone to drill for water, the water might not be found, but the municipality would still be obligated to pay for the drilling).

- The court argued that issues of management control and the authority of municipalities to enter into take-or-pay contracts were colored by the huge size of the projects, the enormous risk to ratepayers, and the fact that the state was vitally interested in the effort to build nuclear power plants. Because of this, the court argued that municipalities (which enjoy some measure of home rule powers in Washington State) needed either an express or implied delegation of power from the legislature in order to build the plants. Some commentators have asked whether such issues as size are relevant to a decision in such a case, noting that such considerations do not appear to have been important in the Oregon Supreme Court case. In the Oregon case the decision seems to have been based less on the novelty of the situation and more on a conservative interpretation of existing law (Falk 1985: 126).

- Finally, a number of commentators have pointed out that the supreme court's interpretation of existing laws was extremely limited in scope. In the words of one legal expert

> One might seek the source of authority in (1) specific provisions for providing electric power, (2) general grants of municipal power, or (3) home rule provisions allowing municipalities to define their own powers. In all three areas, the Oregon court construed municipal authority broadly and the Washington court construed it narrowly" (Falk 1985: 114).

The U.S. Supreme Court. After the second decision by the state supreme court, Chemical Bank, as bond trustee for the Project 4 and 5 bonds, appealed to the U.S. Supreme Court. In its argument, supported by friends of the court briefs submitted by leading investment banking firms, the city of Seattle, and other parties, Chemical Bank lawyers claimed that "The thousands of bondholders, many of them individuals who invested their life savings, suffered a complete forfeiture of their funds while at the same time they were denied elemental due process rights" (*Seattle Times* 1985: 1).

Chemical Bank argued that a constitutional issue, rather than just a matter of state law, was involved because the state supreme court had allowed WPPSS to take investors' money for a public purpose, without the just compensation guaranteed by the right to protection of private property. The U.S. Supreme Court apparently disagreed with this interpretation of the case, as many observers had expected. On April 29, 1985, without comment, the Court declined to review the Washington State Supreme Court rulings.

Conclusion.   It would be a simple matter to conclude any discussion of the Washington State Supreme Court decision with a caution about the autonomy of state law and about the danger of assuming that the legal history of one state can be used to predict the outcomes of court cases in other states. While that is probably true, the Washington decision also points out the fact that some state courts clearly exercise extraordinary judicial discretion in interpreting law and recognizing facts.

Of course, a municipal debt issuer such as WPPSS employs highprice legal advisors to help protect it against just such broad and unexpected interpretations of state law. There were steps that could have been taken to avert the Washington State Supreme Court decision—whether that decision was in fact political in nature or not. However, it should be pointed out that bond attorneys across the country were not seeking precautionary court cases or special legislation when the agreements were originally drawn up.

NOTES TO CHAPTER 4

1.   The war in the press between BPA and WPPSS started roughly in the spring of 1978 (with BPA's announcement of a major rate increase due in large part to the delays on WPPSS Project 2) and lasted until Neil Strand's firing in February 1980 (although the relationship between the two agencies has remained uneasy). The conflict ebbed and flowed, depending primarily on

the occurrence of specific kinds of events such as the announcement of BPA rate increases or the hiring of consultants to do special studies or reports (e.g., the Theodore Barry report or studies by the Institute of Public Administration). Most of the articles appeared over this period in the *Tri-City Herald* (Pasco, Kennewick, and Richland, Washington), the *Aberdeen World*, the *Portland Oregonian*, the *Seattle Times*, and the *Seattle Post-Intelligencer*.

2. For an extensive discussion of the effects of Washington State's economic downturn on ratepayer activism, see Wayne H. Sugai, "Mass Insurgency: The Ratepayers' Revolt and the Washington Public Power Supply System Crisis" (Ph.D. dissertation, University of Washington, 1985).

3. This account follows the discussion in Jeannie Hale, "Chemical Bank Decision—Liability of Washington PUDs and Municipal Participants," memorandum to the Washington State Senate Energy and Utilities Committee from Staff Attorney, June 20, 1983).

REFERENCES

Chemical Bank v. WPPSS. 1983. 99 Wn.2d 772. June.

Carter, Don. 1983. "Mixed Results for Ratepayer Revolt." *Seattle Post-Intelligencer*, February 13, p. B5.

Columbia River Transmission Act. 1974. Public Law No. 93-454, 88 Stat. 1376 (codified as amended at 16 U.S. Code 838-838K (1976 and Supp. V 1981)).

Connelly, Joel. 1982. "A Tiny Utility Takes on WPPSS." *Seattle Post-Intelligencer*, February 20, p. 2.

_____. 1983. "Time—for Someone—to Pay the WPPSS Bill." *Seattle Post-Intelligencer*, February 13, p. B2.

Falk, Theodore C. 1985. "Comparing the State WPPSS Cases: The Municipal Constitution." *Municipal Finance Journal* 6 (Spring): 111-36.

Gleckman, Howard, and Frank Gresock. 1985. "Victory and Defeat." *Credit Markets* (May 7): 57.

Gomena, Peter. 1979. "Mayor Rejects Strand Firing." *Tri-City Herald*, March 6, p. 1.

Institute of Public Administration. 1979a. *Federal, State and Regional Oversight*. Report submitted to the Washington Public Power Supply System Board of Directors. New York: Institute of Public Administration. October.

_____. 1979b. *Organization of Public and Community Relations*. Report submitted to the Washington Public Power Supply System Board of Directors. New York: Institute of Public Administration. October.

_____. 1979c. *Report on Top Management Structure*. Report submitted to the Washington Public Power Supply System Board of Directors. New York: Institute of Public Administration. November 14.

_____. 1980. *Role and Organization of the Board of Directors*. Report submitted to the Washington Public Power Supply System Board of Directors. New York: Institute of Public Administration. January.

Munro, Sterling. 1979. Prepared written testimony delivered before the Water and Power Resources Subcommittee of the House Committee on Interior and Insular Affairs, February 19. Transcript on file at Washington Public Power Supply System offices in Richland, Wash.

Rogers, Harold E. 1984. "What Went Wrong with WPPSS?" *Municipal Finance Journal* 5 (Winter): 81–86.

Scates, Shelby. 1982a. "Politics: The Past and Future of WPPSS." *Seattle Post-Intelligencer*, March 28, p. D9.

_____. 1982b. "Put WPPSS Blame on Bloated Forecasts." *Seattle Post-Intelligencer*, June 1, p. A10.

Seattle Post-Intelligencer. 1982. "Power Surcharge? They Won't Pay," May 11, p. A5.

Seattle Times. 1985. "Court Deals Blow to WPPSS Investors," April 29, p. 1.

Strand, Neil O. 1978. Memorandum to the Washington Public Power Supply System Board of Directors, October 18. Copy on file at Washington Public Power Supply System offices in Richland, Wash.

Theodore Barry & Associates. 1979. *Management Study of the Roles and Relationships of Bonneville Power Administration and Washington Public Power Supply System*. Report submitted to the Bonneville Power Administration. Los Angeles: Theodore Barry & Associates. January.

U.S. Department of the Interior. 1977. *Review of Washington Public Power Supply System Contract Administration and Bonneville Power Administration's Oversight, 1977 Audit Summary*. Washington, D.C.: U.S. Government Printing Office.

U.S. General Accounting Office. 1979. *Impacts and Implications of the Pacific Northwest Power Bill*. Washington, D.C.: U.S. Government Printing Office. September 4.

_____. 1984. *Status of Bonneville Power Administration's Efforts to Improve Its Oversight of Three Nuclear Power Projects*. Washington, D.C.: U.S. Government Printing Office. August 3.

Walkley, Glenn C. 1979. Letter from President of the Washington Public Power Supply System Board of Directors to Dixy Lee Ray, Governor of Washington State. May 18.

Walsh, Annmarie, and David Mammen. 1983. *State Public Corporations: A Guide for Decision Making*. New York: Institute of Public Administration.

Washington Public Power Supply System. 1979. "Minutes of the Washington Public Power Supply System Special Board of Directors' Meeting." Richland, Wash.: Washington Public Power Supply System. April 13.

_____. 1980. "Scope of Work for Theodore Barry & Associates Contract with the Bonneville Power Administration," *Report on Implementation Status of*

Consultant Recommendations—Part I. Report by J.A. Hare, Administrative Auditor. Richland, Wash.: Washington Public Power Supply System. August 8.

Washington Revised Code. 1981a. Chapter 43.52.391.

_____. 1981b. Chapter 45.52.370.

_____. 1981c. Chapter 54.16.150.

Weaver, Jim. 1983. Letter to the Editor. *Wall Street Journal*, August 9, p. 33.

Whitely, Peyton. 1983. "It's a Matter of Pipes and Bolts." *Seattle Times*, May 1, pp. D1-4.

Zonana, Victor F. 1982. "Rebellion Breaks Out in Northwest over Skyrocketing Electricity Rates." *Wall Street Journal*, March 19, p. 29.

5 THE FEDERAL GOVERNMENT

We noted in an earlier chapter that a vacuum of power and responsibility was built into the WPPSS organization, partly because it was a public authority. In many public authorities that vacuum is filled by managing directors and their top executives who rule these organizations without interference from boards of directors or governmental oversight bodies, sometimes in ways that appear to conflict with the public interest. The vacuum itself is not usually the problem. Who or what fills the vacuum is typically the cause of difficulties.

At WPPSS, however, that vacuum was never filled. The organization lacked leadership, it did not serve the public interest, and it may have created more damage than had it been ruled with an iron fist by an aggressive, ambitious, competent chief executive.

The role of the federal government in the WPPSS crisis must also be discussed in terms of a vacuum of power and responsibility. For many reasons and in many different ways Congress, the Atomic Energy Commission (AEC) (later to become the Nuclear Regulatory Commission, or NRC), and other government agencies abdicated responsibility for effectively regulating, coordinating, and controlling power planning in the Pacific Northwest, the financial activities of municipal issuers such as WPPSS, the construction management efforts of the Supply System, and efforts to seek a resolution to the default crisis.

181

Congress, by default, helped to create a power planning environment in the Pacific Northwest that became an ideal marketing arena for the high-powered sales efforts of nuclear equipment vendors. Congress refused, until 1980, to sanction a formal, basinwide power planning process in the Northwest. This refusal created a situation in which regional power planning had to be done by the Bonneville Power Administration, a federal agency to be sure, but one that never had the appropriate authority or mandate to plan for the region's power needs in any way other than one that was haphazard and without popular participation.

Once WPPSS began building its plants, unsuspecting investors were deprived of necessary information about the Supply System because the Securities and Exchange Commission lacked the authority to regulate the disclosure activities of municipal bond issuers.

When the AEC, later the NRC, began to develop and enforce quality assurance standards for nuclear power plants like those under construction by WPPSS during the 1970s, the implementation of those standards only added to the problems facing utilities. The number and kinds of rules imposed by the AEC/NRC constantly changed during the 1970s, exacerbating construction cost increases and schedule delays. Although these regulatory changes were not themselves the primary reasons for WPPSS cost increases, the inability of entities such as WPPSS to implement standards and respond quickly to regulatory changes—as well as to its own violations—were contributory factors to cost increases. As the NRC now admits, its preoccupation with individual violations of standards deflected its attention from the root cause of those violations—inadequate construction management.

Finally, in spite of its own role and that of various federal agencies in the evolving WPPSS crisis, Congress has refused to consider a federal bailout of the Supply System (a measure not easily justified). It has also consistently refused to provide leadership in efforts to discover less dramatic, but more realistic, resolutions to the crisis.

Thus, the federal government contributed to the WPPSS disaster not so much by what it did, as by what it did not do. Vacuums of power and responsibility were created by an absence of federal involvement in areas of activity affecting WPPSS. However, these vacuums were quickly filled by private sector organizations, governmental entities, and bureaucratic procedures driven and shaped by narrow interests and focused primarily on short-run benefits.

NORTHWEST POWER PLANNING[1]

By the time WPPSS defaulted the nuclear power industry was dominated by twenty-four giant transnational corporations that sold over $400 billion worth of products annually. All but 5 ranked among the 150 biggest companies in America. They had close associations with eight of the nation's nine biggest banks, the nation's seven largest insurance companies, and most top investment and law firms (Hertsgaard 1983: 7). They had invested many billions of dollars in their industry and had done everything in their considerable power to persuade individual utilities and joint operating agencies such as WPPSS to buy heavily into nuclear power. The "big four" reactor vendors, General Electric, Westinghouse, Babcock and Wilcox, and Combustion Engineering, were all involved in WPPSS projects as designers or vendors.

A federal regulatory vacuum helped to make possible this nuclear power oligopoly,[2] but another kind of federally induced vacuum was necessary to allow northwestern utilities to embark on the Ten Year Hydro-Thermal Power Program—the grand regional design of which the five WPPSS plants were to be contributing parts.

Background: TVA and CVA

The Public Utility Holding Company Act of 1935 ended the rule of the large holding companies and appeared at first to mark a new era of organized public power planning and development. President Roosevelt promised government ownership of utilities, if necessary, to keep electric rates down, and in 1933 the Tennessee Valley Authority was created and the National Industrial Recovery Act gave the executive branch a strong hand in public works planning.

The Tennessee Valley Authority was, and remains today, one of the U.S. government's most controversial attempts to provide centralized, basinwide power development through a partnership arrangement between government and local citizens. It was envisioned, in Roosevelt's words, as "an agency clothed with the power of government but possessing the flexibility and initiative of private enterprise" (Pritchett 1943: 29). It was created to change life for the better in the Tennessee valley, where a third of the people had malaria,

97 percent had no electricity, and local income was only 45 percent of the national average. With the power to plan, build, own, and operate electrical generating facilities—primarily with its own revenues and generous support from federal tax revenues—TVA made a reputation for itself of selling the cheapest electric power anywhere, even below cost in the early years. The authority was meant to function in part as a yardstick against which the efficiency of private utilities could be measured.

Public power interests across the country pressured for similar agencies in their regions. But TVA had threatened too many public and private interests for Congress to allow it to be reproduced anywhere else in the country. Local private power companies were frightened by the prospect of a huge, powerful entity with the authority of government, the aggressive instincts of private enterprise, and the will to cut electricity costs to bare minimums. The Department of the Interior opposed new TVAs because they would diminish its authority over land resources and management. The Corps of Engineers opposed the TVA concept because it entailed the construction of dams by someone else's engineers and manpower.

With the initiation of the Bonneville and Grand Coulee dam projects in 1933, Congress focused on the obvious need for some kind of federal entity to operate and market the power from those projects. Public utility districts in the Northwest lobbied for a Columbia Valley Authority (CVA). Private interests called for a much more limited federal role, with project operation and sales to be carried out by the Corps of Engineers. But public power interests countered that the Corps was too closely aligned with private interests (Blumm 1983: 199).

The Bonneville Power Administration

In 1936 a compromise was reached. The Corps would control project operation, and a Bonneville Project Administrator would be set up to market power produced by the Bonneville dam, construct transmission lines, and set rates, with preference given to public power utilities in the area.

The notion of a national power planning agency was also briefly revived during the New Deal. In 1934 Franklin D. Roosevelt created the National Power Policy Committee to recommend a unified national power policy, but the Corps of Engineers successfully blocked the committee's planning efforts. The Reorganization Act of 1939 required that future presidential reorganization plans be submitted to Congress for approval and prohibited any further transfer of the Corps' functions. The idea of a national planning agency was dead.

By World War II, Bonneville had established uniform electric rates for the region and promoted the establishment of additional public utility districts. In 1940 Bonneville officially became the Bonneville Power Administration (BPA), and marketing responsibility was extended to cover power produced by Grand Coulee dam. Soon thereafter, BPA began construction of a transmission line between the Bonneville and Grand Coulee dams—the beginning of the vast power transmission grid that would criss-cross the Columbia basin.

Although this transmission grid would make BPA, by default, the most powerful power-planning entity in the region, other Bonneville characteristics would foil an orderly exercise of that power. The result was a history of haphazard power planning, with an almost total lack of public participation and sense of ownership of the regional power plans because of the many behind-the-scenes deals. The abdication of power planning responsibilities by the federal government left a planning vacuum that was quickly, but inadequately, filled. If the chaotic development of the commercial uses of nuclear power created an environment in which entities like WPPSS could be easily sold on nuclear power, the chaotic history of power planning in the Northwest helped to precipitate the actual purchase.

BPA's Growth Cycle

Two characteristics of BPA were especially strong inhibitors of its ability to coordinate regional planning in an orderly fashion: its entrepreneurial drive to expand its service area and stimulate the region's economic growth and the lack of formal congressional approval of the techniques necessary for BPA to carry out its goals.

The construction of the Grand Coulee-Bonneville transmission line had to be paid for with revenues not yet contracted. BPA started a thirty-year process of building generating capacity, searching for customers, producing high estimates of future demand, building additional capacity, and attracting new customers. Each cycle required congressional approval, but Congress quickly adopted a rubber-stamp approach to BPA building and refused to review the many techniques used by BPA to continue the process. Bonneville did not have long-term power purchase capability until 1980, and many of its other powers were vague. It had to enhance its service area with special interpretations of its mandate and through negotiations and deals with its customers, the public and private utilities. This was regional control, to be sure, but exercised outside of the public spotlight and often for only short-run goals.

During the war BPA tried to attract defense industries with cheap power. With the completion of Grand Coulee dam in 1941, BPA had a surplus of power to sell. It did attract industries and began to build more transmission lines. The post-war loss of some defense industries led to another power surplus in 1946.

In 1945 Bonneville Administrator Paul Raver asked his superiors at the Department of the Interior if BPA was supposed to restrict itself to the marketing of power or if it could anticipate needs and help meet them through planning, coordination, and the like. Raver was told that the latter course was acceptable (Blumm 1983: 206). Subsequently, much of BPA's surplus was sold to local aluminum companies, beginning with new industrial sales contracts that year. BPA started to guide and coordinate regional power planning. It organized what later became the Pacific Northwest Utilities Coordinating Committee (PNUCC), a mix of private and public utilities that jointly assembled forecasts, lobbied Congress for new power projects, and so forth. And with BPA's industrial sales and high estimates of new power needs by the individual utilities, additional power capability was again needed. Northwest energy law expert Michael C. Blumm has outlined the essential character of the power planning growth dynamic that helped BPA extend its service area for forty years:

> High forecasts induced more water projects; more projects meant that BPA could market power to industries and private utilities after supplying the needs of its preference customers. Cheap federally produced power became the engine driving regional economic growth (Blumm 1983: 242).

After Truman was elected in 1948, the idea of a Columbia Valley Authority resurfaced. Truman had promised during his campaign to provide the Columbia and Missouri valleys with one agency each that would construct and operate power generating facilities as well as market power. But once again, private utility interests, in alliance with the Corps of Engineers, successfully opposed TVA-like projects in favor of other, individual development projects that would be built by the Corps. The charge of creeping socialism was again used to thwart centralized basinwide power planning.

Eisenhower was elected in 1952, and his administration opposed new federal projects. In 1953, the Secretary of the Interior cancelled the construction of a proposed BPA transmission line in Oregon. Also in that year the Department of the Interior declared that any federal power not committed to northwestern public utilities should be sold to privates on a long-term basis.

Wheeling

With encouragement by the federal government during the 1950s, non-federal power generating capacity underwent tremendous expansion. Since Bonneville already had a transmission system that could be used for the new power, new lines did not have to be built. But BPA's ability to "wheel" power—to transmit it for others—had not yet been formally sanctioned by Congress. Indeed, it probably would have been opposed by the originators of Bonneville's legislation because of their insistence that public power interest receive preference.

Nonetheless, Bonneville was quickly learning how to extend its service area without the explicit permission of Congress, a skill that would become especially valuable when net-billing contracts were created to facilitate the work of WPPSS. In 1940 BPA's General Counsel decided unilaterally that wheeling was an acceptable role for Bonneville. He justified wheeling with the argument that private utilities would be charged for the service, and the resulting revenues would help reduce the costs of power sold to public utilities. The Regional Solicitor backed the counsel's opinion in 1955 and 1956, and in 1957 an appropriation committee agreed with the solicitor. In 1974, after wheeling had been an established practice for twenty years, Congress expressly appropriated money to construct new lines for wheeling (Blumm 1983: 213).

Expanding Industrial Sales

In the late 1950s BPA added a new twist to the cycle of building, marketing, high estimates of future demand, and new building, which had steadily expanded its service area. Largely because of the non-federal power development that its own wheeling made possible, BPA found itself in possession of a huge power surplus but with insufficient revenues to pay its debts. Instead of raising rates, BPA Administrator Charles Luce (later chairman of New York's Consolidated Edison Co.) doubled industrial power sales, a move that was apparently prohibited by the Eisenhower administration's 1953 order to stop promoting such sales. The effect of Luce's action was once again to increase the likelihood of future power shortages. Thus, the BPA growth cycle resulted in renewed pressure to build more generating capacity.

By the early 1960s BPA had become the central power planning entity in the region. The 1961 Columbia River Treaty, signed for the purposes of joint U.S.-Canadian power development, led to another major expansion of BPA's service area (to include California). It also provided BPA with valuable experience in negotiating and gaining special appropriations from Congress.

Exchange Agreements

With the proposal by Washington State Senator Henry Jackson that a Hanford Reservation reactor be used to produce electricity, Bonneville found an opportunity to bypass the growth cycle that it had perfected during the 1940s and 1950s. Congress refused to allow construction of the by-product steam generating plant by a federal entity. WPPSS agreed to build the plant and share the power with private utilities. The role of BPA was to subsidize the cost of the plant through an exchange agreement under which utilities exchanged their share of the project power for equal values of BPA's less expensive hydropower. In effect, the exchange agreement allowed BPA to purchase power, a function specifically denied to BPA in 1937 when it was created, in 1949 when Congress rejected the idea of a CVA, in 1951 when Senator Jackson introduced legislation for BPA to build and operate coal plants in Oregon, and again in 1958.

The exchange agreement concept later evolved into the net-billing contracts that made financing possible for the first three nuclear power plant projects initiated by WPPSS. To justify net billing, BPA relied on opinions and favorable statements by individual members of Congress, as well as advisory opinions from the Interior Solicitor and the Government Accounting Office—essentially the same kinds of informal justification used by BPA to expand its role first into power planning and later into power wheeling. The exchange agreements and net-billing contracts allowed BPA to purchase power capability in a way never expressly authorized by Congress.

The Ten Year Hydro-Thermal Power Program

BPA's ever expanding growth cycle, modified by BPA's ability to purchase power capability through exchange agreements, found its ultimate expression in the Ten Year Hydro-Thermal Power Program. In the late 1960s the Joint Power Planning Council (composed of more than 100 private and public utilities, led by Bonneville), formulated the first phase of the program, a twenty-year construction program including, among other things, the construction of up to twenty nuclear plants. Net-billing contracts were to provide a means for public and private utilities to build the plants and to maintain BPA's position as central actor in regional power planning and development.

By 1972, however, Phase I had stalled. As we have noted, BPA's net-billing capacity had been quickly exhausted by high construction costs. Further credits for additional plants would have exceeded the amount the customers owed BPA. Also, new Internal Revenue Service regulations ended most of the economic advantages of net billing. Phase II of the program was formulated by BPA, and arrangements among participating utilities were negotiated by Bernard Goldhammer, director of power management at BPA. Net billing was no longer possible, but Goldhammer and BPA's outspoken administrator, Donald P. Hodel, convinced the region's utilities that the need for additional generating capacity was great enough to require them to build the necessary plants on their own. There was also the possibility that the Northwest Power Act, already being contemplated by BPA officials and others, would allow BPA to acquire the power from these plants. The new plants were, of course, the ill-fated WPPSS Projects 4 and 5.

The nuclear power industry, thanks to a lack of federal regulation and coordination, was overselling untried technology to unsuspecting utilities in the late 1960s and early 1970s. That industry found a perfect foil in WPPSS, which had become, in effect, a willing agent of the growth cycle that BPA and its utility customers were using to expand their service areas.

The Northwest Power Act

With the collapse of Phase II, Congress finally turned away from its implicit policy of supporting, through acquiescence and appropriations, Northwest power development plans made in relative isolation by BPA and its customers. The passage of the Northwest Power Act in 1980 indicated that Congress wished to narrow rather than expand BPA's statutory mandate. Bonneville was given the purchase authority it had struggled to obtain for over forty years, but that authority could be used to purchase nuclear power only when other alternatives, such as the use of conservation and renewable resources, had been thoroughly exhausted. The act called for more active congressional oversight and public involvement in all future regional power decisions.

The act also reallocated planning power to states in the region through a Northwest Power Planning Council. The governors of Idaho, Montana, Oregon, and Washington were each called on to appoint two members to the panel, which was charged with drafting a twenty-year plan for meeting the Northwest's energy needs. In a 1985 revised version of the council's first plan, adopted in 1983, the council predicted that the Northwest's electricity surplus would continue well into the following decade, perhaps even into the next century. The council concluded that mothballed WPPSS Projects 1 and 3 would not be needed in the forseeable future and should not be included in the region's portfolio of available and reliable energy resources.

Other than the passage of the Northwest Power Act in 1980, neither Congress nor any agency of the federal government has acknowledged the extent of the federal role in the planning that led to the WPPSS disaster. Early in 1984 the General Accounting Office issued a draft report criticizing BPA for a lack of control exercised with regard to WPPSS construction and financing activities. Planning activities, however, were not mentioned.

In August 1984 Donald P. Hodel, administrator of BPA from 1972 to 1977, was asked by a House subcommittee to give his account of BPA's role in the WPPSS decision to build Projects 4 and 5. Hodel, Secretary of Energy in the Reagan administration, appeared during hearings called to determine whether or not BPA should be allowed to purchase power directly from WPPSS Projects 1, 2, and 3, in case the courts void the net-billing agreements. Asked if BPA pressured utilities to participate in Projects 4 and 5, if BPA was aware of the legal questions surrounding participation by sixteen of the utilities, and if BPA staff had concluded in a 1976 internal report that WPPSS had understated costs of the two plants, Hodel replied that he had no recollection of such events (Gleckman 1984a).

MUNICIPAL FINANCIAL DISCLOSURE

Perhaps nowhere is the lack of federal involvement more evident in the activities of WPPSS—at least in so far as investors are concerned—than in connection with the disclosure activities of WPPSS and its underwriters. WPPSS and its underwriters are not subject to the financial disclosure requirements that affect corporate issuers and their underwriters.

The Securities Act of 1933 and the Securities and Exchange Act of 1934 exempted municipal securities, and almost all parties associated with the municipal securities market, from most of their regulations affecting corporate underwriting, buying, selling, and trading. The municipal market was relatively small at that time and considered free from the problems of misrepresentation that plagued the corporate securities markets. The newly formed Securities and Exchange Commission had almost no powers over the municipal markets. Section 17 of the Securities Act does apply to municipal securities, but only in the sense that it prohibits fraudulent omission of facts in official statements provided to potential investors.

In the years following the securities legislation of the 1930s, neither Congress nor the SEC has directly addressed the disclosure problems of municipal issuers and underwriters. But the few existing regulations affecting municipal securities have been modified or interpreted in three ways. First, since 1934 the courts have applied some sections of the Securities and Exchange Act in municipal securities fraud cases. These sections define the nature of due diligence investigations of municipal issuers by those who market the securities. Due diligence refers to the legal requirements for underwriters to verify information appearing in official statements.

Second, court cases in the mid-1970s narrowed the scope of due diligence liability by ruling that any given securities firm was not liable for damage suffered by investors if the firm acted in good faith—even if the firm did not investigate the issuer.

Third, Congress finally amended the Securities and Exchange Act in 1975 to force brokers and dealers to register with the SEC. The Municipal Securities Rulemaking Board (MSRB) was created to register and regulate the activities of brokers and dealers, who were now required to provide investors with certain kinds of information about the securities being sold.

In spite of the legislation, court decisions, and specific activities of the SEC and the MSRB over the years, the root causes of investor misperceptions of the financial capability of issuers have not been addressed. Financial disclosure by issuers has never even been made mandatory. In other words, there is no law or regulation requiring issuers to disclose information in an official statement when bonds are first issued, much less when additional bonds are issued later. In 1975 Missouri Senator Thomas Eagleton proposed legislation that would have applied the same kinds of disclosure requirements to municipal entities that govern corporate issuers. The bill was successfully opposed by the SEC. The next year state and local governments and investment bankers successfully blocked legislation proposed by New Jersey Senator Harrison Williams to establish federal disclosure guidelines for municipal issuers. The Tower amendment, passed in 1976, formally prohibited the MSRB from requiring such disclosure.

Of course, most municipal issuers do indeed publish official statements in order to gain access to the credit markets. Many of these issuers follow voluntary disclosure guidelines developed in 1976 by the Municipal Finance Officers Association (now the Government Finance Officers Association). And in many ways the actual disclosure practices of most municipal issuers yield a quality and quantity of information that is at least as good as that available in other credit markets. But no matter how accurate and extensive municipal disclosure is on average, it is still voluntary. And above all, there is no requirement that underwriters share the responsibility for the disclosure documents issued at the time of a municipal bond sale, as underwriters of corporate securities must do.

In the case of WPPSS this lack of regulated disclosure had a significant impact on the quality of information provided to investors. A series of investigative reports by *Credit Markets* reporter Howard Gleckman uncovered the fact that investor-owned utilities owning shares of WPPSS projects provided their investors with more accurate information about WPPSS after 1979 than did WPPSS itself (Gleckman 1984b and 1984c). Yet WPPSS and the investor-owned utilities shared the same principal underwriter, Merrill Lynch White Weld Capital Markets Group, and the same financial adviser, Blyth Eastman Paine Webber Inc. When working with the investor-owned utilities, the actions of the underwriter and financial adviser were governed by SEC regulations affecting corporate securities. In these cases, the underwriter and financial adviser shared responsibility with the utilities for the information included in the offering statements. Most of these statements included official WPPSS figures on project costs and schedules, but beginning in 1979 the statements included such warnings to investors as: costs are subject to review and may be revised, these dates represent current estimates . . . and future delays are possible, additional delays may result, delays have been experienced and additional delays are possible, consideration is currently being given to revisions of the estimated completion date, and the company's share of construction costs will exceed the last previously announced estimates. Such warnings were not included in WPPSS official statements.

According to Gleckman's investigation, Blyth Eastman helped WPPSS prepare official statements for all of its bond sales during this period, and Merrill Lynch either formally reviewed the official statements, as it did for the large negotiated offering in May 1980, or kept in close contact with Blyth Eastman. Nevertheless, the official statements prepared by WPPSS with the help of these organizations did not include the cautions printed in statements prepared for the investor-owned utilities at virtually the same time, by the same organizations. Gleckman concluded that

> During this period, investors in WPPSS bonds consistently received less accurate information about the true state of the supply system's construction program than did investors in four private utilities which owned shares in the WPPSS units. . . . (Gleckman 1984b: 1).

In December 1983 the SEC revealed that it was investigating the possibility that securities laws had been violated in connection with the sales of WPPSS bonds. Specifically, the investigation was said to involve initial offerings and disclosure by WPPSS, activities of the underwriters, lawyers, accountants and rating firms, and secondary market trading. The general focus of the investigation was fraud, due to the SEC's lack of authority to police disclosure activities in greater depth. Hundreds of subpoenas were issued in the investigation. Among those asked to turn over documents were Merrill Lynch,

Blyth Eastman, Wood, Dawson, Smith & Hellman (formerly Wood & Dawson), and a host of former and current WPPSS officials.

In early 1985, with the WPPSS investigation still underway, SEC Chairman John R. Shad proposed to Congress that the MSRB be given the authority to require municipal disclosure, by insisting that underwriters obtain contractual assurances from issuers as to their intentions to prepare offering statements. New York Senator Alfonse D'Amato, Chairman of the Senate Banking Committee's securities subcommittee, suggested that this modest proposal represented "a further chipping away at the independence of state and local governments" (*Credit Markets* 1985: 41).

THE ASSURANCE OF QUALITY IN PLANT CONSTRUCTION AND DESIGN

In the late 1970s confusion over who was in charge of construction management led to an outbreak of unusually serious problems at WPPSS Project 2. Construction delays were increasing rapidly, but more important from the NRC's point of view, the same quality control regulations were being broken repeatedly on the construction site.

In June of 1980 the NRC found twenty violations in the sacrificial shield wall, a special concrete barrier erected against the possibility of escaping radiation. Contractors had continued to build around the wall even though the Supply System's own quality control inspectors called for repairs as early as 1977. In addition, problems involving clamps for electrical conduit and the separation of electrical cables (necessary to prevent fire hazards), although identified by NRC inspectors in 1978, had not been remedied. In each case, WPPSS contractors had continued installing clamps and cable in apparent violations of NRC standards for over eighteen months.

In June 1980 the NRC ordered WPPSS to stop all construction on Project 2 and fined the Supply System $61,000. Construction was resumed when the NRC was satisfied that WPPSS had completely restructured the construction management system used on the project. A 1984 report by the Office of Technology Assessment noted that the restructuring by WPPSS management included clear and direct lines of responsibility for design and construction, the creation of the position of project director, and the specification of construction management duties, including new review and surveillance procedures. The OTA report noted that the other WPPSS projects were less fortunate in that they were eventually cancelled or mothballed. "The management restructuring came too late to gracefully reverse the effects of early planning decisions" (U.S. Congress, Office of Technology Assessment 1984: 126).

The NRC Investigates Itself

Of course, it is not the mission of the NRC to be concerned directly with construction costs, schedule delays, mothballing, or cancellations, but it was not until the early 1980s that the NRC realized that these problems might be associated with quality assurance problems at nuclear power projects—and the investigation and correction of such problems are indeed part of the NRC's mission. By 1982 questions about quality assurance had surfaced at a number of nuclear power construction projects, including Marble Hill, Midland, Zimmer, South Texas, and Diablo Canyon, as well as WPPSS. In the 1982–1983 Authorization Act for the NRC, Congress called for the agency to investigate its own ability to detect and correct design and construction quality problems of nuclear power plants. The principal conclusion of the staff report, published in 1984, was that

> nuclear construction projects having significant quality-related problems in their design or construction were characterized by the inability or failure of utility management to effectively implement a management system that ensured adequate control over all aspects of the project (U.S. Nuclear Regulatory Commission 1984: 2.2).

In other words, as the report went on to explain, breakdowns in the ability of these utilities to maintain quality in design and construction that was acceptable to the NRC had its root causes in shortcomings of project and corporate management, including breakdowns in planning, scheduling, procurement, and oversight of contractors (U.S. Nuclear Regulatory Commission 1984: 2.2).

The report noted that changes in the political, economic, and regulatory environments of nuclear power plant construction had certainly contributed to construction quality problems, but that the NRC had not adequately assessed the management capability of utilities constructing these plants and probably should not have issued construction permits to a number of utilities. The report called for more careful issuance of construction permits, as well as construction evaluation audits by the NRC and third-party organizations. Above all, "The inspection program should address the issue of management capability and effectiveness on a routine basis" (U.S. Nuclear Regulatory Commission 1984: ix).

WPPSS and Quality Assurance

Ironically, nowhere in the 540-page NRC report is WPPSS mentioned, even though during the preparation of the report the Supply System registered the largest municipal default in history. The irony deepens when one appreciates that the management shortcomings found by the NRC to indicate quality assurance problems were virtually all in evidence at WPPSS during the 1970s. Thus, had the NRC adopted and fully carried out a decade earlier the approach to licensing and inspection that it advocated in the 1984 report, the Supply System's history could have been quite different.

The NRC concluded that the following characteristics are necessary for successful nuclear construction:

- Key project personnel for each of the organizations comprising the project team should have prior nuclear design and construction experience.

- Each team member should assume a project role commensurate with its capability and prior experience. If the owner does not have the experience to manage construction, someone else must do it.

- Even if construction management is the job of some entity other than the utility owner, it is still essential that the utility have strong project management capability within its own organization. The utility should not rely too heavily on an architect-engineer, for example, if the AE does not have the experience or the authority to manage construction.

- Top corporate management must understand and appreciate the complexities and difficulties of nuclear construction and be willing to tailor accordingly financial, organizational, and staffing support; planning and scheduling; and close management oversight of the project and project contractors. Above all, in this regard, top management should not take a fossil approach to nuclear construction. The use of fixed-price construction contracting is usually not appropriate, nor is the employment of contractors simply because they may have worked on previous fossil projects (U.S. Nuclear Regulatory Commission 1984: 2.3).

• Top management must be involved in the project. NRC case studies "confirmed the phenomenon of top corporate management setting the tone for a project, and affecting the emphasis of its subordinates, both managers and workers. In this regard, management's actions have much more influence than their words" (U.S. Nuclear Regulatory Commission 1984: 2.4).

• Effective information flows must link top management, intermediate layers of management, and first-line supervisors and foremen.

• Top management must be committed to quality and quality assurance, ideally viewing NRC standards as minimums of construction performance.

The NRC admitted that during the 1970s its inspection program had shared with the top management of most troubled utilities a weakness in detecting the real reason for quality problems—an "inability to recognize that recurring problems in the quality of construction were merely symptoms of much deeper, underlying programmatic deficiencies in the project, including project management" (U.S. Nuclear Regulatory Commission 1984: 3.9).

Another Call for Improved Management Quality

In keeping with Congress's long-term commitment to help the nuclear power industry, House and Senate committees asked the Office of Technology Assessment in 1983 to examine the question of what Congress could do to make nuclear power technology "more attractive to all the parties of concern" (U.S. Congress, Office of Technology Assessment 1984: 8). The OTA report concluded that technological complexity and change, along with a rapidly changing regulatory environment contributed to the management challenges facing utilities that undertake nuclear power plant construction. The report suggested that these conditions might be changed to ease the pressures on utilities, but noted that "The most important improvement required is in the internal management of nuclear utilities" (U.S. Congress, Office of Technology Assessment 1984: 19).

The OTA staff found that managerial problems often stemmed from a lack of nuclear experience on the part of utility top management, little or no appreciation of the uniqueness and complexity of nuclear construction, the absence of clear lines of authority and specific allocation of responsibility in such projects, and a general failure of top management to become directly involved in their project and to offer coordination and motivation of staff and contractors.

Anticipating the conclusion of the NRC study, published a few months later, the OTA staff recommended that the quality of management become a focus of regulatory efforts and that the NRC certify utilities as to their fitness to build as well as operate nuclear plants. "Certification could force the poor performers to either improve their management capabilities, obtain the expertise from outside, or choose other types of generating capacity" (U.S. Congress, Office of Technology Assessment 1984: 20). The OTA staff pointed out that the managerial problem bears not only on the ability of nuclear power projects to meet NRC safety guidelines. Solving the problem is necessary also to convince investors and the general public that the nuclear power industry should survive. "If the efforts to improve utility management described thus far are insufficient to satisfy all these actors, it is unlikely that new plants will be ordered" (U.S. Congress, Office of Technology Assessment 1984: 135).

FEDERAL LEADERSHIP IN CRISIS RESOLUTION: THE PROSPECTS FOR A FEDERAL BAILOUT

Although the federal government must bear a significant measure of blame for the WPPSS default, a federal bailout appears highly unlikely. Ignorance or denial of the role of Congress and various federal agencies in the evolution of the Supply System's problems and an awareness of the important role played by WPPSS management shortcomings contribute to congressional resistance to a dramatic WPPSS financial rescue. These same factors also account for a lack of congressional interest in providing leadership for crisis resolution, which would be a much more appropriate kind of involvement in the affairs of WPPSS.

As we have seen, congressional inaction in such matters as planning and regulation is a decades-old stance. But the tradition of federal unwillingness to become involved in bailouts at the state level is even more longstanding. In May of 1843 the Reverend Sydney Smith sent a letter to the U.S. House of Representatives that included the following plea:

> I petition your honorable House to institute some measures for the restoration of American credit, and the repayment of debts incurred and repudiated by several of the States. Your Petitioner lent to the State of Pennsylvania a sum of money, for the purpose of some public improvement. The amount, though small, is to him important, and is a saving from a life income, made with difficulty and privation. If their refusal to pay (from which a large number of English families are suffering) had been the result of war, produced by the unjust aggression of powerful enemies; if it had arisen from civil discord; if it had proceeded from an improvident application of means in the first years of self-government; if it were the act of a poor State struggling against the barreness of nature — every friend of America would have been contented to wait for better times; but the fraud is committed in the profound peace of Pennsylvania, by the richest State in the Union, after the wise investment of the borrowed money in roads and canals, of which the repudiators are every day reaping the advantage. It is an act of bad faith which (all its circumstances considered) has no parallel, and no excuse (Smith 1844: 3).

Neither Smith's many eloquent protests (for which he became famous) nor any other tactics by investors succeeded in persuading Congress to authorize a federal assumption of state debts after several state defaults occurred during the mid-nineteenth century. The moral outrage of Smith and others helped to force negotiated settlements in most cases, and ever since a sense of moral responsibility has been part of the public borrowing process (Walsh 1978: 20).

Partly because of such settlements, the federal government has consistently maintained a hands-off policy with regard to municipal defaults. The only recent exceptions to that policy have been cases in which federal money has been used to ensure the continued provision of crucial municipal services (e.g., police and fire protection) to large city populations. The most notable example of this was the federal offer to New York City of up to $2.3 billion in seasonal, short-term loans to help forestall the city's impending bankruptcy in late 1975.

Suggestions for a WPPSS Bailout

The moral outrage of WPPSS 4 and 5 bondholders certainly matches that of Sydney Smith. But the Washington State Supreme Court decision seems to have ruled out the possibility of a settlement negotiated by WPPSS or the state of Washington with Project 4 and 5 bondholders. Some of these bondholders expect legal action to help them recover their investments, but this will not happen unless they can document intentional efforts to defraud by WPPSS or other parties involved in bond sales. Many other investors are hoping, as Sydney Smith once did, that Congress will agree to a federal assumption of municipal debts. But Congress, true to its tradition of leaving the states to fend for themselves in such matters, has shown little enthusiasm for such ideas.

As early as 1982 American Express Co., at the request of WPPSS participants, devised a direct federal rescue plan for the Supply System, involving the use of a federally subsidized loan to BPA or some other agency to purchase new bonds issued by WPPSS. Earnings produced by the bond sale would be invested and used to pay off WPPSS 4 and 5 debt service. Congress never gave the proposal serious consideration.

In January 1983 Howard Sitzer, of Thomson McKinnon, suggested that the state of Washington could create a public corporation to issue termination bonds backed by federal guarantees. The cost of the guarantees would be recovered through billing to BPA customers. The bond proceeds would equal annual debt service on WPPSS Projects 4 and 5 bonds.

In March of 1983, just prior to the Washington State Supreme Court decision invalidating the take-or-pay contracts, members of the Washington Public Utility Districts Association (most of whom were WPPSS participants) suggested a number of options. One possibility offered was a regionalization plan that would spread the debt through BPA billings to its northwestern customers, including non-WPPSS participants and direct service industries.

In early 1984 another plan was suggested by a special commission appointed by the Washington governor and headed by Charles Luce, one-time Bonneville administrator and former chairman of Consolidated Edison. The Luce Commission recommended the creation of a new federally chartered regional financing agency to sell bonds to pay off WPPSS Project 4 and 5 debt and finance final construction on Projects 1, 2, and 3. Oregon Representative Jim Weaver called the Luce Commission findings "the biggest flop I've ever heard of in my life" (*Credit Markets* 1984: 6).

Writing in the *Wall Street Journal* in August 1983, economists James T. Bennett and Thomas J. DiLorenzo argued that any kind of federal rescue of WPPSS

> . . . can only make matters worse by signaling that fiscal irresponsibility will not be penalized by default and bankruptcy, but instead will be rewarded by a taxpayer bailout. The appropriate policy is not to invent another way of cross-subsidizing a failing enterprise, but to let sleeping failures lie (Bennett and DiLorenzo 1983: 14).

WPPSS and the National Nuclear Epidemic

Some advocates of a federal bailout link their arguments with a defense of WPPSS management. They argue that WPPSS and its creditors should not be punished because the organization clearly was caught in a nationwide epidemic of nuclear power plant failures in the 1970s and 1980s. In other words, it is suggested that an analysis of cost and schedule statistics shows that WPPSS management was actually not much worse than that of Marble Hill, Midland, Seabrook, Shoreham, South Texas, Zimmer, and a host of other troubled nuclear projects. This argument has been couched in impressive social science jargon (absolute versus relative mismanagement models) by Professor Robert E. Berney, formerly of the Washington State University Department of Economics, and member of the executive board of directors of WPPSS (Berney n.d.). Advocates of a federal bailout argue that because WPPSS was caught in a nationwide problem beyond its control, the federal government should be part of the solution.

There can be no doubt that a national problem has existed for some time. The following facts from the 1984 study by the Office of Technology Assessment provide sobering evidence of the size and extent of the nuclear epidemic:

- Over 100 nuclear units were cancelled from 1972 to 1983, twice the number of coal plants. Those nuclear plants represent almost $10 billion in investment costs (in 1982 dollars). At least another sixteen units could be cancelled by 1990.

- No nuclear plant now in operation or under construction has been ordered since 1974. By 1990 most plants under construction now will have been completed or cancelled, and no new domestic orders are expected.

- Average construction costs of nuclear plants more than doubled during the 1970s and are expected to increase at least another 80 percent during the 1980s.

- At the beginning of the 1970s, 80 percent of electric utilities had bond ratings of AA or AAA (Standard & Poor's). By 1981 no electric utilities were rated AAA and only 25 percent were rated AA.

The Mismanagement Factor

Evidence of the Supply System's managerial failings has been abundantly documented. And a growing body of evidence, accumulated during the early 1980s by the NRC, the OTA, and others, suggests that managerial deficiencies have been the primary cause of many problems experienced by other utilities as well. The OTA study found that variations in construction costs among nuclear utilities were due in part to regional differences in the cost of labor and materials, the weather, and regulatory changes, "but more to differences in the experience and ability of utility and construction managers" (U.S. Congress, Office of Technology Assessment 1984: 14).

Indications of problems at the Long Island Lighting Company's Shoreham plant led the New York State Public Service Commission to undertake a five-year study of LILCO's management practices. The result was a series of unprecedented prudency hearings to determine whether the utility should be penalized for imprudent management decisions. The PSC concluded that

> LILCO management has failed to address adequately the management responsibilities entrusted by its shareholders, ratepayers and regulators. LILCO's management actions in aggregate have been deficient and unreasonable. The project management organization, inconsistently supported by top management and the Board of Directors, have afforded [sic] inadequate leadership to the project team. This deficiency not only allowed, but caused significant inadequacies in the performance of engineering and construction of the Shoreham project. The contributions of Stone & Webster as Architect/ Engineer and Construction Manager were deficient both within the scope of

the work under its internal control, and as a result of improper management by LILCO (New York State, Department of Public Service 1984: 6).

As a penalty for imprudent management decisions, the commission staff recommended that LILCO be prohibited from including in its rate base a minimum of $1.55 billion in plant costs. In other words, the utility and its stockholders, rather than ratepayers, were expected to bear the financial costs of mismanagement.

Increasingly, public service commissions or public utility commissions are finding poor management practices to blame for utility cost increases. Arkansas, Florida, New York, Iowa, and Virginia have disallowed costs (i.e., refused to allow them to be covered in the rate base) that were judged to be over and above the costs of efficient operations. Ohio and New Jersey have joined New York in questioning the prudence of management decisions during construction. This discovery that many nuclear power plant construction problems may be due in large part to mismanagement decreases the likelihood that Congress will provide utilities with the kind of help they are seeking.

Prospects for a Federal Bailout

If the New York State Public Service Commission's line of reasoning were applied to WPPSS, then perhaps Project 4 and 5 bondholders would have no right to expect a federal bailout or any other kind of settlement that places the burden of WPPSS costs directly on rate payers or taxpayers. WPPSS and its investors would be responsible for the organization's mistakes. Although bondholders are not investors in the same sense as are stockholders of investor-owned utilities, there is nevertheless a public perception that bondholders must accept some risk for the failure of their debtor utilities.

Whether or not Congress passes legislation to rescue WPPSS bondholders depends of course on how legislators evaluate the balance of interests involved in the crisis—what groups are identified by members of Congress as their proper constituencies. Whatever happens, a number of factors will mitigate against congressional action to provide direct subsidies to WPPSS or to allow regionalization of WPPSS debt. These factors include the following:

- *The basic inertia of Congress.* The story of the federal government's action relating to nuclear power development, regional power planning, and WPPSS itself is one of inaction. There is no particular reason for Congress to act differently now, or to act at all.

- *The lack of an injured party, other than bondholders.* No massive unemployment or disruption of crucial municipal services has resulted from a WPPSS default. Nor does it appear that the economic interests of the Northwest will be significantly harmed by the default. Bondholders (as lenders) are not owners in the sense that LILCO stockholders are, but many voters associate bondholding with risk-taking investments. It is difficult for legislators to justify help for individuals perceived as having gambled and lost. Perhaps just as important, the votes of disgruntled bondholders are dispersed across the country. Votes of ratepayers affected by WPPSS, on the other hand, are focused in two states, Washington and Oregon, that tend to swing between the two major political parties from election to election.

- *The clearly documented case against WPPSS management.* There is much evidence that the primary cause of the Supply System's problems were caused by poor management. In other words, project failure (if not the long-term default itself) does not appear to have been beyond the control of WPPSS management, and therefore special outside assistance is not easily justified.

- *The dangerous precedent of a federal bailout.* With so many nuclear utilities experiencing problems for so many of the same reasons, Congress may put itself in a position of obligation to all by recognizing an obligation to WPPSS.

- *The lack of key political support.* For example, Representative Jim Weaver, an Oregon Democrat, chairs the House Interior Committee's Subcommittee on Mining, Forest Management, as well as the Bonneville Power Administration. This subcommittee probably would have jurisdiction over any federal legislation required to implement federal assistance to WPPSS through BPA. Weaver was one of the first critics of WPPSS in the Northwest, at a time when such criticism was not popular. He has since become a strong and effective champion of Oregon ratepayers. In late May 1985 Representative Weaver reaffirmed his opposition to federal imposition of a WPPSS bailout through BPA, by proposing that control of Bonneville be turned over to the Northwest Power Planning Council, the regional power planning board created by the Northwest Power Act.

These are only a few of the factors that disincline Congress to take radical action in the interests of WPPSS or its bondholders, no matter what has been the federal role in the WPPSS disaster. Facing a similar situation over 150 years ago, disgruntled bondholder Sydney Smith concluded a letter to the editor of a Pennsylvania newspaper with what he considered to be the only course of action left open to him. Smith's indignant sarcasm describes the position taken by many WPPSS Project 4 and 5 bondholders:

> And now, having eased my soul of its indignation, and sold my stock at 40 percent discount, I sulkily retire from the subject, with a fixed intention of lending no more money to free and enlightened republics, but of employing my money henceforth in buying up Abyssinian bonds, and purchasing into the Turkish Fours, or the Tunis-Three-and-a-half per Cent funds (Smith 1844: 13).

NOTES TO CHAPTER 5

1. This account follows the discussion in Michael C. Blumm, "The Northwest's Hydroelectric Heritage: Prologue to the Pacific Northwest Power Planning and Conservation Act," *Washington Law Review* 58 (1983): 175–244; and Kai N. Lee, Donna Lee Klemka, and Marion E. Marts, *Electric Power and the Future of the Pacific Northwest* (Seattle: University of Washington Press, 1980).
2. For an account of the federal government's failure to provide leadership in the area of the general development and regulation of nuclear power see Mark Hertsgaard, *Nuclear Inc.: The Men and Money Behind Nuclear Energy* (New York: Pantheon Books, 1983), and Daniel Ford, "A Reporter at Large—Nuclear Plant Safety—Part I," *The New Yorker* (October 25, 1982): 107–59.

REFERENCES

Bennett, James T., and Thomas J. DeLorenzo. 1983. "Beefy Bailouts: First Big Mac and Now a Whopper?" *Wall Street Journal*, August 26, p. 14.

Berney, Robert E. n.d. "The Management of WPPSS: Success or Failure." Washington State University Department of Economics Working Paper No. 884–1, Pullman, Wash.

Blumm, Michael C. 1983. "The Northwest's Hydroelectric Heritage: Prologue to the Pacific Northwest Power Planning and Conservation Act." *Washington Law Review* 58 (April): 175–244.

Credit Markets. 1984. "GAO Criticizes Bonneville Role in Overseeing WPPSS Activities" (March 19): 6.

_____. 1985. "Registering and Opinion" (March 25): 41.

Gleckman, Howard. 1984a. "Energy Secretary Parries House Questions on His Role in WPPSS." *Credit Markets* (August 6): 3.

_____. 1984b. "Investors in Private Utilities Knew of Problems at WPPSS Before System Bondholders." *Credit Markets* (September 10): 1.

_____. 1984c. "Lack of Municipal Disclosure Rules Plays Major Part in WPPSS Crisis." *Credit Markets* (September 17): 3.

Hertsgaard, Mark. 1983. *Nuclear Inc.: The Men and Money Behind Nuclear Energy.* New York: Pantheon.

New York State, Department of Public Service. 1984. "Investigation of the Shoreham Nuclear Power Station, Executive Summary Testimony." Albany, N.Y.: New York State Department of Public Service. February.

Pritchett, C. Herman. 1943. *The Tennessee Valley Authority.* Chapel Hill: University of North Carolina Press.

Smith, Sidney. 1844. *Letters on American Debts.* New York: J. Winchester, New World Press.

U.S. Congress, Office of Technology Assessment. 1984. *Nuclear Power in an Age of Uncertainty.* Washington, D.C.: U.S. Government Printing Office. February.

U.S. Nuclear Regulatory Commission. 1984. *Improving Quality and the Assurance of Quality in the Design and Construction of Nuclear Power Plants—A Report to Congress.* Washington, D.C.: U.S. Government Printing Office. May.

Walsh, Annmarie H. 1978. *The Public's Business: The Politics and Practices of Government Corporations.* Cambridge, Mass.: MIT Press.

6 ROLES AND RESPONSIBILITIES

All of the actors we have discussed must share the blame for the WPPSS crisis because, in a very real sense, each of those actors is an essential part of WPPSS as a whole. WPPSS is a series of concentric yet interacting rings whereby WPPSS management and the board of directors are linked to various other groups such as the state of Washington, Bonneville, members of the investment community, the region's voters, and ratepayers by formal and informal chains of power and influence.

With regard to the most immediate problem facing WPPSS, the prolongation of the crisis, all of the WPPSS actors have carefully evaded blame for any of the Supply System's problems. That frantic effort has meant that no leadership has been available to help resolve the default equitably. Thus while avoiding blame, these actors have become responsible in a larger and more important way.

This avoidance of responsibility, or in some cases during the 1970s, ignorance of their particular responsibilities, has been an ongoing characteristic of these actors. In fact it has made all of them accessories in the project failure that pushed WPPSS toward default. The struggle to avoid responsibility for WPPSS and its problems has been rather like the frenzied attempts of children to avoid standing after the music stops in a game of musical chairs.

The game has been underway since the nuclear projects were initiated. From the outset, top executives assumed that policy planning

207

(particularly the assessment of demand for the plants) was the job of the board, public utility districts, and the regional planning system; that project management was the job of private contractors, particularly the architect-engineers; and that quality assurance was the job of the Nuclear Regulatory Commission. The board left planning to the Bonneville Power Administration and regional utility groups. Simply assuming that top management could effectively run the organization, the board occupied itself almost exclusively with details, such as individual change order approvals, without looking at the broader implications involved. The state government, which had no appointment powers over WPPSS, viewed WPPSS as the responsibility of BPA and member utilities and went out of its way to avoid involvement in WPPSS affairs until it was too late. BPA assumed WPPSS could adequately manage its projects but made no effort to confirm that assumption until the question arose of paying debt service for Project 2 bonds. The manner in which BPA tried to gain more influence over WPPSS affairs, beginning at that time, seems to indicate that the federal agency was just as interested in absolving itself of responsibility for WPPSS problems as in making constructive contributions to the solution of those problems. When electric rates started to go up, ratepayers realized that they were responsible for the actions of their utility representatives. Ratepayer activism sparked a sense of that responsibility in utility officials, who in turn started court actions to pass it along to bondholders.

During the financing of the WPPSS projects, bond salesmen and analysts attached disclaimers to published reports on the WPPSS bonds to avoid responsibility for statements that were sometimes little more than good promotional copy. Underwriters and financial advisers concentrated on selling bonds at increasing interest rates, leaving to WPPSS the responsibility of understanding and solving the underlying problems that were undermining its creditworthiness. Bond fund managers and institutional investors carefully reviewed legal opinions to reassure themselves that all responsibility for WPPSS debts would rest squarely with the project participants. But in a ruling that many observers labeled still another example of the avoidance of responsibility, the Washington State Supreme Court decided that those legal opinions were mistaken. While the music has stopped temporarily, all of the chairs are occupied and the bondholders are left standing.

But the real question is, of course, why did everyone so assiduously avoid responsibility for WPPSS—why has there been such an appalling lack of leadership with regard to the activities of that organization, beginning even before the magnitude of its problems were apparent?

This avoidance of involvement can be explained by what Wall Street calls the tar baby syndrome. In 1979, when the Supply System's problems began to attract nationwide public attention, everyone involved with WPPSS quickly became afraid of being associated with, and even more, responsible for, those problems—of being stuck to the tar baby. This syndrome was exacerbated by the growing suspicion by many of the groups, inside and outside of the WPPSS organization, that the Supply System's problems would not be solved without some kind of congressional action. Those suspicions, along with rumors that federal officials were considering bail-out scenarios, increased the players' reluctance to try to resolve things at the local level.

Earlier, during the middle and late 1970s, oversight groups including the state and BPA recognized some of the danger signals of serious problems, but they still did not want to interfere. At this point, the problems still seemed soluble. Nevertheless, these oversight bodies also recognized that considerable effort and commitment would be required to gain more direct and effective involvement in WPPSS activities. The authority they had was not quickly converted into power. In such a situation, outside groups must carry out their oversight responsibilities either by expanding their formal power or by using informal channels of influence. In either case they are effectively expanding their involvement in (and association with) problems in order to carry out the responsibilities they have had all along.

Oversight bodies often believe that the likely results of circumventing the institutional checks on their power do not justify the effort required to do so. In the case of WPPSS, however, the situation deteriorated rapidly and demanded action. By the time WPPSS problems seemed serious, and effort to become involved essential, WPPSS was dangerously close to being a tar baby. This probably explains the ambivalence, especially of BPA, toward WPPSS in the late 1970s. BPA wanted to address the WPPSS problems, and it was willing to make the effort to gain some control over the Supply System, but it also wanted to distance itself from the problems.

Of course, the irony of this predicament is that Washington State made possible the eventual transformation of WPPSS into a tar baby by severely limiting its own ability to control WPPSS when the joint operating agency legislation was passed. BPA did much the same thing later when it failed to write into Project 1, 2, and 3 agreements the kinds of formal oversight powers that it had exercised on the Supply System's Hanford project.

Part of the reason for the early failure of the state to insist on a stronger oversight role is that when joint action agency legislation was passed, no one envisioned that such entities would undertake such an ambitious project as the simultaneous construction of five nuclear power plants. Just as WPPSS was managed as if it were still a small organization during the late 1970s, the legislation creating WPPSS was appropriate for a much smaller and far less consequential governmental entity.

BPA was willing to ease the controls it had over WPPSS activities on the Hanford plant when the nuclear plants were begun. It did so because of friction between BPA and WPPSS on the earlier project and because such controls were deemed excessive in the relatively stable operating environment of the 1970s.

Members of the investment community also had a kind of over-sight relationship with WPPSS, but their failure to take responsibility for the Supply System's problems is more clear cut. Members of that community are always sensitive to the development of tar babies. Most Wall Street firms have considerable expertise in avoiding re-sponsibility in situations like that created by the WPPSS default. Their job is to minimize risk and maximize profit, not to seek out and solve problems before they lead to tar babies. As we have already noted, the oldest adage on Wall Street is simply, "if it's legal, and the price is right, it's good business."

WHO IS TO BLAME FOR WHAT?

None of these concentric circles of power and influence can com-pletely escape blame for the WPPSS disaster because, in the sense described above, they are all elements of the WPPSS phenomenon. The courts will determine the legal liability for the financial damages caused by default, based on review of existing contracts and agree-ments and on any laws relating to the WPPSS situation. But the courts are not likely to draw public policy conclusions from the WPPSS disaster. For this reason, it is more than just an academic exercise to try to determine who among these actors made the most significant contributions to the Supply System's problems. Without someone to blame in that non-legal sense, it is impossible to locate the points of leverage at which pressure can be applied to help avoid the next WPPSS.

The following summary highlights the findings discussed in previous chapters concerning the performance of the various actors in the WPPSS drama.

WPPSS Management and the Board of Directors

The nature of their roles, and the way they carried out those roles, make WPPSS management and the board of directors primarily responsible for cost increases, schedule delays, and project failure in general—the aspect of the WPPSS crisis that led to court tests of participant responsibilities. Many other groups, including and especially BPA, but also the private financial advisers and private contractors, pressured WPPSS into making poor decisions. Nevertheless, these decisions were ultimately the responsibility of the board and top management.

Many other utilities now face problems similar to those of WPPSS. And regulatory changes, inflation, labor problems, and acts of God negatively affected WPPSS, as they have many other utilities. However, based on the actual ways in which the WPPSS organization was managed, as documented in the minutes of the board meetings, in the reports of various management consultants, and in a host of other studies, it is clear that WPPSS was badly mismanaged. It is also clear that this was the result primarily of a chain of inexperience that extended from the board through top management down to many of the construction and engineering personnel. In essence, these actors never identified their proper role in the fast growing WPPSS organization, either with regard to each other or with regard to the individuals and organizations outside of WPPSS.

The Washington State Senate Energy and Utilities Committee was well founded in its judgment that "WPPSS mismanagement has been the most significant cause of cost overruns and schedule delays on the WPPSS projects" (Washington State Senate Energy and Utilities

Committee 1981: 40). The Supply System's own administrative auditor admitted that during the crucial years, 1971-1979, "the type of staff required to manage the growing giant of a program was simply 'not in place'" (Washington Public Power Supply System 1980: 1-1). These conclusions seem even more appropriate in the mid-1980s, with the ever increasing number of revelations by state public service commissions about mismanagement at other nuclear power utilities experiencing similar construction cost increases and schedule delays.

Washington State

Inaction on the part of Washington State government officials played a significant part in the Supply System's slide into project failure. That inaction continues today and contributes to the prolongation of default through the failure of state officials to effect a bailout or negotiated settlement that would distribute the cost of the default in an equitable, or at least acceptable, manner.

Part of this inaction has resulted from a lack of strong political leadership in the state and from the fact that although WPPSS is a public authority of the state, unlike most subsidiary corporations of state government, it was not normally subject to state oversight. Nor were its directors appointed by state authority. Although WPPSS was created by state law, it was the creature of county utility districts with project participants in several states and subject to contractual oversight by a federal agency. The formula for fragmented responsibility is clear.

The state's disinterest in bailout efforts also arises from the belief that state leadership of such a rescue would likely commit the state to more than its fair share of financial participation—at least more than might otherwise be lost if no bailout occurred and the state's credit rating was lowered. And of course, part of the inaction has resulted simply from the reluctance of state politicians to take action that would be highly unpopular with voters. In fact, the threatened limits on municipal borrowing by Washington State and its localities, promised by the investment community as an inevitable result of default, have for the most part not materialized. In this sense, the state government's inaction has been justified.

The Bonneville Power Administration

BPA played a significant role in pressuring WPPSS participants into building Plants 4 and 5 and helped to coordinate the faulty power forecasts that were used to justify all aspects of the Ten Year Hydro-Thermal Power Program. BPA also failed to recognize WPPSS problems early enough, lacked the capacity to contribute to project management improvement, and became obsessed with trying to control administrative details when problems became obvious. BPA only increased WPPSS difficulties when it began what appears to have been a public relations campaign against the Supply System in the late 1970s.

Although BPA eventually fought for influence over WPPSS decisions, it was also careful never to assume any more legal responsibility for WPPSS actions than was detailed in the net-billing contracts for Projects 1, 2, and 3. The reactions of BPA officials to the WPPSS crisis were necessarily colored by the fact that they serve a clientele that includes individuals and organizations not directly associated with WPPSS. The WPPSS board was in error when it assumed through the early and middle 1970s that BPA could be relied on for managerial advice or constructive input. Bondholders and the financial community were mistaken when they believed that BPA's involvement was the kind of federal presence that would somehow prevent or resolve the WPPSS default.

Wall Street Investment Banks and Dealers

With regard to WPPSS, Wall Street acted as it always has, ignoring or downplaying complicated issues involving power demand and management shortcomings. Advice to WPPSS from financial advisers and underwriters was framed primarily in terms of how to sell more bonds. Rating firms seemed slow to appreciate what some other analysts were recognizing about the declining credit quality of WPPSS bonds. Investment houses used every tactic at their disposal to sell bonds, especially to individual investors through bond funds and unit trusts. And with an eye on future profits, the investment community meekly backed away from its threat to punish the state of Washington for a WPPSS default by denying access to the bond markets.

Wall Street firms are competitive and aggressive in search of profits. There is a basic conflict of interest in a public authority paying for financial advice from firms that stand to profit eventually from certain financial decisions of the board. But WPPSS officials should have understood exactly what the role of the financial community did and did not entail.

Legal Counsel

WPPSS legal counsel must take a share of the responsibility for the effects of the Washington State Supreme Court decision. Those attorneys were paid to review proposed contracts and to recommend precautions against just such a decision. The take-or-pay contracts obligating participants to pay back Project 4 and 5 debts were thought to be valid under Washington State law by the vast majority of knowledgeable observers.

Courts

The state supreme court decision invalidating the take-or-pay contracts made long-term default inevitable, but it is important to remember that default, possibly long term, would have resulted in any case. The WPPSS board was already preparing for some form of default in May, a month before the court decision. In addition, events since the default indicate that at least some of the WPPSS Project 4 and 5 participants never could have raised their electric rates high enough to pay for their shares of the project expenses without losing crucial industrial customers (to natural gas, for example) and eventually going bankrupt. Bankruptcies by a few key rural electric cooperatives would precipitate a revenue shortfall that could not be covered by contract step-up provisions. Long-term default would occur even if the validity of the contracts had been upheld in court.

But these facts in no way explain the June 15, 1983, decision by the Washington State Supreme Court. No court decision better illustrates the lack of a clear line separating politically motivated court decisions from decisions based solely on legal considerations. The decision was unexpected by almost everyone. The dissenting justices were respected veterans of the elected court, with far longer tenures on that bench than five of the seven justices who rendered the majority opinion. In the eyes of most legal observers immune from the political and economic crisis conditions in Washington State during the early 1980s, the majority decision stands on a poor foundation in existing law. A reading of the critical commentary and a common sense review of Washington law clearly suggest that the decision was, at the very least, an extreme example of what is euphemistically referred to as judicial discretion.

The News Media and the Activist Ratepayers

With regard to the role of the news media, Shelby Scates, a respected *Seattle Post-Intelligencer* staff columnist, has admitted that "Never in this newsman's 25 years experience, has a story so big been missed by so much of the news media. Our tardy arrival with inquiry rivals, I suspect, WPPSS own mismanagement" (Scates 1982: D-10). The press did not begin in-depth investigative reporting on WPPSS until BPA rate hikes in the late 1970s created public interest in stories on the Supply System. When such reporting began, it focused on the public bickering and embarrassing news leaks that fueled the growing hostilities between WPPSS and BPA. By the early 1980s many journalists were concentrating on contract fraud and easily documented managerial incompetence. These were surface manifestations of much deeper and more profound WPPSS management shortcomings, but also important facts — and the aspects of a complicated issue most easily understood by the general reading public.

Activist ratepayers were also the subject of increasing news media attention during the late 1970s and early 1980s. In fact, media attention was probably responsible for the influence of these groups, beyond the point when many of them had ceased being very active. Whatever the case, ratepayer activism, as covered by the local press, helped spark a statewide (and then a nationwide) crisis in confidence with regard to WPPSS.

No one can claim that the journalistic treatment of WPPSS and its problems was entirely thorough or objective. Nor were activist ratepayers always fair or even sensible. But both groups acted predictably given the circumstances. The mismanagement of public relations during the 1970s by WPPSS executives was a natural result of their overall misunderstanding about what management of the Supply System entailed.

Vendors of Equipment and Services

Of course, WPPSS construction could never have begun without vendors of equipment and services. The firms that sold power plant component systems—Babcock & Wilcox, General Electric, Combustion Engineering, Westinghouse, and so on—represent the core of the U.S. power construction industry. The architect-engineers included Burns and Roe, Bechtel, Ebasco, and United Engineers & Constructors, some of the largest and most experienced engineering firms in the world. The consulting engineer, R.W. Beck and Associates, has served in that role on many major U.S. nuclear projects.

These organizations have invested billions of dollars in the development and continued public and private use of nuclear power to generate electricity. They worked actively to persuade BPA and WPPSS to build as many nuclear plants as possible.

The participation of R.W. Beck in the projects is a typical example. Consulting engineers are routinely brought in to estimate a project's total cost by combining estimates of construction costs, debt service requirements, and future power demand. Beck officials admitted in sworn testimony in 1982 what Beck engineers had told a few probing investment analysts as early as 1979—that they did not independently verify power need figures, construction cost estimates, or interest rate assumptions because they never had a budget line or authorization to test out the raw data supplied by WPPSS members. Beck officials may never have pressed for such authorization; to do so could have jeopardized their continued involvement as a consultant in the largest public power financing ever undertaken. Nevertheless, by 1978 the weakness of the estimates that Beck was routinely reviewing for bond prospectuses was obvious to any interested observer (the estimates were repudiated every quarter).

The Federal Government

Congress and federal regulatory agencies such as the Nuclear Regulatory Commission and the Securities and Exchange Commission remained in the wings while most of the WPPSS drama took place. Their absence created vacuums of power and responsibility in areas of industrial nuclear power development, regional power planning, municipal financial disclosure, quality assurance in nuclear power plant construction, and default crisis resolution. These vacuums were filled by other groups whose activities were not coordinated and whose interests not broad enough to serve public purposes adequately.

The federal government did not cause the WPPSS crisis, but its inaction shaped the political and economic environment that proved to be fertile ground for the Supply System's problems.

HOW TO AVOID THE NEXT WPPSS

In the terms defined in Chapter 2 on management, WPPSS was badly managed. Thus, the Supply System was particularly vulnerable to the many serious problems associated with the construction of nuclear power plants during the 1970s, as well as to the shortcomings of the other actors in the WPPSS drama. Some of the roles and responsibilities of those actors are now being revised, partly as a result of the WPPSS crisis.

- Formalized regional power planning is now a reality in the Pacific Northwest.

- The NRC is refocusing some of its attention to management quality.

- The SEC is investigating the possibility of new regulations for the investment community.

- Bond attorneys across the country are testing contracts before they are signed, or recommending precautionary legislation.

- Rating agencies have developed more sophisticated criteria to evaluate the overall track records of public authorities.

- Bondholders are more wary of investment risks than ever before.

- More insured bond issues are being sold—insurance is now available for individual bond portfolios.

- Voters and ratepayers in the Pacific Northwest are more carefully monitoring the activities of their public officials.

- The nuclear power industry groups have initiated their own inspection programs to evaluate the quality of nuclear power plant construction.

- No new nuclear power plants are being ordered.

- Consideration is being given to the sale of BPA to regional power planning interests.

Thus, many of the vague and informal relationships among the concentric rings of power and influence that make up the WPPSS phenomenon have been tightened, and in some cases formalized. These changes may assure that another WPPSS-like disaster does not occur. But they may not. The various programs and proposals to inspect, evaluate, and regulate do not directly or adequately address the central problem of WPPSS—the need for state governments to ensure that their subsidiary public authorities adequately manage their own business, while maintaining their independent legal character.

The Status of Public Authorities

The public authority is a branch of state or local government with corporate status, that is, with some built-in ambiguity. Their administrative independence provides flexibility to act in a businesslike fashion, to finance, to construct, and often to operate the revenue-producing enterprises of government (Walsh and Leigland 1983: 7). But with such independence, authorities that are not well managed can cause a great deal of harm to bondholders, ratepayers, and citizens of the states in which the authorities reside. Even when authorities are well managed, they may develop policies and priorities that serve the organization's interests rather than public interest. And these priorities can be protected by their incorporation into bond resolutions—legal contracts with bondholders that cannot be changed by legislation.

New York State Attempts at Reform

The pros and cons of public control over public authorities have been considered before in the context of a serious public authority default. In 1975 New York State's Moreland Act Commission presented a series of interrelated public authority reform measures in the wake of the statewide financial devastation triggered by the default of the Urban Development Corporation (UDC), a New York State public authority, and the necessity for the state to provide large sums of money to bail out UDC and other moral obligation authorities. The nature of the recommendations made, some of which are applicable to WPPSS, and the fate of those recommendations offer an informative perspective on why appropriate reform measures may never be taken by officials in any state.

After reviewing half a million documents and hearing from more than 100 witnesses, the commission called for a subtle, but extremely complicated, network of changes in New York State laws and administrative procedures. Rather than advocate a host of new, centralized, formal controls on the activities of New York State authorities, the Moreland commission suggested treating those authorities as if they were indeed corporate subsidiaries of the state. Instead of tighter control, the commission suggested better state management of authorities, including more effective delegation of authority and greater incentives for the authorities to better manage their own affairs. The commission stated one of its most important findings in the following way:

> Public authorities must be restructured so that it is clear that directors are accountable for their actions on behalf of the authority, that they must exercise their powers with regard for their primary role in the authority structure, and that they are responsive to the needs of the State and to the bondholders. Consistent with these principles, directors must be encouraged to be actively involved in the affairs of the authority and not act merely as advisers to powerful management (New York State Moreland Act Commission 1976: 62).

The commission was well aware that it was dealing with a crucial, but difficult to understand problem that resulted from the "necessarily confused dual nature of the public authority" (New York State Moreland Act 1976: 64). Put very simply, authority boards had to be able and allowed to exercise more managerial control over their organizations. But at the same time, they had to develop a stronger sense of responsibility to elected officials. The commission concluded that Urban Development Corporation board members had never developed an ability to manage or control their organization, and consequently they had failed to develop a sense of responsibility for the organization's actions. New York State officials were not in a position to monitor effectively the day-to-day operations of the UDC or any other public authority. The lack of clear lines of accountability and authority allowed UDC to rush headlong into financial and administrative chaos.

The commission recommended ways to increase the willingness and ability of directors to control authorities like UDC in an accountable manner. If our analysis of WPPSS management weakness is generally accurate, at least two of these measures, listed and explained below, might have helped forestall the WPPSS crisis.

1. The governor should appoint private citizens to the board. They should have experience relevant to the business of the authority. A majority should serve at the pleasure of the governor. A minority should serve for a term greater than a single term of the governor (New York State Moreland Act Commission 1976: 63).

The commission wanted highly experienced directors with no vested interest in the state bureaucracy, yet still accountable to the governor. Serving "at the pleasure of" means that the governor can dismiss directors whenever he so desires, without the consent of the legislature. To have the majority of directors serve this way would assure the governor meaningful control over public authority policy— and a significant share of responsibility if problems arise. The remaining directors, with terms longer than the governor's, could help with long-range planning and provide continuity during transition periods.

2. Members of a public authority board should be held accountable to a statutory standard of performance and their responsibilities should be clearly defined (New York State Moreland Act Commission 1976: 64).

This recommendation supplemented the first one. Expertise is not enough; directors must be motivated to use it carefully. One problem with public authorities nationwide is that directors do not have traditional corporate performance incentives or standards. Public authorities pursue economic self-sufficiency, consistent with their public purposes, rather than profit. Most important, bondholders cannot replace directors in the same way that stockholders of private sector corporations can, and governors and other state officials such as treasurers or controllers are usually too far removed to monitor day-to-day decisionmaking.

Given all of this, the commission suggested that New York State's Public Authorities Law be rewritten to include the same kind of duty of care provision found in the New York Business Corporation Law. In other words, directors would be made "personally liable" for what could be found legally to constitute "improper management," including the failure to provide adequate supervision of the officers and agents of the corporation, the failure to act competently, the failure to keep reasonably informed about the activities of the corporation, and the failure to keep abreast of the corporation's financial status (New York State Moreland Act Commission 1976: 66, 72, n. 12). (At the same time the commission recommended indemnification against personal financial loss. The purpose of its recommendations was to inform and motivate directors and those who appoint them, rather than to punish.)

In any case, almost all of the Moreland commission recommendations were ignored or seriously compromised.[1] By the late 1970s the New York State Legislature had begun to act in a way directly opposed to that suggested by the Moreland commission: It was increasing the indemnification provisions covering actions of public authority personnel without making any corresponding increase in personal liability. In 1978 the legislature rewrote the Public Officers Law to create an even broader indemnification provision. In 1979 the legislature passed laws extending Public Officers Law coverage to directors of UDC and a subsidiary authority, the Battery Park Construction Authority, as a response to lawsuits against board members because of troubled construction projects undertaken by those authorities.

In 1981 the legislature created a special new section of the Public Officers Law that explicitly outlined broad indemnification coverage for directors, officers, and employees of public authorities. The section was designed to supersede all other provisions for indemnification. The only condition to be satisfied before this extended coverage could be applied was for the board of directors of a given authority to formally adopt it.

The Moreland Act Commission was trying to improve the management of public authorities in two fundamental ways, both of which could be used profitably in other states. First, it is necessary that a highly visible state official take responsibility for selecting appropriate directors and overseeing their activities. The more visible the official, and the more directors he is allowed to appoint, the better.

A governor may indeed make appointments for political purposes, but to a certain extent his office is responsible for those appointees—and he is in a better position to appoint a competent director for a large public authority than are ratepayers in public utility districts.

Second, it is necessary that authority directors realize they are responsible for the quality of management of the organization. It was not until a 1980 consulting report on the role and organization of the board of directors that WPPSS directors understood the full range of their responsibilities and operational options as members of a board (Institute of Public Administration: 1980). People with different kinds of skills and experience were needed at WPPSS, and they should have been informed and responsible. The board should be thought of as the point of leverage where a relatively small application of pressure can help public authorities avoid deep difficulty.

The kinds of reforms mentioned above could easily be augmented with additional measures, depending on a given authority's function, size, and so on. Selection and compensation guidelines for a given state's authority directors could be established. Capital planning by authorities could be coordinated with state agency planning. Authorities could be required to use consistent financial accounting and reporting formats or construction cost estimating procedures. They might be required to produce annual business plans developed by authority staff, signed by directors, and discussed in public meetings. Special staff units could be created within the governor's office to collect and evaluate information on state authorities and their activities. A number of other measures could be added to encourage better oversight of authorities without compromising their independence and flexibility with overly detailed state controls.[2]

In the Aftermath of Default

At least one of the measures recommended by the Moreland commission for New York was partially carried out in Washington State in connection with WPPSS. In October 1981 state law was changed to require WPPSS to appoint four outside directors, presumably with considerable business experience, to a reconstituted eleven-member WPPSS executive board. But three of the outside directors appointed resigned because the Executive Board had statutory authority only over management of construction; other major decisions, including whether or not to terminate plants, reverted to the traditional twenty-three-member board. The three outside members argued that this division of responsibility was unworkable, and that in any case they were not fully enough protected against personal liability lawsuits for good faith decisions.

In the spring of 1982 the law was changed again. This time, six outside directors were called for, three to be appointed by the governor and three by the full board. The division of responsibilities between the executive board and the traditional board was maintained, but outside directors were declared "immune from civil liability for good faith errors in judgment" (Washington State Legislature 1982: 211).

In the second board reform bill, the legislature also addressed its own liability, and in doing so reaffirmed its unwillingness to take any real responsibility for the Supply System: "The state specifically disclaims any liability for any WPPSS' obligations" (Washington State Legislature 1982: 211). Board members were already immune from liability for good faith actions and would be reimbursed for legal costs, and the like. The legislature further broadened the protection of state public authority directors in the spring of 1985 by requiring that fraud be proven before damages of any kind could be awarded.

The Political Realities of Reform

The fate of the Moreland commission recommendations corresponds to the lack of thoughtful attention in Washington State and other states to the problem of how public authorities can be encouraged to better manage themselves, without diminishing their ability to function. It is difficult enough for busy state legislators to understand and fully appreciate these kinds of complicated reform measures, much less try to fight for them or even explain them to constituents. It is often hard to justify strengthening a governor's power, even in a constructive way. A final and very important reason for the lack of action on public authority reform in many states is that so many people benefit from public authorities just as they are, even when they are poorly managed. As we have seen, this accounts in large part for the extended agonies of WPPSS. The public authority concept is like the tar baby syndrome in reverse—too many individuals and groups are already stuck to the concept as it is. They would prefer to not make any changes.

BONDHOLDERS AND THE FUTURE OF WPPSS

Changes in how the public's business is conducted may seem more crucial to officials in the Pacific Northwest in light of efforts made by Project 4 and 5 bondholders and the bond fund trustee, Chemical Bank, to recover the $2.25 billion loaned to WPPSS. If incompetence, negligence, or fraud on the part of WPPSS officials can be proven in court, or if legal costs grow too high for WPPSS participants, some kind of financial settlement with the bondholders might be possible. The consideration being given by the federal government in 1986 to the sale of the Bonneville Power Administration to Northwest power planning interests might eventually lead to the refunding of outstanding WPPSS obligations, including Project 4 and 5 bonds. (Bondholders will also try to recover damages from WPPSS underwriters, engineers, advisers, and others.)

As legal expenses mount, and particularly if a settlement with bondholders becomes a possibility, citizens and public officials in the Northwest will have special incentive to consider some fundamental public policy problems of which the WPPSS disaster was only a surface manifestation. One issue involves the roles and responsibilities of state government corporations. Who should appoint the officers of such corporations, and how should the duties of those officers be defined? Who is responsible for overseeing the activities of those corporations? What should be the responsibility of parent governments if their subsidiaries cannot live up to their financial obligations? In Washington State, what role should public utility districts play in regional power planning and development? If the Bonneville Power Administration is sold to regional interests, how should it be structured to maintain accountability and financial integrity?

Another issue involves the efforts by public entities to "privatize" economic development activities by contracting them out to private businesses. How can these kinds of complex contracts be managed by public officials who possess little relevant technical experience? How can highly technical work be supervised by such officials? Should this kind of privatization be encouraged, and if so, how should state laws regarding public agency contracting and debt issuance be amended to facilitate the process? If the efforts by bond-holders to recover their money can spur discussion of these kinds of issues, then the benefit of their activism would extend far beyond the thousands of individuals and organizations who purchased the bonds.

Such activism is to be expected in any case. Of all of the groups and individuals discussed in this book, the bondholders must be considered the principal victims of the WPPSS default. Northwest rate-payers may have been deceived and misrepresented, but they have been released from their commitment (made by their utility representatives) to pay for Projects 4 and 5. Their financial loss, even with the prospect of huge legal fees, pales in comparison with the $2.25 billion principal (plus interest) owed bondholders. That money most likely will never be repaid in full, whether or not a settlement is reached.

Since 1983 bondholders and Chemical Bank have been working to overcome the effects of the decision by the Washington State Supreme Court that allowed for the legal victimization of bond-holders. One of the largest obstacles to political and legal efforts to recover bondholder money is the misunderstanding by public officials as well as the general public about who the WPPSS bondholders are, and the roles and responsibilities of bondholders in general. This misunderstanding may have influenced efforts by Northwest rate-payers and utilities to escape their responsibilities for the terminated plants, and may even have influenced the decision by the Washington State Supreme Court that invalidated the take-or-pay contracts. Most damaging to bondholders, this misunderstanding may inhibit future efforts by state and federal political leaders to resolve equitably the WPPSS default.

Part of the misunderstanding has arisen from the fact that, unlike the other concentric circles making up WPPSS, the bondholders have only recently organized themselves into groups such as the National WPPSS 4 and 5 Bondholders Committee, which raises money, surveys and informs bondholders, lobbies for congressional support, pursues legal action, and generally represents the interests of its membership. Like all tax-exempt municipal securities sold during the 1970s and early 1980s, the defaulted bonds were bearer bonds— there was no formal, comprehensive registration of who owned them. Only after the default, with the first attempts by Chemical Bank in October of 1983 to identify and organize bondholders, did most of the purchasers of Project 4 and 5 bonds begin to realize who their fellow bondholders were.

By that time, however, bondholders were already far behind in the public relations war over who should take responsibility for WPPSS. They had already suffered a redefinition of their role in the WPPSS crisis from bondholder to shareholder, or investor in the most technical sense. Bondholders are creditors who loan money on the condition that it be repaid in full, along with interest, in a timely fashion. Bondholders do not purchase a share of ownership in the hope that it will increase in value, and they have neither obligation nor right to play an active part in the internal operation of a company.

The importance of the distinction between bondholder and shareholder becomes apparent by comparing the WPPSS situation to that of other utilities with cancelled nuclear projects. Consumers Power of Michigan and Public Service of Indiana are both privately owned utilities that began construction of nuclear power plants financed by shareholder funds and taxable bonds. Each utility terminated the construction of nuclear power plants, and because those plants could never generate the revenues pledged to pay back the utilities' debts, funds had to be found elsewhere. Disputes arose between shareholders and ratepayers about who should shoulder the loss.

At no point in this ongoing debate has serious consideration been given to the idea that bondholders should be responsible for the financial burden. If the plants had been completed, the ratepayers would have paid for them through electric rates. Because the plants were terminated, the transfer of cost to shareholders from ratepayers is politically attractive. Such a transfer is consistent with the risk/renewal relationship accepted as a principle underlying investment activity, and it is also consistent with the view of some state public service commissions that owners of utilities, rather than their relatively captive customer bases, should take financial responsibility for certain kinds of management and planning errors.

But when WPPSS terminated Projects 4 and 5 there were no shareholders and there was no shareholders' equity. The take-or-pay contracts entered into by the eighty-eight project participants were viewed by the investment community and potential bond purchasers as a substitute for such equity. As a result, and because a terminated plant could not generate cash through the production of power, the participating utilities and their ratepayers faced enormous losses when the construction on Projects 4 and 5 was cancelled.

The political and legal efforts by utilities and ratepayers to avoid such losses were aided by the transformation of bondholders in the public mind from creditors to shareholders. The media and public debate characterized bondholders as "investors" who, like private utility shareholders, were hoping to shift financial responsibility to unsuspecting ratepayers. In hearings before his House subcommittee, Representative Jim Weaver dismissed one bondholder's complaint by asking rhetorically if he believed that "in capitalism there is supposed to be risks when you invest your money" (U.S. House of Representatives 1985: 44). Bondholders may have been especially damaged by the redefinition of their role by at least one Washington State Supreme Court Justice during the court's deliberations on the Project 4 and 5 take-or-pay contracts. In concurring with the majority decision that held those contracts invalid, Justice Dore wrote that if general obligation bonds had been involved in the project financing, "citizens" would have had to pay back the debt. "Because the bonds are labeled as revenue bonds, however, the risk of project failure should be on the investors who bought the bonds knowing the sole source of payment was to be the revenues from the sale of electricity which was expected to be generated" (*Chemical Bank v. WPPSS 1983*: 805).

Justice Dore's remarks ignore the original purpose of the take-or-pay contracts and make purchasers of revenue bonds appear to be speculators consciously gambling on risky ventures in the hope of profit. WPPSS bondholders, whether individuals or institutions, were not investors in this sense. Tax-exempt securities are purchased for a variety of reasons. They help wealthy individuals and organizations like banks and insurance companies shelter income, and they help individuals and families keep pace with inflation and provide income for retirement. Indeed, there is always some risk involved in the purchase of municipal bonds, but those securities are rarely bought simply because risk suggests the potential of high return. Above all, municipal bonds represent a secure, steady, tax-exempt stream of income rather than a gamble for high stakes.

Nor is it possible to claim that all or even most Project 4 and 5 bondholders are wealthy individuals, banks, or insurance companies who can easily afford to lose their investments. Many institutional bondholders tried to clear their portfolios of WPPSS Project 4 and 5 bonds beginning in 1981, when the ratings on those bonds began to drop and analysts began to wonder how long WPPSS could maintain market access. A 1985 sample of 10,000 Project 4 and 5 bondholders by the National WPPSS 4 and 5 Bondholders Committee reveals the following characteristics:

- Two-thirds of these bondholders are over sixty years old, and forty-nine percent are over sixty-five years old.
- Fifty-two percent are retired.
- Eighty-six percent expected the income from the bonds to represent a significant supplement to their social security income.
- Two-thirds of these bondholders purchased only one or two $5,000 WPPSS bonds (Lehmann 1986).

Almost 20 percent of these bondholders admitted to never having bought a municipal bond before, but no matter what their prior experience with tax-exempt securities, most individual WPPSS bondholders have learned important and painful lessons from their experience with the Supply System. Many of them now recognize that they were naive to believe that they would be recommended only those bonds that salespeople or investment houses considered truly creditworthy. It is the job of sales representatives to sell, and most make commissions whether or not their clients make money. Individual investors have always been more intensely marketed by investment houses when knowledgeable institutional investors begin to shy away from certain kinds of bonds. Most investment houses had stopped buying WPPSS bonds for themselves long before they stopped recommending them to retail customers. Of the WPPSS bondholders surveyed by the National WPPSS 4 and 5 Bondholders Committee, 67 percent said they would never again buy bonds associated with Washington State. Forty-two percent said they would buy only insured or insurable bonds in the future. Indeed, the WPPSS disaster led one WPPSS bondholder to found the Bond Investors Association, a non-profit group that provides portfolio insurance to individual bondholders (Lehmann 1986).

In spite of their education at the hands of bond salespeople, Northwest ratepayers, utilities, politicians, and judges, many WPPSS Project 4 and 5 bondholders continue to misunderstand some crucial dimensions of the problems they face. Many are frustrated and confused because they do not fully realize what is at stake for the Pacific Northwest. To many bondholders the default is particularly galling because the Northwest still enjoys the lowest electric rates in the country. This leads them to conclude that rates could be increased relatively painlessly to raise money to repay bondholders. The total electric rate necessary to enable this repayment would be less, in many cases, than annual rate increases experienced recently by bondholders living in other parts of the country. Costly lawsuits could be resolved quickly, a settlement made, and WPPSS forgotten.

But what appears as a mean-spirited or even irrational refusal to raise rates must be understood in relation to other important factors, many of which are not well appreciated by bondholders. First, a significant portion of the industrial base in the Northwest arose because of the availability of cheap power. Substantial rate increases would threaten the growth and continuity of those industries. Shutdowns and relocations by the aluminum industry are already occurring.

Second, the low price of electricity has influenced the way homes are built and how electricity is used in the Northwest. Energy needs supplied in other regions of the country more efficiently by oil or gas, such as home heating, are supplied in the Northwest by electricity. Home insulation and energy-efficient appliances, which have been widely used in the rest of the country for a decade, have only recently become attractive to Northwest residents. As a result, the per capita electric consumption in the region is significantly above that of the rest of the nation. In such a situation, rate increases are a much more serious prospect than many bondholders realize.

Third, rate increases necessary to pay off WPPSS debt, unlike fuel costs, represent a fixed cost that must be recovered no matter what the demand for electricity. Such increases in the Northwest would likely lead to conservation, industry pullouts, and switches to natural gas, which in turn would lead to more rate increases because the fixed cost would then be spread over a smaller base. As noted above, this cycle probably would have led to a long-term default even if the state supreme court decision had not invalidated the Project 4 and 5 contracts.

In other words, what many bondholders do not understand is that, although a settlement is possible, it is likely to result only from a protracted struggle, a legal and political war of attrition that by the end of 1985 was not even half over, even though over $100 million had already been spent on lawsuits by the many different legal combatants. And even if a settlement is reached, it may involve only a fraction of the money owed to bondholders, or a long payout period extending over many years.

In order to reach a settlement—much less one that most bond-holders will consider to be acceptable—bondholders and their voluntary associations must remain active and organized and must continue to educate politicians and the general public, as well as themselves, about the complex tangle of issues that WPPSS has become. Without this activist stance bondholders will be unable to reach a satisfactory conclusion to their problems with WPPSS and government officials and the general public will have less incentive to ask and attempt to answer some of the fundamental questions raised by the WPPSS default.

NOTES TO CHAPTER 6

1. For a more extensive discussion of the New York case, see James Leigland, "Reforming the State's Public Authorities," *New York Affairs* 9, no. 2 (1985): 50–57.
2. For a more extensive discussion of these and other public authority reform measures, see Annmarie H. Walsh, *The Public's Business: The Politics and Practices of Government Corporations* (Cambridge: MIT Press, 1978).

REFERENCES

Chemical Bank v. WPPSS. 1983. 99 Wn. 2d 772. June.

Institute of Public Administration. 1980. *Role and Organization of the Board of Directors.* Report submitted to the Washington Public Power Supply System Board of Directors. New York: Institute of Public Administration. January.

Lehmann, C. Richard. 1986. Interview with the Treasurer of the National WPPSS 4 and 5 Bondholders Committee. February 13.

New York State Moreland Act Commission on the Urban Development Corporation and Other State Financing Agencies. 1976. *Restoring Credit and Confidence: A Reform Program for New York State and Its Public Authorities.* Report to the Governor of New York. Albany, N.Y.: New York State Moreland Act Commission. March 31.

Scates, Shelby. 1982. "WPPSS Critics Get Caught in the Flack." *Seattle Post-Intelligencer*, March 28, p. D10.

U.S. House of Representatives, Committee on Interior and Insular Affiars, Subcommittee on Mining, Forest Management, and Bonneville Power Administration. 1985. *WPPSS Bond Default: Who Pays?* Oversight hearing held
on January 26, 1984. Washington, D.C.: U.S. Government Printing Office.

Walsh, Annmarie, and James Leigland. 1983. "The Only Planning Game in
Town." *Empire State Report* (May): 6–12.

Washington Public Power Supply System. 1980. *Report on Implementation
Status of Consultant Recommendations — Part I.* Report by the Office of
Administrative Auditor. Richland, Wash.: Washington Public Power Supply
System. August 8.

Washington State Energy and Utilities Committee. 1981. *Causes of Cost Overruns and Schedule Delays on the Five WPPSS Nuclear Power Plants,* Volume 1. Report to the Washington State Senate and the 47th Legislature.
Olympia, Wash.: Washington State Energy and Utilities Committee. January
12.

Washington State Legislature. 1982. "Senate Bill 4996, Chapter 43." *Legislative Report, Final 1982.* Olympia, Wash.: Washington State Legislature,
pp. 210–11.

SELECT BIBLIOGRAPHY

Anderson, D. Victor. *Illusions of Power.* New York: Praeger, 1985.

Arthur Andersen and Co. *Washington Public Power Supply System Project Planning and Measurement Review.* Report submitted to F.D. McElwee, Assistant Director of Projects, Washington Public Power Supply System. New York: Arthur Andersen and Co., 1978.

Austen, Eileen Titmuss. *Washington Public Power Supply System.* New York: Drexel Burnham Lambert Inc., June 3, 1981.

_____. *The Ides of March.* New York: Drexel Burnham Lambert Inc., January 1983.

Beers, Roger, and Terry R. Lash. *Choosing an Electrical Energy Future for the Pacific Northwest: An Alternative Scenario.* Palo Alto, Calif.: Natural Resources Defense Council, Inc., January 1977.

Bennett, James T., and Thomas J. DiLorenzo. "How the Government Evades Taxes." *Policy Review* 19 (Winter 1982): 71–89.

_____. "Beefy Bailouts: First Big Mac and Now a Whooper?" *Wall Street Journal,* August 26, 1983, p. 14.

_____. *Underground Government: the Off-Budget Public Sector.* Washington, D.C.: Cato Institute, 1983.

Bennett, R.R., and D.J. Kettler. *Dramatic Changes in the Costs of Nuclear and Fossil-fueled Plants.* New York: EBASCO Services, Inc., September 1978.

Berney, Robert E. "The Management of WPPSS: Success or Failure." Washington State University Department of Economics Working Paper No. 884-1, Pullman, Wash., n.d.

Blumm, Michael C. "The Northwest's Hydroelectric Heritgage: Prologue to the Pacific Northwest Power Planning and Conservation Act." *Washington Law Review* 58 (April 1983): 175–244.

233

Blyth Eastman Pain Webber Public Power Finance Group. *Presentation to Washington Public Power Supply System: A Balanced Financing Program.* New York: Blyth Eastman Pain Webber Inc., April 1980.

Boeing Engineering and Construction Company. *Boeing Engineering and Construction Company Presentation to the WPPSS Board of Directors.* Seattle: Boeing Engineering and Construction Company, November 2, 1979.

Bonneville Power Administration. *A Ten Year Hydro-Thermal Power Program for the Pacific Northwest.* Portland, Ore.: Bonneville Power Administration, 1969.

_____. *About BPA.* Portland, Ore.: Bonneville Power Administration, 1974.

_____. *The Role of the Bonneville Power Administration in the Pacific Northwest Power Supply System: Including its Participation in the Hydro-Thermal Power Program—A Program Environmental Statement and Planning Report.* Portland, Ore.: Bonneville Power Administration, 1977.

_____. *Population, Employment and Households, Projection to 2000 for Washington.* Portland, Ore.: Bonneville Power Administration, July 1979.

_____. *Final Environmental Impact Statement on 1979 Wholesale Rate Increase.* Portland, Ore.: Bonneville Power Administration, October 1979.

Boulton, William R. "The Evolving Board: A Look at the Board's Changing Roles and Information Needs." *Academy of Management Review* 3 (October 1978): 827–36.

Buchart, L. E. *Presentation to Management Review Board, Washington Public Power Supply System.* Seattle: Boeing Engineering and Construction Co., February 1, 1980.

Caro, Robert. *The Power Broker: Robert Moses and the Fall of New York.* New York: Random House, 1975.

Carter, Don. "Mixed Results for Ratepayer Revolt." *Seattle Post-Intelligencer,* February 13, 1983, p. B5.

Chemical Bank v. WPPSS. 99 Wn.2d 772, June 1983.

Clifford, Donald K. *Managing the Threshold Company.* New York: McKinsey & Co., 1973.

Columbia River Transmission Act (1974). Public Law No. 93–454, 88 Stat. 1376 (codified as amended at 16 U.S. Code 838–838K (1976 and Supp. V 1981)).

Connelly, Joel. "A Tiny Utility Takes on WPPSS." *Seattle Post-Intelligencer,* February 20, 1982, p. 2.

_____. " 'Mr. Public Power' Blames the Experts." *Seattle Post-Intelligencer,* March 28, 1982, p. D7.

_____. "Time—for Someone—to Pay the WPPSS Bill." *Seattle Post-Intelligencer,* February 13, 1983, p. B2.

Conner, Richard D. "Contracting for Construction Management Services." *Law and Contemporary Problems* 46 (Winter 1983): 5–23.

Coopers and Lybrand. *Review of Contract Administration and Project Accounting.* Report submitted to F.D. McElwee, Assistant Director of Projects, Washington Public Power Supply System. New York: Coopers and Lybrand, May 17, 1978.

"Court Deals Blow to WPPSS Investors." *Seattle Times*, April 29, 1985, p. 1.

Cresap, McCormick and Paget Inc. *Study of Management Organization and Related Issues, Washington Public Power Supply System.* Report submitted to the Washington Public Power Supply System, Executive Committee. San Francisco: Cresap, McCormick and Paget Inc., August 1976.

Daniels, Paul R. *Termination is Good News for WPPSS and its Bondholders.* Chicago: John Nuveen & Co., January 27, 1982.

Davis, Edward R., and Lindsay White. "How to Avoid Construction Headaches." *Harvard Business Review* 2 (March/April 1973): 87–93.

Decision Planning Corporation. *A Report on the Implementation of BPA Oversight Activities on WNP-1, WNP-2 and WNP-3.* A report to the Bonneville Power Administration. Costa Mesa, Calif.: Decision Planning Corporation, April 30, 1980.

Dibner, David R. "Construction Management and Design-Build: An Owner's Experience in the Public Sector." *Law and Contemporary Problems* 46 (Winter 1983): 137–44.

Duisin, Xenia W. *Government Corporations, Special Districts, and Public Authorities: Their Organization and Management, A Selected, Annotated Bibliography.* New York: The Institute of Public Administration, 1985.

Falk, Theodore C. "Prelude to the State WPPSS Cases: The BPA as Broker." *Municipal Finance Journal* 6 (Winter 1985): 41–60.

_____. "Comparing the State WPPSS Cases: The Municipal Constitution." *Municipal Finance Journal* 6 (Spring 1985): 111–36.

Feldstein, Sylvan G.; Frank Fabozzi; and Irving Pollack, eds. *Handbook of Municipal Bonds*, Volume II. Homewood, Ill.: Dow Jones Irwin, 1983.

Foote, Jeffrey P.; Alan S. Larsen; and Rodney S. Maddox. "Bonneville Power Administration: Northwest Power Broker." *Environmental Law* 6 (1976): 831–57.

Ford, Daniel. "A Reporter at Large—Nuclear Plant Safety—Part 1." *The New Yorker*, October 25, 1982, pp. 107–59.

_____. "A Reporter at Large—Nuclear Plant Safety—Part 2." *The New Yorker*, November 1, 1982, pp. 45–103.

"GAO Criticizes Bonneville Role In Overseeing WPPSS Activities." *Credit Markets*, March 19, 1984, p. 6.

Gleckman, Howard. "Energy Secretary Parries House Questions on His Role in WPPSS." *Credit Markets*, August 6, 1984, p. 3.

_____. "Investors in Private Utilities Knew of Problems at WPPSS Before System Bondholders." *Credit Markets*, September 10, 1984, p. 1.

_____. "Lack of Municipal Disclosure Rules Plays Major Part in WPPSS Crisis."
    Credit Markets, September 17, 1984, p. 3.
_____. *WPPSS: From Dream to Default.* New York: Credit Markets, 1984.
Gleckman, Howard, and Frank Gresock. "Victory and Defeat." *Credit Markets*,
    May 7, 1985, p. 57.
Gomena, Peter. "Mayor Rejects Strand Firing." *Tri-City Herald*, March 6,
    1979, p. 1.
Gotschall, Mary G. "John Mitchell, Dean of Bond Counsel, Discusses the Old
    Power Elite." *Credit Markets*, November 19, 1984, p. 13.
Greenbaum, Elliot A. *Washington Public Power Supply System.* Municipal credit
    report. Basking Ridge, N.J.: Michael A. Weisser, Inc., February 15, 1979.
Gurwitz, Aaron S., and Daniel E. Chall. "Nuclear Power Plant Construction:
    Paying the Bill." *Federal Reserve Bank of New York Quarterly Review* 9
    (Summer 1984): 48-57.
Hale, Jeannie. "Chemical Bank Decision—Liability of Washington PUDs and
    Municipal Participants." Memorandum to the Washington State Senate Energy
    and Utilities Committee from Staff Attorney, June 20, 1983.
Henriques, Diana. *The Machinery of Greed: The Abuse of Public Authorities
    and What to Do About It.* Princeton: Princeton University Press, 1982.
Hertsgaard, Mark. *Nuclear Inc.: The Men and Money Behind Nuclear Energy.*
    New York: Pantheon Books, 1983.
Hinman, George; Paul Swanidass; and Walter Butcher. *Energy Projections for
    the Pacific Northwest.* Pullman, Wash.: Environmental Research Center,
    Washington State University, 1975.
Hodel, Donald P. "The Prophets of Shortage." Speech delivered to the City
    Club of Portland, July 11, 1975. Portland, Ore.: Bonneville Power Adminis-
    tration, 1975.
Institute of Public Administration. *Survey of WPPSS Board.* Report to the
    Washington Public Power Supply System Board of Directors, Committee on
    Management Consultant. New York: Institute of Public Administration, July
    1979.
_____. *Federal, State and Regional Oversight.* Report submitted to the Wash-
    ington Public Power Supply System Board of Directors. New York: Institute
    of Public Administration, October 1979.
_____. *Organization of Public and Community Relations.* Report submitted to
    the Washington Public Power Supply System Board of Directors. New York:
    Institute of Public Administration, October 1979.
_____. *Report on Top Management Structure.* Report submitted to the Wash-
    ington Public Power Supply System Board of Directors. New York: Institute
    of Public Administration, November 14, 1979.
_____. *Role and Organization of the Board of Directors.* Report submitted to
    the Washington Public Power Supply System Board of Directors. New York:
    Institute of Public Administration, January 1980.

_____. "Memorandum to Committee on Management Consultant, WPPSS Board of Directors." New York: Institute of Public Administration, July 16, 1980.

Jones, L. R. "Resolving the WPPSS Crisis: Bankruptcy, Bailout or Negotiated Workout?" Municipal bond research report prepared for Harris Trust and Savings Bank. Chicago: Harris Trust and Savings Bank, April 5, 1983.

Knight/Bonniwell. *What Would Be the Potential Financial and Economic Impacts on the Northwest Should WPPSS Default on Plants 4 & 5?* Final Report to the Office of the Governor, State of Washington. Chicago: Knight/Bonniwell, March 29, 1983.

Koenen, Austin V., and John W. Gillespie. *Public Power Finance After the WPPSS Default: A Return to Fundamentals.* New York: Public Power Finance Group, Public Finance Department, Lehman Brothers Kuhn Loeb Inc., February 1984.

Komanoff, Charles. *Power Plant Cost Escalation: Nuclear and Coal Capital Costs, Regulation and Economics.* New York: Van Nostrand Reinhold Co., 1982.

_____. *WPPSS Costs Versus the Industry Norm.* Report to the Washington State Attorney General. New York: Komanoff Energy Associates, June 1982.

Lamb, Robert, and Stephen P. Rappaport. *Municipal Bonds: The Comprehensive Review of Tax-Exempt Securities and Public Finance.* New York: McGraw-Hill Co., 1980.

Landau, Martin, and Russell Stout. "To Manage is Not to Control: Or the Folly of Type II Errors." *Public Administration Review* 39 (March/April 1979): 148–56.

Lee, Kai N. "The Path Along the Ridge: Regional Planning in the Face of Uncertainty." *Washington Law Review* 58 (April 1983): 317–42.

Lee, Kai N.; Donna Lee Klemka; and Marion E. Marts. *Electric Power and the Future of the Pacific Northwest.* Seattle: University of Washington, Press, 1980.

Lehmann, C. Richard. Interview conducted with the Treasurer of the National WPPSS 4 and 5 Bondholders Committee, by James Leigland, February 13, 1986.

Leigland, James. "The Public-Private Alliance: The Case of WPPSS and the Investment Community." Unpublished research paper presented at the Annual Meeting of the American Political Science Association, Washington, D.C., August 30, 1984.

_____. "WPPSS: Some Lessons for Public Management." *IPA Report* 1, no. 1 (1984): 3–7.

_____. "Reforming the State's Public Authorities." *New York Affairs* 9, no. 2 (1985): 50–7.

Leighland, James, and Laura R. Malkin. "Causes and Consequences of Management Failure in Public Enterprise: The Case of the Washington Public Power Supply System." Unpublished research paper presented at the Annual Meeting of the International Association of the Schools and Institutes of Administration, Tunis, September 1985.

Lepinski, Jerry. *Washington Public Power Supply System: Its Role and its Credit*. Nuveen Research Comment. Chicago: John Nuveen & Co., June 29, 1979.

Linden, Susan M., and Leon J. Karvelis. *Washington Public Power Supply System: State of Washington (Nuclear Projects Nos. 4 and 5)*. New York: Merrill Lynch Pierce Fenner & Smith Inc., Fixed Income Research Department, February 12, 1979.

Management Analysis Company. *Manpower Staffing Diagnostic of Projects WNP-2, WNP-1/4, and WNP-3/5*. Report submitted to N. O. Strand, Managing Director of Washington Public Power Supply System. San Diego: Management Analysis Company, January 1980.

Marion, Joseph, and Francis J. Quinn. *Competitive and Negotiated Offerings: The Relative Merits of the Negotiated Method*. A report prepared for the Washington Public Power Supply System. New York: Merrill Lynch White Weld Capital Markets Group, Merrill Lynch Pierce Fenner & Smith Inc., November 24, 1980.

Mellem, Roger D. "Darkness to Dawn? Generating and Conserving Electricity in the Pacific Northwest: A Primer on the Northwest Power Act." *Washington Law Review* 58 (April 1983): 245–78.

Metz, Robert. "Power Bonds in Northwest." *The New York Times*, December 7, 1981, p. IV-8.

Munro, Sterling. Prepared written testimony delivered before the Water and Power Resources Subcommittee of the House Committee on Interior and Insular Affairs, February 19, 1979. Transcript on file at Washington Public Power Supply System offices, Richland, Wash.

New York State Assembly Committee on Corporations, Authorities and Commissions. *Agency Out of Control: A Critical Assessment of the Finances and Mission of the Port Authority of New York and New Jersey*. Albany, N.Y.: New York State Assembly Committee on Corporations, Authorities and Commissions, June 1982.

New York State Moreland Act Commission on the Urban Development Corporation and other State Financing Agencies. *Restoring Credit and Confidence: A Reform Program for New York State and Its Public Authorities*. Albany, N.Y.: New York State Moreland Act Commission, March 31, 1976.

Nolan, Robert B. " 'Take-or-Pay' Contracts: Are They Necessary for Municipal Project Financing?" *Municipal Finance Journal* 4 (Spring 1983): 111–15.

Northwest Energy Policy Project. *Energy Futures Northwest*. Portland, Ore.: Northwest Energy Policy Project, May 1978.

Northwest Environmental Technology Laboratories. *Energy 1990 Consultants' Report*. Bellevue, Wash.: Northwest Environmental Technology Laboratories, 1976.

"Nuveen Sued for Fraud Over Sales of Unit Trusts with WPPSS Bonds." *Credit Markets*, July 23, 1984, p. 4.

O'Brien, Brendan. Deposition given in *DeFazio et al. v. Washington Public Power Supply System et al.*, September 29, 1982. Transcript on file in staff office of the Washington State Senate Energy and Utilities Committee, Olympia, Wash.

Olsen, Darryll, and Walter R. Butcher. "The Regional Power Act: A Model for the Nation?" *Public Policy Notes*. Seattle: Institute for Public Policy and Management, University of Washington, 1984.

Oregon Department of Energy. *Oregon's Energy Future*. Salem, Ore.: Oregon Department of Energy, January 1, 1977.

Patterson, Donald C. Letter to James Perko, Assistant Director of Finance and Treasurer, Washington Public Power Supply System, from the Senior Vice President of Blyth Eastman Paine Webber, WPPSS financial adviser, February 27, 1980.

Peach, J. Dexter. Letter from the director of the U.S. General Accounting Office to U.S. Representative James H. Weaver, accompanying U.S. GAO report, *Analysis of Estimated Cost for Three Pacific Northwest Nuclear Power Plants* (Washington, D.C.: U.S. Government Printing Office, July 30, 1979), July 30, 1979.

"Power Surcharge? They Won't Pay." *Seattle Post-Intelligencer*, May 11, 1982, p. A5.

Pritchett, C. Herman. *The Tennessee Valley Authority*. Chapel Hill: University of North Carolina Press, 1943.

Redman, Eric. "Nonfirm Energy and BPA's Industrial Customers." *Washington Law Review* 58 (April 1983): 279–316.

"Registering an Opinion." *Credit Markets*. March 25, 1985, p. 41.

Rogers, Harold E. "What Went Wrong with WPPSS?" *Municipal Finance Journal* 5 (Winter 1984): 81–6.

Scates, Shelby. "Politics: The Past and Future of WPPSS." *Seattle Post-Intelligencer*, March 28, 1982, p. D9.

_____ . "WPPSS Critics Get Caught in the Flack." *Seattle Post-Intelligencer*, March 28, 1982, p. D10.

_____ . "Put WPPSS Blame on Bloated Forecasts." *Seattle Post-Intelligencer*, June 1, 1982, p. A10.

Seligman, Dan. "The Washington Public Power Supply System." Unpublished research report prepared for the Institute for Environmental Studies, University of Washington, July 1978.

Sitzer, Howard, and Leon J. Karvelis. *Washington Public Power Supply System: At the Crossroads*. New York: Merrill Lynch Pierce Fenner & Smith Inc., Fixed Income Research Department, July 24, 1981.

Skidmore, Owings, and Merrill. *Electric Energy Conservation Study*. Report prepared for the Bonneville Power Administration. Portland: Skidmore, Owings, and Merrill, July 1976.

Smith, James E. Letter to Paul S. Tracy, Jr., Vice President of First National City Bank, New York, from Comptroller of the Currency, August 27, 1975.

Smith, Sydney. *Letters on American Debts.* New York: J. Winchester, New World Press, 1844.

Squires, William R., and Michael Murphy. "The Impact of Fast Track Construction and Construction Management on Subcontractors." *Law and Contemporary Problems* 46 (Winter 1983): 55–67.

Standard & Poor's. *Standard & Poor's Ratings Guide.* New York: McGraw-Hill, 1979.

Stone & Webster Engineering Corporation. *Final Report: Assessment of 1980 Project Construction Budgets.* Report submitted to the Washington Public Power Supply System, Executive Committee of the Board of Directors. Boston: Stone & Webster, November 16, 1979.

Strand, Neil O. Memorandum to the Washington Public Power Supply System Board of Directors, October 18, 1978. Copy on file at Washington Public Power Supply System offices in Richland, Wash.

Sugai, Wayne H. "The WNP 4 and 5 Participation Decision: Seattle and Tacoma—A Tale of Two Cities." *The Northwest Environmental Journal* 1 (Autumn 1984): 45–95.

_____. "Mass Insurgency: The Ratepayers' Revolt and the Washington Public Power Supply System Crisis." Unpublished Ph.D. dissertation, University of Washington, Seattle, 1985.

The Bond Buyer's Municipal Statbook 1984. New York: The Bond Buyer, 1985.

"The Fallout From 'Whoops.' " *Business Week*, July 11, 1983, pp. 80–7.

Theodore Barry & Associates. *Management Study of the Roles and Relationships of Bonneville Power Administration and Washington Public Power Supply System.* Report submitted to the Bonneville Power Administration. Los Angeles: Theodore Barry & Associates, January 1979.

_____. *A Survey of Organizational and Contractual Trends in Power Plant Construction.* Los Angeles: Theodore Barry & Associates, March 1979.

Tuttle, Martha Z. *Joint Action Agencies: What Are They and How Do They Work?* New York: L. F. Rothschild, Unterberg, Towbin, Municipal Research Department, October 4, 1982.

U.S. Congress, Office of Technology Assessment. *Nuclear Power in an Age of Uncertainty.* Washington, D.C.: U.S. Government Printing Office, February 1984.

U.S. Department of Energy. *Management Review: Burns and Roe Contract Administration and Estimating Procedures, and Related WPPSS Responsibilities for Processing Change Orders on the WPPSS Nuclear Project No. 2, 1978 Audit Summary.* Washington, D.C.: U.S. Government Printing Office, April 10, 1978.

_____. *Nuclear Plant Cancellations: Causes, Costs and Consequences.* Washington, D.C.: U.S. Government Printing Office, April 1983.

_____ . *The Future of Electric Power in America: Economic Supply for Economic Growth.* Washington, D.C.: U.S. Government Printing Office, June 1983.

U.S. Department of the Interior. *Review of Washington Public Power Supply System Contract Administration and Bonneville Power Administration's Oversight, 1977 Audit Summary.* Washington, D.C.: U.S. Government Printing Office, 1977.

U.S. General Accounting Office. *Region at the Crossroads—the Pacific Northwest Search for New Sources of Electric Energy.* Washington, D.C.: U.S. Government Printing Office, August 10, 1978.

_____ . *Analysis of Estimated Cost for Three Pacific Northwest Nuclear Power Plants.* Washington, D.C.: U.S. Government Printing Office, July 30, 1979.

_____ . *Impacts and Implications of the Pacific Northwest Power Bill.* Washington, D.C.: U.S. Government Printing Office, September 4, 1979.

_____ . *Financial Community's Perceived Impacts Which Could Result From Default or Successful Legal Challenge by Participants in Washington Public Power Supply System Nuclear Projects Nos. 4 and 5.* Washington, D.C.: U.S. Government Printing Office, July 2, 1982.

_____ . *Bonneville Power Administration and Rural Electrification Administration Actions and Activities Affecting Utility Participation in Washington Public Power Supply System Plants 4 and 5.* Washington, D.C.: U.S. Government Printing Office, July 30, 1982.

_____ . *Status of Bonneville Power Administration's Efforts to Improve Its Oversight of Three Nuclear Power Projects.* Washington, D.C.: U.S. Government Printing Office, August 3, 1984.

U.S. House of Representatives, Committee on Interior and Insular Affairs, Subcommittee on Mining, Forest Management, and Bonneville Power Administration. *WPPSS Bond Default: Who Pays?* Oversight hearing held on January 26, 1984. Washington, D.C.: U.S. Government Printing Office, 1985.

U.S. Nuclear Regulatory Commission. *Reducing Nuclear Powerplant Leadtimes: Many Obstacles Remain.* Report to Congress. Washington, D.C.: U.S. Government Printing Office, 1978.

_____ . *Regional Evaluation of Licensee Performance: Washington Nuclear Project No. 2.* Report No. 50-397/80-11. San Francisco: Nuclear Regulatory Commission, Region V, August 12, 1980.

_____ . *Improving Quality and the Assurance of Quality in the Design and Construction of Nuclear Power Plants—A Report to Congress.* Washington, D.C.: U.S. Government Printing Office, May 1984.

Vann, Harold E. *Performance Evaluation and Recommendations for Improving Future Performance on WNP-1/WNP-4.* Philadelphia: United Engineers and Constructors, August 25, 1978.

Walkley, Glenn C. Letter to Washington Governor Dixy Lee Ray from the President of the Washington Public Power Supply System Board of Directors, May 18, 1979.

Walsh, Annmarie H. *The Public's Business: The Politics and Practices of Government Corporations.* Cambridge: MIT Press, 1978.

Walsh, Annmarie, and James Leigland. "The Only Planning Game in Town." *Empire State Report,* May 1983, pp. 6–12.

_____. "The Authorities: $24 Billion Debt and Still Growing." *Empire State Report,* July 1983, pp. 33–8.

Walsh, Annmarie, and David Mammen. *State Public Corporations: A Guide for Decision Making.* New York: Institute of Public Administration, 1983.

Washington Energy Research Center, Office of Applied Energy Studies. *Independent Review of Washington Public Power Supply System Nuclear Plants 4 and 5: Final Report to the Washington State Legislature.* Seattle: Washington Energy Research Center, Washington State University/University of Washington, March 15, 1982.

Washington Public Interest Research Group. *Electricity Forecasts and Alternatives for the Pacific Northwest — Considerations for Washington State.* Seattle: Washington Public Interest Research Group, October 1977.

Washington Public Power Supply System. *Supply System Projects: Questions and Answers.* Richland, Wash.: Washington Public Power Supply System, February 1979.

_____. "Minutes of the Washington Public Power Supply System Special Board of Directors' Meeting." Richland, Wash.: Washington Public Power Supply System, April 13, 1979.

_____. "Minutes, WPPSS Regular Executive Committee Meeting." Richland, Wash.: Washington Public Power Supply System, June 27, 1980.

_____. *Report on Implementation Status of Consultant Recommendations — Parts I, II, and III.* Consolidation of 3-Volume Report, by J. A. Hare, Administrative Auditor. Richland, Wash.: Washington Public Power Supply System, August 8, 1980.

Washington State Senate Energy and Utilities Committee. *Causes of Cost Overruns and Schedule Delays on the Five WPPSS Nuclear Power Plants,* Volumes 1 and 2. A report to the Washington State Senate and the 47th Legislature. Olympia, Wash.: Washington State Senate Energy and Utilities Committee, January 12, 1981.

Washington State Legislature. "Senate Bill 4996, Chapter 43." *Legislative Report, Final 1982.* Olympia, Wash.: Washington State Legislature, 1982, pp. 210–11.

Weaver, Jim. Letter to the Editor. *Wall Street Journal,* August 9, 1983, p. 33.

Whitely, Peyton. "It's a Matter of Pipes and Bolts." *Seattle Times,* May 1, 1983, pp. D1–4.

Wilson, Hugh A., and Regina S. Axelrod. "The Shoreham Debacle: Public/Private Issues." Unpublished research paper presented at the Annual Meeting of the American Political Science Association, Washington, D.C., August 30, 1984.

Winders, John J. "Are Bond Counsel Obliged to Serve Others in Addition to Their Clients?" *Weekly Bond Buyer*, August 25, 1980. p. 1.

"WPPSS Looks to Curb Escalating Legal Costs." *Weekly Bond Buyer*, June 6, 1983, p. 3.

Zonana, Victor F. "Rebellion Breaks Out in Northwest over Skyrocketing Electricity Rates." *Wall Street Journal*, March 19, 1982, p. 29.

INDEX

245

Consultants, 27, 29–36, 68, 154–155, 211; and board of directors of WPPSS, 213; and Bonneville Power Administration, 27, 177 n. 1, 147–148, 149–156; and credit analysis, 103, 126–127
Consumers Power of Michigan, 226
Contractors, 25, 61–66; and budgeting, 42, 46, 50, 54; and contracts, 46, 49, 50, 54, 63, 64–65, 197; fraud, 163–164, 215
Cornell Law Review, 174
Corporate culture, 26–27, 73–74, 75, 166–167
Cost overruns, 5, 10–11, 110; and contractor fraud, 163-164, 215; and management of WPPSS, 23, 24, 38, 41–68, 126–127, 211–212; *see also* Administrative costs; Construction costs
Cost-plus contracts, 54, 64–65
Costs. *See* Administrative costs; Cost overruns; Construction costs
Courts, 1, 144, 167–176, 210–211; and board of directors of WPPSS, 174–175; and Initiative 394, 14; and municipal bond disclosure, 191; and net billing, 191; and take or pay contracts, 87, 167–176, 214–215; *see also* King County Superior Court; lawsuits; Washington State Supreme Court
Crabshell Alliance, 35
Credit analysis, 89–94, 120–130; and administrative costs, 103, 124–125, 126–127; and bond counsels, 92–98; and demand estimates, 98–103, 123; economic factors, 98–103, 123–124; legal factors, 92–98, 121–122, 125–126; and management, 124, 126–127; and marketing of bonds, 116–117; and rating firms, 84–92, 95, 116, 217; and underwriters, 109, 112–113
Credit Markets, 192, 194
Cresap, McCormick and Paget, Inc., 29–31, 32; and board of directors of WPPSS, 34–35, 36, 151; and budgeting, 39, 41; and costs, 49, 50, 54; and engineering staff of WPPSS, 56; and project management failures, 58, 59, 61

Daniels, Paul R., 125, 126, 127
Davis, Edward, 53
Dawson, John, 86
Demand for power: and Bonneville Power Administration, 9-10, 96, 101–102, 127–128, 160, 185; and conservation, 123, 126; and credit analysis, 98–103, 123; and Northwest Regional Planning Council, 160; and price, 99–101, 123–124, 214, 229–230; projections, 9, 11–12, 13–14, 98–103, 106, 127–128, 160
Design-built construction. *See* Fast-track construction
Design refinements: and construction costs, 11, 49–50, 124; management review of, 40, 56, 194–195; and quality control, 194–198
Diablo Canyon nuclear facility, 195
DiLorenzo, Thomas J., 68, 201
Don't Bankrupt Washington Committee, 164
Dore, Justice, 227
Draw Day, 165–166
Drexel Burnham Lambert, 12, 112–113
Duke Power Co., 45

Eagleton, Thomas, 192
Ebasco Services, 45, 67, 216
Eisenhower, Dwight D., 4, 5, 187, 188
Ellensburg, Washington, 4, 9, 165
Environmental concerns, 24, 25, 159–160
Environmental Research Center (University of Washington), 25, 102
Envirosphere Co., 36
Ernst & Ernst v. *Hochfelder*, 114
Exchange agreements, 5, 93, 188–189

Falk, Theodore C., 98, 170, 175
Fast-track construction, 49–50, 53–55, 62, 63, 64
Federal Census of Governments, 140
Federal government, 1–2, 181–205, 216–217; and bailout of WPPSS, 182, 198–205, 209; and municipal financial disclosure, 191–194; and Northwest Power Planning, 183–191; and quality control, 110-111, 182, 198; supposed guar-

ABOUT THE AUTHORS

James Leigland is Director of Public Enterprise Studies at the Institute of Public Administration in New York City. He has written extensively on public enterprise and public authorities in the United States and abroad and has served as a consultant on public enterprise to state and local governments.

Dr. Leigland earned B.A. degrees in political science and philosophy from the University of Washington and a Ph.D. in political science from Columbia University in New York, where he taught at Columbia College for three years.

Robert Lamb is Professor of Finance and Management at the New York University Graduate School of Business Administration. He has written sixteen books, including *Municipal Bonds: A Comprehensive Review of Tax-Exempt Securities and Public Finance*, and is the founder and editor-in-chief of the *Journal of Business Strategy.* He has been a management consultant to major banks and investment banks, to the U.S. government, and to various government authorities, and he is presently serving as an Expert Witness before the U.S. Supreme Court on behalf of the U.S. government. Professor Lamb is an adviser to the Federal Reserve Board, the Justice Department, the Treasury Department, and the Federal Trade Commission. He has taught at Columbia University and the Wharton School of Finance.